Middle School 2-2

기말고사 완벽대비

적중 100

영어 기출 문제집

중 **2**

천재 | 이재영

Best Collection

구성과 특징

교과서의 주요 학습 내용을 중심으로 학습 영역별 특성에 맞춰 단계별로 다양한 학습 기회를 제공하여 단원별 학습능력 평가는 물론 중간 및 기말고사 시험 등에 완벽하게 대비할 수 있도록 내용을 구성

Words & Expressions

Step1 Key Words 단원별 핵심 단어 설명 및 풀이
Key Expression 단원별 핵심 숙어 및 관용어 설명
Word Power 반대 또는 비슷한 뜻 단어 배우기
English Dictionary 영어로 배우는 영어 단어

Step2 실력평가 단원별 수시평가 대비 주관식, 객관식 문제풀이

Step3 서술형 대비 학업성취도 및 수행능력평가 대비 서술형 문제풀이

Conversation

Step1 핵심 의사소통 의사소통에 필요한 주요 표현 방법 요약
핵심 Check 기본적인 표현 방법 및 활용능력 확인

Step2 대화문 익히기 상황에 따른 대화문 활용 및 연습

Step3 기본평가 시험대비 기초 학습 능력 평가

Step4 실력평가 단원별 수시평가 대비 주관식, 객관식 문제풀이

Step5 서술형 대비 학업성취도 및 수행능력평가 대비 서술형 문제풀이

Grammar

Step1 주요 문법 단원별 주요 문법 사항과 예문을 알기 쉽게 설명
핵심 Check 기본 문법사항에 대한 이해 여부 확인

Step2 기본평가 시험대비 기초 학습 능력 평가

Step3 실력평가 단원별 수시평가 대비 주관식, 객관식 문제풀이

Step4 서술형 대비 학업성취도 및 수행능력평가 대비 서술형 문제풀이

Reading

Step1 구문 분석 단원별로 제시된 문장에 대한 구문별 분석과 내용 설명
확인문제 문장에 대한 기본적인 이해와 인지능력 확인

Step2 확인학습A 빈칸 채우기를 통한 문장 완성 능력 확인

Step3 확인학습B 제시된 우리말을 영어로 완성하여 작문 능력 키우기

Step4 실력평가 단원별 수시평가 대비 주관식, 객관식 문제풀이

Step5 서술형 대비 학업성취도 및 수행능력평가 대비 서술형 문제풀이
교과서 구석구석 교과서에 나오는 기타 문장까지 완벽 학습

Composition

|영역별 핵심문제|

단어 및 어휘, 대화문, 문법, 독해 등 각 영역별 기출문제의 출제 유형을 분석하여 실전에 대비하고 연습할 수 있도록 문제를 배열

|서술형 실전 및 창의사고력 문제|

학교 시험에서 점차 늘어나는 서술형 시험에 집중 대비하고 고득점을 취득하는데 만전을 기하기 위한 학습 코너

|단원별 예상문제|

기출문제를 분석한 후 새로운 시험 출제 경향을 더하여 새롭게 출제될 수 있는 문제를 포함하여 시험에 완벽하게 대비할 수 있도록 준비

|단원별 모의고사|

영역별, 단계별 학습을 모두 마친 후 실전 연습을 위한 모의고사

INSIGHT on the textbook

교과서 파헤치기

- **단어Test1~2** 영어 단어 우리말 쓰기와 우리말을 영어 단어로 쓰기
- **대화문Test1~2** 대화문 빈칸 완성 및 전체 대화문 쓰기
- **본문Test1~5** 빈칸 완성, 우리말 쓰기, 문장 배열연습, 영어 작문하기 복습 등 단계별 반복 학습을 통해 교과서 지문에 대한 완벽한 습득
- **구석구석지문Test1~2** 지문 빈칸 완성 및 전문 영어로 쓰기

이책의 차례

Contents

Lesson **7** **A Life Full of Fun** 05~56

Lesson **8** **Viva, South America!** 57~108

Special Lesson **The Two Stones** 109~124

〈Insight on the textbook〉 교과서 파헤치기 01~52

〈책 속의 책〉 정답 및 해설 01~33

A Life Full of Fun

🎙 의사소통 기능

- 경험 묻고 답하기
  A: Have you ever touched a snake?
  B: No, I haven't.
- 절차 묻고 답하기
  A: Do you know how to make fried rice?
  B: Sure. It's easy. First, cut the vegetables into
      small pieces. Next, ...

🎙 언어 형식

- 현재완료
  Ms. Green **has studied** Spanish for three years.
- 명사를 수식하는 현재분사와 과거분사
  Look at the **falling** leaves.

교과서
Words & Expressions

Key Words

- □ **alive** [əláiv] ⑱ 살아 있는
- □ **among** [əmʌ́ŋ] ⑳ ~ 중에
- □ **amusing** [əmjúːziŋ] ⑱ 재미있는, 즐거운
- □ **animated movie** 만화영화
- □ **appear** [əpíər] ⑧ 나타나다, 등장하다
- □ **boil** [bɔil] ⑧ 끓이다, 끓다
- □ **box office** 극장 매표소
- □ **caricature** [kǽrikətʃər] ⑲ 캐리커쳐, (풍자) 만화
- □ **cartoon** [kɑːrtúːn] ⑲ 만화
- □ **cartoonist** [kɑːrtúːnist] ⑲ 만화가
- □ **chef** [ʃef] ⑲ 요리사
- □ **choose** [tʃuːz] ⑧ 고르다, 선택하다
- □ **comic strip** 신문 연재만화
- □ **common** [kámən] ⑱ 공통의
- □ **creative** [kriéitiv] ⑱ 창의적인, 독창적인
- □ **develop** [divéləp] ⑧ 개발하다, 만들다
- □ **dirty** [dɔ́ːrti] ⑱ 더러운
- □ **drawing** [drɔ́ːiŋ] ⑲ 그림
- □ **education** [èdʒukéiʃən] ⑲ 교육
- □ **fascinating** [fǽsənèitiŋ] ⑱ 매력적인
- □ **fry** [frai] ⑧ 볶다, 튀기다
- □ **lastly** [lǽstli] ⑨ 마지막으로
- □ **machine** [məʃíːn] ⑲ 기계

- □ **movement** [múːvmənt] ⑲ 움직임
- □ **pepper** [pépər] ⑲ 고추
- □ **plate** [pleit] ⑲ 접시
- □ **pollute** [pəlúːt] ⑧ 오염시키다
- □ **pour** [pɔːr] ⑧ 붓다
- □ **probably** [prábəbli] ⑨ 아마도
- □ **publish** [pʌ́bliʃ] ⑧ 출판하다
- □ **recipe** [résəpi] ⑲ 조리법, 비법
- □ **remain** [riméin] ⑧ 계속 ~이다
- □ **sauce** [sɔːs] ⑲ 소스
- □ **select** [silékt] ⑧ 선택하다, 고르다
- □ **showtime** [ʃóutaim] ⑲ 상영 시간
- □ **silly** [síli] ⑱ 어리석은
- □ **simple** [símpl] ⑱ 간단한, 단순한
- □ **sneaker** [sníkər] ⑲ 운동화
- □ **spread** [spred] ⑧ 펴 바르다
- □ **sunscreen** [sʌ́nskriːn] ⑲ 자외선 차단제
- □ **taste** [teist] ⑧ 맛보다, 먹다
- □ **translate** [trænsléit] ⑧ 번역하다
- □ **type** [taip] ⑲ 형태
- □ **usual** [júːʒuəl] ⑱ 평소의, 보통의
- □ **washing powder** (세탁용) 세제, 가루비누
- □ **well-known** ⑱ 유명한, 잘 알려진

Key Expressions

- □ **be made into** ~로 만들어지다
- □ **can't wait to** ~가 기대되다
- □ **catch one's interest** ~의 관심을 끌다
- □ **come together** 합쳐지다
- □ **cut A into pieces** A를 조각으로 자르다
- □ **jump out at** ~에게 금방 눈에 띄다, ~에게 분명히 보이다
- □ **make fun of** ~을 놀리다

- □ **of all ages** 모든 연령의
- □ **pay for** ~에 대한 돈을 내다
- □ **play a role** 역할을 하다
- □ **take a look** 살펴보다
- □ **ups and downs** 기복
- □ **watch out** 조심하다

Word Power

※ 서로 반대되는 뜻을 가진 어휘

- □ **appear** (나타나다) ↔ **disappear** (사라지다)
- □ **dirty** (더러운) ↔ **clean** (깨끗한)
- □ **silly** (어리석은) ↔ **clever, bright** (영리한)
- □ **kind** (친절한) ↔ **unkind** (불친절한)

- □ **alive** (살아 있는) ↔ **dead** (죽은)
- □ **usual** (평소의, 보통의) ↔ **unusual** (특이한)
- □ **first** (처음(으로), 맨 먼저) ↔ **lastly** (마지막으로)
- □ **high** (높은) ↔ **low** (낮은)

※ 요리와 관련된 어휘

- □ **cut** (자르다)
- □ **boil** (끓이다)

- □ **put** (놓다)
- □ **fry** (볶다, 튀기다)

- □ **pour** (붓다)
- □ **spread** (바르다)

- □ **add** (더하다)
- □ **bake** (굽다)

English Dictionary

- □ **amusing** 재미있는, 즐거운
  → causing laughter
  웃음을 유발하는

- □ **appear** 나타나다
  → to start to be seen
  보이기 시작하다

- □ **caricature** 풍자만화
  → a funny drawing of somebody that exaggerates some of their features
  누군가의 어떤 특징들을 과장하는 재미있는 그림

- □ **develop** 개발하다, 만들다
  → to invent something new
  새로운 무언가를 고안하다

- □ **education** 교육
  → a process of teaching and learning
  가르치고 배우는 과정

- □ **fascinating** 매력적인
  → extremely interesting
  매우 흥미로운

- □ **fry** 볶다, 튀기다
  → to cook something in hot fat or oil
  뜨거운 지방 또는 기름으로 무언가를 요리하다

- □ **movement** 움직임
  → the act of moving
  움직이는 행동

- □ **publish** 출판하다
  → to make information available to people in a book, magazine, or newspaper
  책, 잡지, 또는 신문으로 사람들에게 이용 가능한 정보를 만들다

- □ **remain** 계속 ~하다
  → to stay in the same place or in the same condition
  같은 장소 또는 같은 상태에 머무르다

- □ **silly** 어리석은
  → showing little thought; foolish
  생각이 거의 없음을 보여주는; 바보 같은

- □ **sunscreen** 자외선 차단제
  → a type of lotion that you put on your skin to protect it from being damaged by the sun
  태양에 의해 손상되는 것으로부터 피부를 보호하기 위해 피부에 바르는 로션의 한 유형

- □ **translate** 번역하다
  → to be changed from one language to another
  하나의 언어에서 다른 언어로 바뀌다

- □ **usual** 평소의, 보통의
  → normal; happening most often
  보통의; 가장 자주 일어나는

01 다음 단어들 중 요리와 관련이 없는 것은?

① pour
② bake
③ fry
④ cook
⑤ publish

02 다음 중 단어의 명사형이 틀린 것은?

① educate – education
② pollute – pollution
③ suggest – suggestion
④ translate – translation
⑤ agree – agreetion

03 다음 영영풀이가 가리키는 것을 고르시오.

> to be changed from one language to another

① translate
② publish
③ remain
④ pour
⑤ taste

04 다음 중 밑줄 친 부분의 뜻풀이가 바르지 않은 것은?

① Cindy is a creative storybook writer. 창의적인
② Korean people think education for children is important for the future. 교육
③ Do you know how to use this washing machine? 기계
④ It's fascinating to see how babies grow into children. 당황스러운
⑤ Cartoonists often work with writers who create ideas. 만화가

05 다음 우리말에 맞게 빈칸에 알맞은 말을 쓰시오.

(1) 마지막으로, 뜨거운 물을 붓고 기다리세요.
➡ _____, pour hot water and wait.

(2) 나는 빵에 버터와 잼을 발랐다.
➡ I _____ butter and jam on the bread.

(3) 접시 위에 어떤 음식도 남기지 마라.
➡ Don't leave any food on your _____.

(4) 콩으로 간장을 담근다.
➡ Soybean _____ _____ _____ soy sauce.

(5) 이 그림은 나의 관심을 끌었다.
➡ This picture _____ _____ _____.

(6) 지도 좀 함께 보자.
➡ Let's _____ _____ _____ at the map together.

06 다음 주어진 문장의 밑줄 친 spread와 같은 의미로 쓰인 것은?

> I need a knife to spread butter on bread.

① I'll spread strawberry jam on the toast for you.
② I saw the bird spread its wings.
③ Before the party, we need to spread a cloth on the table.
④ Virus spread rapidly during the holidays.
⑤ The fire spread to the building before the fire fighters arrived.

01 다음 짝지어진 단어의 관계가 같도록 빈칸에 알맞은 말을 쓰시오.

> clean : dirty = _____ : alive

02 다음 문장의 빈칸에 들어갈 말을 〈보기〉에서 골라 쓰시오.

> ┤ 보기 ├
>
> usual / well-known / creative / silly / cartoonist

(1) She came up with a _____ solution to the problem.

(2) The _____ is good at drawing cute animals.

(3) I hope I didn't make any _____ mistakes.

(4) There was more rainfall than _____ this summer.

(5) Stephen Hawking is one of the most _____ scientists.

03 다음 우리말에 맞게 빈칸에 알맞은 말을 쓰시오.

(1) 극장의 극장 매표소 옆에 매점이 있다.
  ➡ There is a snack bar next to the _____ _____ in the theater.

(2) 다른 상영 시간을 골라줄 수 있나요?
  ➡ Can you pick another _____?

(3) 책에 얼마의 돈을 냈나요?
  ➡ How much did you _____ _____ the book?

04 다음 우리말과 일치하도록 주어진 어구를 모두 배열하여 완성하시오.

(1) 너는 네 친구들을 놀려서는 안 된다.
   (make / friends / your / you / should / of / fun / not)
   ➡ _____

(2) Lucy는 삶의 기복에서 항상 침착하다.
   (Lucy / downs / life's / calm / always / is / through / and / ups)
   ➡ _____

(3) 나는 매일 그날의 웹툰을 살펴본다.
   (take / at / a look / the webtoons / I / the day / of)
   ➡ _____

05 다음 〈보기〉에 주어진 단어를 사용하여 빈칸을 완성하시오.

> ┤ 보기 ├
>
> agreement / suggestion / amusement / education / pollution

> <The Best Animated Movie for Children's _____>
> Animals welcome to the city's plan to build an _____ park in the forest. However, they soon suffer from serious _____. An old elephant makes a _____. The animals and the city reach an _____ to create a better world for everyone.

Conversation

① 경험 묻고 답하기

> **A** Have you ever touched a snake? 뱀을 만져 본 적 있니?
>
> **B** No, I haven't. 아니. 없어.

- 'Have you ever + 과거분사 ~?'는 경험을 묻는 표현으로 'Have you ever been to ~?'는 '~에 가 본 적이 있니?'라는 의미이다. 이에 대한 대답으로 긍정일 때는 'Yes, I have.', 부정일 때는 'No, I haven't.'로 대답한다. Have you?는 상대방에게서 받은 질문을 다시 상대방에게 묻는 표현으로 반복된 부분은 생략한다.

■ 경험 묻고 답하기

- 현재까지의 경험을 물을 때 현재완료 시제를 사용하므로 'Have you ever + 과거분사 ~?' 형태에 유의한다.
- 경험하지 못한 것으로 '전혀 ~해 본 적이 없다.'라고 강조하기 위해 'No, I've never ~'로 대답할 수 있다.
- 과거의 경험은 과거 시제를 이용한다.

ex) Did you touch the snake? – 과거에 뱀을 만졌는지 묻는 표현

Have you ever touched the snake? – 과거부터 현재까지 뱀을 만져 본 적이 있는지 묻는 표현

핵심 Check

1. 다음 우리말과 일치하도록 빈칸에 알맞은 말을 쓰시오.

(1) **A:** Have you ever _____ a sport star? (스포츠 스타를 만나 본 적 있어?)

　　B: No, I _____. _____ you? (아니. 없어. 너는?)

　　A: Yes, I _____. (나는 만나 본 적이 있어.)

(2) **A:** _____ _____ _____ _____ to Dokdo? (독도에 가 본 적 있니?)

　　B: Yes, I _____ _____ there. (응. 거기에 가 보았어.)

　　A: Wow, when _____ you go there? (와. 언제 그곳에 갔었니?)

② 절차 묻고 답하기

> **A** Do you know how to make fried rice? 어떻게 볶음밥을 만드는지 아니?
>
> **B** Sure. It's easy. First, cut the vegetables into small pieces. Next, ...
> 물론이죠. 쉬워요. 첫째, 채소를 작은 조각으로 자르세요. 다음 ....

■ 서수를 사용하여 어떤 절차의 순서를 열거할 수 있다. 이때, 'Second, Third' 대신에 'Next, Then'을 쓸 수 있다.

• first / first of all: 먼저, 우선

• then / next: 다음에는

• lastly / finally: 마지막으로

■ **절차 묻고 답하기**

• How can I buy a subway ticket from a machine? 기계로부터 지하철 표를 어떻게 살 수 있나요?

1. First, select "Language." 첫째, 언어를 선택하세요.

2. Second, choose where to go. 둘째, 어디로 갈지 선택하세요.

3. Lastly, pay the fare, and get the ticket. 마지막으로, 요금을 지불하고, 표를 받으세요.

핵심 Check

2. 다음 우리말과 일치하도록 빈칸에 알맞은 말을 쓰시오.

(1) **A:** Do you know _____ _____ make *ramyeon*? (어떻게 라면을 만드는지 아니?)

B: Sure. It's easy to make. _____, boil water in a pot. _____, put noodles in the pot. (물론이지. 만들기 쉬워. 첫째, 냄비에 물을 끓여. 둘째, 면을 냄비에 넣어.)

A: Okay. What should I do _____? (알겠어. 그 다음에는 무엇을 해야 하니?)

B: _____ them for 3-4 minutes. (그것을 3–4분 동안 끓여.)

(2) **A:** Do you know how to _____ _____ _____?
(너는 어떻게 쉽게 잠이 드는지 알고 있니?)

B: _____ _____ _____, take a warm bath and drink a glass of milk. _____, stretch and relax your body. _____, read a boring book. (우선, 따뜻한 목욕을 하고 우유 한 잔을 마셔. 다음, 몸을 스트레칭하고 휴식을 취해. 마지막으로, 지루한 책을 읽어.)

A: I see. Thank you for your advice. (알겠어. 조언해 주어 고마워.)

A. Communication: Listen –Dialog 1

Jane: Kevin, you look ❶down.

Kevin: Nothing ❷serious. Sometimes my feelings change a lot.

Jane: I understand. Many teens have ❸ups and downs in their feelings.

Kevin: Oh, really?

Jane: ❹Have you watched the ❺animated movie "Shining Days"?

Kevin: ❻No, I haven't. Why do you ask?

Jane: ❼It is about a teenager's feelings. ❼It will help you ❽understand your feelings better.

Kevin: That sounds good! I'll watch ❼it.

Jane: Kevin, 너 기분이 안 좋아 보이는구나.

Kevin: 별거 아니에요. 때때로 제 감정이 많이 바뀌어요.

Jane: 이해한단다. 많은 십 대가 감정의 기복이 있지.

Kevin: 아, 정말요?

Jane: 'Shining Days'라는 만화 영화를 본 적이 있니?

Kevin: 아니요, 본 적이 없어요. 왜 물으세요?

Jane: 그건 십 대의 감정에 관한 거야. 그건 네가 네 감정을 더 잘 이해하도록 도와줄 거야.

Kevin: 괜찮은 거 같네요! 그걸 볼게요.

❶ down: 우울한 = depressed = blue　　　❷ serious: 심각한

❸ ups and downs: 기복

❹ Have you ever p.p. ~?: '~해 본 적이 있니?'라고 경험을 묻는 표현이다.

❺ animated movie: 만화영화

❻ 경험 유무를 묻는 질문에 'Yes, I have.' 또는 'No, I haven't.'로 대답한다.

❼ It은 모두 "Shining Days"를 가리킨다.

❽ help의 목적격 보어로 원형부정사 understand가 쓰였다.

Check(√) True or False

(1) Kevin looks down because of serious problems.　　　　T ☐ F ☐

(2) Kevin hasn't watched the animated movie "Shining Days".　　T ☐ F ☐

B. Wrap Up – Listening ❺

Judy: ❶Have you ever been to Sokcho?

Minsu: Yes, I have. ❷Actually my uncle lives ❸there, so I visit ❹him every year.

Judy: Really? Then, you've climbed Mt. Seorak, ❺haven't you?

Minsu: Yes, I've climbed to the top of the mountain ❻twice.

Judy: 너는 속초에 가 본 적이 있니?

Minsu: 응, 가 본 적이 있어. 사실은 내 삼촌이 거기 살아서, 나는 매년 그를 방문해.

Judy: 정말? 그러면, 너는 설악산을 올라 본 적이 있지. 그렇지 않니?

Minsu: 응, 그 산의 정상에 올라간 적이 두 번 있어.

❶ Have you ever been to ~?: ~에 가 본 적이 있니?　　❷ actually: 사실은, 실제로

❸ there는 Sokcho를 가리킨다.　　　　❹ him은 Minsu's uncle을 가리킨다.

❺ 부가의문문으로 '그렇지 않니?'라며 다시 한 번 확인하는 표현이다.

❻ twice: 두 번

Check(√) True or False

(3) Minsu's uncle lives in Sokcho.　　　　T ☐ F ☐

(4) Minsu climbs to the top of Mt. Seorak every year.　　T ☐ F ☐

Communication: Listen – Dialog 2

Emily: Oh, look at the long line at the ❶box office.

Tony: Yeah, there's a ticket machine over there. Let's buy the tickets from the machine.

Emily: All right. Do you know how to use the machine?

Tony: Sure. It's easy. ❷First, select a movie and a showtime.

Emily: Okay. We can watch the seven o'clock show. Then what?

Tony: Well, ❸select ❹the number of tickets and choose our seats.

Emily: Okay. Two tickets, and I want to sit in the back.

Tony: No problem. ❺Lastly, ❻pay for the tickets.

Emily: It's very simple.

❶ box office: 극장 매표소
❷ 절차를 답하는 표현으로 first(첫째), second(둘째), next(다음) 등을 사용한다.
❸ 명령문이므로 동사원형으로 시작한다.
❹ the number of: ~의 수, cf. a number of: 많은
❺ lastly: 마지막으로
❻ pay for: ~에 대한 돈을 내다

 Communication – Listen more

Suji: Good morning, ❶Chef Garcia!

Garcia: Hello, Suji. ❷Have you ever made nacho pizza?

Suji: Nacho pizza? ❸No, I haven't.

Garcia: Kids will love ❹it, and I'll tell you how to make ❹it.

Suji: Sounds good!

Garcia: It's easy to make. First, ❺put nacho chips on a plate and ❻spread pizza sauce on ❼them.

Suji: Okay. Let me help you with the pizza sauce.

Garcia: Thanks. Next, put some ham, onions, and ❽peppers on top.

Suji: Okay. Then?

Garcia: Add cheese and bake for about 12 minutes in the oven.

Suji: I ❾can't wait to taste it!

❶ chef: 요리사
❷ Have you ever ~?: '~해 본 적이 있니?'라며 경험을 묻는 질문이다.
❸ 경험이 없을 때는 No, I haven't., 경험이 있을 때는 'Yes, I have.'라고 대답한다.
❹ it은 모두 'nacho pizza'를 가리킨다.
❺ put A on B: A를 B 위에 놓다
❻ spread: 바르다
❼ them은 nacho chips를 가리킨다.
❽ pepper: 고추
❾ can't wait to ~: ~가 기대되다

 Communicate: Speak

Anna: Do you know how to make ❶fried rice?

Jinsu: Sure. It's easy. First, ❷cut the vegetables into small ❸pieces.

Anna: Okay. What do you do next?

Jinsu: Put some oil in the pan. ❹Then, fry the vegetables with rice.

Anna: Wow, it's really simple.

❶ fried rice: 볶음밥
❷ cut A into B: A를 B로 자르다
❸ piece: 조각
❹ Next 또는 After that 등으로 바꾸어 쓸 수 있다.

 Wrap Up – Listen ❻

Mike: Today, I'll tell you how to ❶draw a bear's face. First, draw a big circle for the face. ❷Next, make two circles on top of the face. ❸After that, draw two circles for its eyes and ❹color ❺them black. Then, draw a small circle for the nose. Lastly, make a mouth.

❶ draw: 그리다
❷ Next는 Second로 바꾸어 쓸 수 있다.
❸ After that은 Third 또는 Next로 바꾸어 쓸 수 있다.
❹ color는 동사로 '색칠하다'를 뜻한다.
❺ them은 two circles를 가리킨다.

● 다음 우리말과 일치하도록 빈칸에 알맞은 말을 쓰시오.

Communication: Listen – Dialog 1

Jane: Kevin, you look _____.

Kevin: Nothing _____. Sometimes my feelings change _____ _____.

Jane: I understand. Many teens have _____ _____ _____ in their feelings.

Kevin: Oh, really?

Jane: _____ _____ _____ the animated movie "Shining Days"?

Kevin: No, _____ _____. _____ do you ask?

Jane: It is about a teenager's _____. It will help you _____ your feelings _____.

Kevin: That _____ good! I'll _____ it.

해석

Jane: Kevin, 너 기분이 안 좋아 보이는 구나.
Kevin: 별거 아니에요. 때때로 제 감정 이 많이 바뀌어요.
Jane: 이해한단다. 많은 십 대가 감정의 기복이 있지.
Kevin: 아, 정말요?
Jane: 'Shining Days'라는 만화영화를 본 적이 있니?
Kevin: 아니요, 본 적이 없어요. 왜 물으 세요?
Jane: 그건 십 대의 감정에 관한 거야. 그건 네가 네 감정을 더 잘 이해 하도록 도와줄 거야.
Kevin: 괜찮은 거 같네요! 그걸 볼게요.

Communication: Listen – Dialog 2

Emily: Oh, look at the long _____ at the box office.

Tony: Yeah, there's a _____ _____ over there. Let's buy the tickets _____ the _____.

Emily: All right. Do you know _____ _____ _____ _____ _____?

Tony: Sure. It's easy. First, _____ a movie and a showtime.

Emily: Okay. We can _____ the seven o'clock show. Then _____?

Tony: Well, _____ the number of tickets and choose our _____.

Emily: Okay. Two tickets, and I want to sit in the _____.

Tony: No problem. _____, _____ _____ the tickets.

Emily: It's very _____.

Emily: 아, 극장 매표소에 길게 늘어선 줄을 좀 봐.
Tony: 네, 저쪽에 발매기가 하나 있어요. 저 기계에서 표를 사요.
Emily: 좋아. 그 기계를 어떻게 쓰는지 아니?
Tony: 그럼요. 쉬워요. 먼저, 영화와 상 영 시간을 골라요.
Emily: 알았어. 우리는 7시 영화를 볼 수 있겠네. 그리고 뭘 하니?
Tony: 음, 표 매수를 선택하고 우리의 좌석을 골라요.
Emily: 좋아. 표 두 장, 그리고 나는 뒤 에 앉고 싶어.
Tony: 좋아요. 마지막으로 표 값을 내요.
Emily: 정말 간단하구나.

Communication: Listen More

Suji: Good morning, Chef Garcia!

Garcia: Hello, Suji. _____ _____ _____ _____ nacho pizza?

Suji: Nacho pizza? _____, _____ _____.

Garcia: Kids will love it, and I'll tell you _____ _____ _____ it.

Suji: Sounds good!

Garcia: It's easy to make. _____, _____ nacho chips _____ a plate and _____ pizza sauce on them.

Suji: Okay. Let me _____ you _____ the pizza sauce.

Garcia: Thanks. _____, put some ham, onions, and _____ on top.

Suji: Okay. Then?

Garcia: _____ cheese and _____ for about 12 minutes in the _____.

Suji: I can't _____ to _____ it!

Communicate: Speak

Anna: Do you know how to make _____ _____?

Jinsu: Sure. It's easy. First, _____ the vegetables _____ small pieces.

Anna: Okay. What do you do _____?

Jinsu: _____ some oil in the pan. Then, _____ the vegetables with rice.

Anna: Wow, it's really _____.

Wrap Up – Listening ❺

Judy: _____ you ever _____ to Sokcho?

Minsu: Yes, I _____. _____ my uncle lives there, so I visit him every year.

Judy: Really? Then, _____ _____ Mt. Seorak, _____ _____?

Minsu: Yes, I've climbed to the top of the mountain _____.

Wrap Up – Listening ❻

Mike: Today, I'll tell you _____ _____ _____ a bear's face. _____, draw a big _____ for the face. _____, make two circles on top of the face. After that, _____ two circles for its eyes and _____ them black. Then, draw a small _____ for the nose. _____, make a mouth.

해석

Suji: 안녕하세요, Garcia 셰프님!
Garcia: 안녕하세요, 수지 씨. 나초 피자를 만들어 본 적 있나요?
Suji: 나초 피자요? 아뇨, 만들어 본 적 없어요.
Garcia: 아이들이 그걸 매우 좋아할 거예요. 그럼 제가 어떻게 만드는지 알려 드리죠.
Suji: 좋아요!
Garcia: 만들기 쉬워요. 첫째로 접시 위에 나초 칩을 올려놓고 그것들 위에 피자 소스를 바르세요.
Suji: 네, 피자 소스를 제가 도와드릴게요.
Garcia: 고맙습니다. 다음으로 햄, 양파, 피망을 위에 올리세요.
Suji: 네. 그다음에는요?
Garcia: 치즈를 올리고 오븐에서 약 12분 동안 구우세요.
Suji: 빨리 맛보고 싶군요!

Anna: 너는 볶음밥을 만드는 법을 아니?
Jinsu: 물론이야. 그건 쉬워. 먼저 채소를 작은 조각으로 잘라.
Anna: 알았어. 다음엔 뭘 하니?
Jinsu: 팬에 기름을 둘러. 그러고는 채소를 밥과 함께 볶아.
Anna: 와, 정말 간단하구나.

Judy: 너는 속초에 가 본 적이 있니?
Minsu: 응, 가 본 적이 있어. 사실은 내 삼촌이 거기 살아서, 나는 매년 그를 방문해.
Judy: 정말? 그러면, 너는 설악산을 올라 본 적이 있지, 그렇지 않니?
Judy: 응, 그 산의 정상에 올라간 적이 두 번 있어.

Mike: 오늘 나는 곰의 얼굴을 그리는 방법을 네게 말해 줄게. 첫 번째로, 얼굴에 해당하는 큰 원을 그려. 다음에, 얼굴 위에 두 개의 원을 그려. 그 후에 눈에 해당하는 두 개의 원을 그리고 그것들을 검게 색칠해. 그리고 코에 해당하는 작은 원을 그려. 마지막으로 입을 만들어.

[01~02] 다음 설명을 읽고 물음에 답하시오.

Mike: Today, I'll tell you how to draw a bear's face. First, draw a big circle for the face. Next, make two circles on top of the face. After that, draw two circles for its eyes and color them black. Then, draw a small circle for the nose. Lastly, make a mouth.

01 How many circles do Mike need to draw a bear's face?

➡ _____

02 위 설명의 내용과 일치하지 <u>않는</u> 것은?

① Mike는 곰의 얼굴을 그리는 법을 설명하고 있다.
② 첫 번째로, 얼굴에 해당하는 큰 원을 그린다.
③ 두 번째로, 얼굴 위에 두 개의 원을 그린다.
④ 세 번째로, 눈에 해당하는 두 개의 원을 그리고 검게 색칠한다.
⑤ 마지막으로, 코에 해당하는 작은 원을 그린다.

[03~04] 다음 대화를 읽고 물음에 답하시오.

Anna: <u>너는 볶음밥을 만드는 법을 아니?</u> (fried, how)
Jinsu: Sure. It's easy. First, cut the vegetables into small pieces.
Anna: Okay. What do you do next?
Jinsu: Put some oil in the pan. Then, fry the vegetables with rice.
Anna: Wow, it's really simple.

03 위 대화의 밑줄 친 우리말을 주어진 단어를 사용하여 영작하시오.

➡ _____

04 위 대화에서 언급한 볶음밥을 만드는 법을 간략히 우리말로 설명하시오.

➡ _____

05 다음 우리말을 주어진 단어를 모두 배열하여 영작하시오.

(1) 나는 전에 Baltimore에 가 본 적이 없다. (been / I've / before / Baltimore / never / to)
➡ _____

(2) 너는 중국에 가 보았니? (ever / China / you / to / have / been)
➡ _____

[01~03] 다음 대화를 읽고 물음에 답하시오.

> Jane: Kevin, you look (A)<u>down</u>.
>
> Kevin: Nothing serious. Sometimes my feelings change a lot.
>
> Jane: I understand. Many teens have ups and downs in their feelings.
>
> Kevin: Oh, really?
>
> Jane: (B)<u>"Shining Days"라는 만화영화를 본 적이 있니?</u>
>
> Kevin: _____(a)_____ Why do you ask?
>
> Jane: It is about a teenager's feelings. It will help you understand your feelings better.
>
> Kevin: That sounds good! I'll watch it.

01 위 대화의 빈칸 (a)에 들어갈 말로 적절한 것은?

① No, I'm not.   ② No, I haven't.
③ No, I don't.   ④ No, I have.
⑤ No, I didn't.

02 위 대화의 밑줄 친 (A)와 바꾸어 쓸 수 있는 것은?

① depressed   ② happy
③ satisfied   ④ excited
⑤ pleased

03 위 대화의 밑줄 친 (B)의 우리말을 다음 〈보기〉의 주어진 어구를 모두 배열하여 영작하시오.

> ┌─ 보기 ┐
>
> watched / the / have / animated / you / movie "Shining Days"

➡ _____

_____

[04~05] 다음 대화를 읽고 물음에 답하시오.

> Emily: Oh, look at the long line at the box office.
>
> Tony: Yeah, there's a ticket machine over there. Let's buy the tickets from the machine.
>
> Emily: All right. Do you know (A)[how / what] to use the machine?
>
> Tony: Sure. It's easy. First, select a movie and a showtime.
>
> Emily: Okay. We can watch the seven o'clock show. Then what?
>
> Tony: Well, select the number of tickets and (B)[to choose / choose] our seats.
>
> Emily: Okay. Two tickets, and I want to sit in the back.
>
> Tony: No problem. (C)[Lately / Lastly], pay for the tickets.
>
> Emily: It's very simple.

04 위 대화의 빈칸 (A)~(C)에 들어갈 말로 적절한 것끼리 짝지어진 것은?

	(A)	(B)	(C)
①	how	to choose	Lately
②	how	choose	Lately
③	how	choose	Lastly
④	what	choose	Lastly
⑤	what	to choose	Lately

05 위 대화의 내용과 일치하지 <u>않는</u> 것은?

① 극장 매표소에 줄이 길게 늘어서 있다.
② Emily와 Tony는 발매기에서 표를 샀다.
③ 발매기에서 표를 사기 위해 먼저 영화와 상영 시간을 골라야 한다.
④ 표 값을 지불 한 후 표 매수와 좌석을 고를 수 있다.
⑤ Emily는 뒷좌석에 앉고 싶어 한다.

[06~07] 다음 대화를 읽고 물음에 답하시오.

Suji: Good morning, Chef Garcia!

Garcia: Hello, Suji. Have you ever made nacho pizza?

Suji: Nacho pizza? No, I haven't.

Garcia: Kids will love it, and I'll tell you how to make it.

Suji: Sounds good!

Garcia: It's easy to make. First, ___ⓐ___ nacho chips on a plate and spread pizza sauce on them.

Suji: Okay. Let me ___ⓑ___ you with the pizza sauce.

Garcia: Thanks. Next, put some ham, onions, and peppers on top.

Suji: Okay. Then?

Garcia: Add cheese and ___ⓒ___ for about 12 minutes in the oven.

Suji: I can't ___ⓓ___ to taste it!

서답형

06 다음 〈보기〉에 주어진 단어를 위 대화의 빈칸에 알맞게 쓰시오.

┌─── 보기 ───┐
put / bake / wait / help
└────────────┘

➡ ⓐ _____ ⓑ _____
ⓒ _____ ⓓ _____

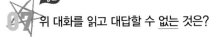

07 위 대화를 읽고 대답할 수 없는 것은?

① What is Garcia talking about?

② What do Garcia and Suji need to make the nacho pizza?

③ How long should Garcia and Suji bake the pizza in the oven?

④ What should Garcia and Suji do after spreading pizza source on the nacho chips?

⑤ What ingredient should Garcia and Suji prepare to make pizza source?

서답형

08 다음 대화가 자연스럽게 이어지도록 순서대로 배열하시오.

(A) Okay. What do you do next?

(B) Wow, it's really simple.

(C) Sure. It's easy. First, cut the vegetables into small pieces.

(D) Put some oil in the pan. Then, fry the vegetables with rice.

(E) Do you know how to make fried rice?

➡ _____

서답형

[09~10] 다음 대화를 읽고 물음에 답하시오.

Judy: (a)속초에 가 본 적이 있니?

Minsu: Yes, I have. Actually my uncle lives there, so I visit him every year.

Judy: Really? Then, you've climbed Mt. Seorak, ___(A)___?

Minsu: Yes, I've climbed to the top of the mountain twice.

09 위 대화의 빈칸 (A)에 들어갈 부가의문문을 완성하시오.

➡ _____

10 밑줄 친 (a)의 우리말을 영작하시오.

➡ _____

서답형

11 다음 주어진 우리말과 일치하도록 주어진 단어를 모두 배열하여 완성하시오.

(1) 독도에 가 본 적이 있니?
(ever / to / you / have / Dokdo / been)

➡ _____

(2) 나는 해리포터 시리즈를 읽어 본 적이 있다.
(have / the / I / read / series / Harry Potter)

➡ _____

[01~04] 다음 대화를 읽고 물음에 답하시오.

Suji: Good morning, Chef Garcia!

Garcia: Hello, Suji. Have you ever made nacho pizza?

Suji: Nacho pizza? No, I haven't.

Garcia: Kids will love it, and I'll tell you how to make it.

Suji: Sounds good!

Garcia: It's easy to make. First, put nacho chips on a plate and spread pizza sauce on them.

Suji: Okay. Let me help you with the pizza sauce.

Garcia: Thanks. Next, put some ham, onions, and peppers on top.

Suji: Okay. Then?

Garcia: Add cheese and bake for about 12 minutes in the oven.

Suji: I can't wait to taste it!

01 대화에 맞게 조리 순서를 빈칸에 쓰시오.

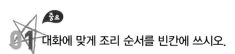

➡ _____

02 What will the cook make?

➡ _____

03 What did the cook do first to make the dish?

➡ _____

04 What ingredients did the cook put on the chips?

➡ _____

05 다음 대화에서 (A)~(E)가 자연스럽게 이어지도록 순서대로 배열하시오.

Emily: Oh, look at the long line at the box office.

Tony: Yeah, there's a ticket machine over there. Let's buy the tickets from the machine.

Emily: All right. Do you know how to use the machine?

(A) Okay. Two tickets, and I want to sit in the back.

(B) No problem. Lastly, pay for the tickets.

(C) Second, select the number of tickets and choose our seats.

(D) Sure. It's easy. First, select a movie and a showtime.

(E) Okay. We can watch the seven o'clock show. Then what?

➡ _____

[06~07] 다음 대화를 읽고 물음에 답하시오.

Judy: Have you ever been to Sokcho?

Minsu: Yes, I have. Actually my uncle lives there, so I visit him every year.

Judy: Really? Then, you've climbed Mt. Seorak, haven't you?

Minsu: Yes, I've climbed to the top of the mountain twice.

06 Has Minsu climbed Mt. Seorak?

➡ _____

07 Why does Minsu visit Sokcho every year?

➡ _____

교과서

Grammar

> - They **have known** each other for five years. 그들은 5년째 서로를 알고 있다.
> - **Have** you **been** to Japan? 일본에 가 본 적이 있니?

■ 현재완료는 과거의 사건이 현재까지 영향을 미칠 때 사용한다. 'have[has]+p.p.'의 형태로, 부정형은 'have[has] not+p.p.'이며, 의문형은 'Have[Has]+주어+p.p. ~?'로 나타낸다.

- She **has talked** with him for an hour. 그녀는 그와 한 시간 동안 대화를 나누었어.
- I **have seen** the play once. 나는 그 연극을 한 번 본 적이 있어.

■ 현재완료는 '완료, 경험, 계속, 결과'의 네 가지 용법으로 쓰인다. 완료 용법은 'just, already, yet'과 같은 부사와 주로 함께 쓰이며, 경험은 'ever, never, once, before' 등과 같은 부사와 함께 쓰인다. 'How long ~?'으로 묻는 질문이나 'for+기간', 'since+특정 시점'은 현재완료의 계속 용법에 속한다. 결과 용법은 특별한 부사와 어울리지 않고 과거에 발생한 사건으로 인하여 현재까지 영향을 미치고 있는 상태를 나타내는 용법이다.

- Diana **has finished** her laundry. Diana는 그녀의 빨래를 끝냈다. 〈완료〉
- Paul **has made** bread since 2 o'clock. Paul은 두 시부터 빵을 만들어 왔다. 〈계속〉
- They **have** never **been to** China. 그들은 중국에 가 본 적이 없어. 〈경험〉
- The boys **have gone to** their home. 그 소년들은 집에 가고 없어. 〈결과〉

* have been to와 have gone to의 사용에 유의한다. '~에 가 본 적이 있다'는 경험은 have been to로 표현하고, '~에 가고 없다'는 결과는 have gone to로 표현한다.

■ 현재완료는 과거의 일이 현재까지 영향을 미칠 때 쓰는 시제이므로 과거를 나타내는 어구인 yesterday, last year, ~ ago 등과 함께 쓸 수 없다.

- When have you eaten the food? (×)
- When **did** you **eat** the food?　　(○)

핵심 Check

1. 다음 우리말과 일치하도록 빈칸에 알맞은 말을 쓰시오.

(1) Jason은 세 시간 동안 깨어 있다.

➡ Jason ＿＿＿＿＿ ＿＿＿＿＿ awake for three hours.

(2) 그 기차는 막 떠났다.

➡ The train ＿＿＿＿＿ just ＿＿＿＿＿.

(3) 나는 지금까지 너에게 여러 번 전화했어.

➡ I ＿＿＿＿＿ ＿＿＿＿＿ you so many times until now.

② 명사를 수식하는 현재분사와 과거분사

> • Be quiet. There is a **sleeping** baby. 조용히 해. 자고 있는 아기가 있어.
>
> • Pick up a **fallen** leaf. 떨어진 잎 하나를 주워라.

■ 분사는 Ving 형태를 취하는 현재분사와, p.p. 형태를 취하는 과거분사로 나뉘며, 모두 명사를 수식하거나 설명하는 형용사 역할을 한다. 현재분사는 '~하는'이라는 의미로 주로 해석되어 능동이나 진행의 의미를 나타내고, 과거분사는 '~된'이라는 의미로 주로 해석되어 수동이나 완료의 의미를 나타낸다.

  • I saw **singing** girls. 나는 노래하는 소녀들을 봤어.

  • The **disappointing** behavior made my mom upset. 그 실망스러운 행동은 우리 엄마를 화나게 했다.

■ 분사가 단독으로 명사를 수식할 때에는 일반적으로 명사 앞에서 수식하지만, 분사가 다른 어구와 함께 명사를 수식할 때에는 명사 뒤에서 수식한다.

  • Do you see the boys **playing** basketball? 농구하는 소년들이 보이나요?

  • Kevin found a vase **broken** by Sally. Kevin은 Sally에 의해 깨진 꽃병을 발견했다.

  • People **living** in the town felt happy. 그 마을에 사는 사람들은 행복했다.

■ '사역동사(have, make)+목적어+과거분사', '지각동사+목적어+과거분사', 'get+목적어+과거분사'는 목적어와 목적보어의 관계가 수동인 경우 쓰인다.

  • Jason **had** the woman **ask** some questions. Jason은 그 여자가 몇 가지 질문을 하게 했다.
    = Jason **had** some questions **asked** by the woman.

■ 'Ving'로 형태가 같은 현재분사와 동명사의 차이를 구별해야 한다. 현재분사는 '~하는', '~하는 중인'이라고 해석되고, 동명사는 '~하는 것'이라고 해석되거나 'V를 용도로 하는 명사'로 해석된다.

  • There is a woman **waiting** for someone. 누군가를 기다리는 여자가 있습니다. – 현재분사

  • I can't find the **waiting** room. 나는 대기실을 찾을 수 없어요. – 동명사 (기다리는 용도로 쓰이는 방 – 대기실)

핵심 Check

2. 다음 주어진 동사를 어법에 맞게 빈칸에 쓰시오.

   (1) 무언가를 타이핑하는 그 소녀를 아니?

     ➡ Do you know the girl _____ something? (type)

   (2) Adam은 우리에게 지루한 이야기를 해줬어.

     ➡ Adam told us a _____ story. (bore)

   (3) 그것은 BTS에 의해 불러진 노래야.

     ➡ It is a song _____ by BTS. (sing)

01 다음 문장에서 어법상 <u>어색한</u> 부분을 바르게 고쳐 쓰시오.

(1) My father hasn't gone to the museum until now.

_____ ➡ _____

(2) We saw the program several times until now.

_____ ➡ _____

(3) I did nothing since yesterday.

_____ ➡ _____

(4) We have work for this company for five years.

_____ ➡ _____

02 다음 주어진 단어를 어법에 맞게 빈칸에 쓰시오.

(1) People _____ in the town felt happy. (live)

(2) Do you know a baby _____ over there? (cry)

(3) I read the book _____ by a famous author. (write)

(4) Nick was holding a spoon _____ of gold. (make)

(5) Watch out for the _____ dog. (bark)

03 주어진 단어를 바르게 배열하여 다음 우리말을 영어로 쓰시오. 필요하다면 어형을 바꾸시오.

(1) 여섯 살 이후로 나는 책을 500권 읽었다. (read / since / was / I / have / 500 books / six / I)

➡ _____

(2) 그 소년은 벌써 우유를 마셨어. (the milk / the boy / drink / has / already)

➡ _____

(3) 이것은 구워진 감자인가요? (this / is / bake / a / potato)

➡ _____

(4) 너의 침낭을 찾았니? (bag / sleep / find / did / you / your)

➡ _____

(4) sleeping bag: 침낭

01 다음 빈칸에 들어갈 말로 가장 적절한 것은?

> The man has worked for the company _____ 2010.

① at   ② in   ③ for
④ since   ⑤ during

02 다음 빈칸에 들어갈 말로 적절하지 <u>않은</u> 것은?

> Have you ever _____ Jenny before?

① called   ② met
③ saw   ④ played with
⑤ talked with

03 다음 빈칸에 들어갈 말이 바르게 짝지어진 것은?

> • I saw something _____ in the kitchen.
> • A girl _____ Jessica came to see you.

① burned – name
② burned – named
③ burning – named
④ burning – naming
⑤ burning – to name

04 다음 중 어법상 바르지 <u>않은</u> 것은?

① Have you ever taken first prize before?
② When did he go out last night?
③ People have stoped buying our products recently.
④ They made her go there alone.
⑤ We have never seen the boys and girls before.

05 다음 중 밑줄 친 부분과 쓰임이 같은 것은?

> I <u>have been</u> to Mexico several times.

① Colin <u>has gone</u> to the theater without an umbrella.
② We <u>have</u> just <u>made</u> some cookies.
③ Terry <u>hasn't called</u> her friends yet.
④ He <u>has played</u> the guitar since he was an elementary school student.
⑤ They <u>have visited</u> the museum four times.

06 다음 빈칸에 들어갈 말로 가장 적절한 것은?

> He _____ her for three years until now.

① met   ② is meeting
③ meets   ④ has met
⑤ is met

07 다음 중 빈칸에 들어갈 말로 적절하지 <u>않은</u> 것은? (2개)

> My parents _____ the fence fixed.

① had   ② saw
③ got   ④ helped
⑤ seemed

서답형
08 적절한 시제를 활용하여 다음 두 문장을 하나의 문장으로 표현하시오.

> Eunji started to live in Busan when she was five years old. She still lives in Busan.

➡ _____

_____

09 다음 문장의 밑줄 친 부분과 쓰임이 같은 것은?

The <u>boring</u> movie made students fall asleep.

① <u>Writing</u> a letter is easy.
② Did you enjoy <u>baking</u> bread?
③ I am not interested in <u>playing</u> computer games.
④ She kept <u>yelling</u> at me.
⑤ Who is the girl <u>raising</u> her hand?

10 다음 중 어법상 틀린 것은?

A: ①<u>Has</u> your brother ②<u>climbed</u> Mt. Seorak?
B: Yes, he ③<u>does</u>. He ④<u>has climbed</u> Mt. Seorak two times ⑤<u>before</u>.

①   ②   ③   ④   ⑤

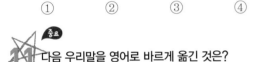

11 다음 우리말을 영어로 바르게 옮긴 것은?

① 웃고 있는 저 소녀를 아니?
  ➡ Do you know that smile girl?
② 그 부상당한 남자는 어디에 있니?
  ➡ Where is the injuring man?
③ 언제 그녀를 처음 만났니?
  ➡ When have you met her first?
④ 그 책을 몇 번이나 읽었니?
  ➡ How many times have you read the book?
⑤ 나는 이곳에서 3년 동안 살고 있어요.
  ➡ I have lived here since three years.

서답형
12 현재완료 시제와 주어진 단어를 활용하여 다음 우리말을 영어로 쓰시오.

나는 지금 막 냉동피자 한 조각을 먹었어.
(freeze / just / have / piece)

➡ _____

13 (A)~(C)에 들어갈 말이 바르게 짝지어진 것은?

• The (A)[exciting / excited] game made us pleased.
• I (B)[played / have played] the guitar since I was five years old.
• (C)[Have you found / Did you find] your wallet yesterday?

① excited – have played – Have you found
② excited – played – Did you find
③ exciting – have played – Have you found
④ exciting – played – Have you found
⑤ exciting – have played – Did you find

14 다음 대화의 빈칸에 들어갈 말로 가장 적절한 것은?

A: _____ this movie?
B: Yes. I have seen it once.

① Have you made
② Have you heard about
③ Have you seen
④ Did you see
⑤ Did you want to see

15 빈칸에 들어갈 말을 바르게 짝지은 것은?

Tom is Paul's English teacher. Tom _____ Paul since he was ten years old. Tom _____ Paul very well.

① teaches – has known
② will teach – knew
③ is teaching – is knowing
④ has taught – knows
⑤ has taught – has known

서답형

16 주어진 단어를 활용하여 다음 우리말을 영어로 쓰시오.

> 나는 중고차 한 대를 샀어.

➡ _____

중요

17 다음 중 빈칸에 들어갈 말이 다른 하나는?

① I haven't seen her _____ yesterday.

② Jina has danced ballet _____ she was very young.

③ He has talked with someone _____ an hour.

④ Julie has knitted a hat _____ last month.

⑤ My sisters have ridden their bikes _____ this morning.

18 다음 밑줄 친 두 문장을 하나의 문장으로 바르게 바꾼 것은?

> A: Where is your brother?
> B: He went out to a mall. He is not here.

① He used to be in a mall.

② He has been here.

③ He wanted to go to a mall.

④ He has been in a mall.

⑤ He has gone to a mall.

중요

19 빈칸에 들어갈 말이 바르게 짝지어진 것은?

> He _____ all day under the _____ sun since this morning. He is very tired.

① is working – burned

② works – burning

③ worked – burned

④ has worked – burning

⑤ has worked – burned

중요

20 다음 중 어법상 바르지 않은 것은?

> A: How long ①have you played the drums?
> B: I ②have played the drums ③for 5 years.
> A: Do you like playing them?
> B: Yes. Playing the drums ④makes me ⑤amusing.

①   ②   ③   ④   ⑤

서답형

21 주어진 단어를 활용하여 다음 우리말을 영어로 쓰시오.

> 그 놀라운 소식은 사실이 아니야.
> (surprise / true)

➡ _____

22 다음 우리말을 영어로 옮길 때 세 번째와 일곱 번째 오는 단어를 바르게 짝지은 것은?

> 나는 전에 내 남동생과 싸운 적이 있어요.

① have – with   ② have – brother

③ with – before   ④ fought – brother

⑤ fought – before

서답형

23 주어진 단어를 바르게 배열하여 다음 우리말을 영어로 쓰시오. 두 개의 단어는 어법에 맞게 변형하시오.

> 부서진 창문을 통해 집 안으로 찬바람이 불어 왔다. (the / house / the / break / into / through / window / cold / blow / winds)

➡ _____

_____

서답형

24 excite를 어법에 맞게 빈칸에 쓰시오.

> A: The concert was _____!
> B: I agree. The _____ fans rushed into the stadium.

01 다음 우리말 의미에 맞게 주어진 단어를 빈칸에 쓰시오.

> bake / slice / sleep / cheer / rise / dance

(1) 우리는 아침 일찍 해변에서 일출을 봤습니다.
➡ Early in the morning, we saw the _____ sun at the beach.

(2) 잠자는 고양이 앞에 있는 구운 감자가 보이니?
➡ Do you see the _____ potatoes in front of the _____ cat?

(3) 나의 친구들은 무대에서 춤추는 소녀들이야.
➡ My friends are the girls _____ on the stage.

(4) 나는 환호하는 군중들 중 한 명이었어.
➡ I was one of the _____ crowds.

(5) 이 자른 치즈를 어디에 두어야 하나요?
➡ Where should I put this _____ cheese?

02 적절한 시제를 활용하여 다음 두 문장을 하나의 문장으로 표현하시오.

> • Jenny made friends with Christina in 2010.
> • They are still friends.

➡ _____

03 주어진 단어를 활용하여 다음 대화를 영어로 쓰시오.

> A: 볶음밥을 요리해 본 적이 있니?
> (cook / ever / fry)
> B: 응, 나는 그것을 여러 번 요리해 봤어.
> (many times)

➡ A: _____
B: _____

04 주어진 단어를 활용하여 다음 우리말을 영어로 쓰시오.

> 전에 다른 나라에 가 본 적이 있니?
> (before / other)

➡ _____

05 주어진 동사를 내용과 어법에 맞게 빈칸에 쓰시오.

> be / rain / lose / drive / read

(1) My uncle _____ the car in 2009.
(2) The weather _____ warm recently. It's still warm.
(3) It _____ since last night.
(4) Clara _____ her key the other day.
(5) Zach _____ the book several times until now.

06 주어진 어구를 바르게 배열하여 다음 우리말을 영어로 쓰시오. 필요하다면 어형을 바꾸시오.

> 빨간 모자를 쓰고 있는 소년을 보아라.
> (a red cap / the boy / at / wear / look)

➡ _____

07 주어진 단어를 활용하여 다음 우리말을 영어로 쓰시오.

> 나의 남동생은 어젯밤부터 아파요. (sick)

➡ _____

08 다음 밑줄 친 부분이 현재분사인지 동명사인지 구별하고, 그렇게 구별한 이유를 서술하시오.

> (1) Look! There is a <u>swimming</u> baby.
> (2) Where can we find a <u>swimming</u> pool?

➡ (1) _____ 이유: _____

_____

(2) _____ 이유: _____

_____

09 주어진 어구를 활용하여 다음 우리말을 영어로 쓰시오.

(1) 나는 지금까지 제주도에 두 번 가봤어요.
(Jejudo / twice / until now)

➡ _____

(2) 나는 어제 그 유리창을 깼어요. (break)

➡ _____

(3) 우리는 아직 그 영화를 보지 못했습니다.
(have)

➡ _____

10 다음 상황을 읽고 빈칸에 알맞은 말을 쓰시오.

> Jason was born in Canada in 2001. He moved to Seoul in 2011. He started to learn *taekwondo* as soon as he arrived in Seoul. He is eighteen years old now. He still learns *taekwondo*. He likes *taekwondo*.

> Jason _____(live) in Seoul since _____. He took his first *taekwondo* lesson in _____. He _____(learn) *taekwondo* _____ eight years.

11 다음 상황을 설명하는 문장을 한 문장으로 바꿔 쓰시오.

> My grandmother broke her right arm last month. She can't use it now.

➡ _____

12 주어진 단어를 바르게 배열하여 다음 우리말을 영어로 쓰시오. 필요하다면 어형을 변형하시오.

> 그녀는 내게 삶은 달걀 하나와 다진 당근을 가져오게 하였다.
> (carrot / she / make / boil / chop / a / and / egg / bring / me)

➡ _____

13 다음 대화의 빈칸에 알맞은 말을 쓰시오.

> A: Does James work for this company?
> B: Yes, he does. Actually he _____ for this company for five years.

➡ _____

14 다음 문장에서 어법상 어색한 부분을 찾아 바르게 고쳐 쓰시오.

(1) I am boring with his lecture.

_____ ➡ _____

(2) This is a bag making in China.

_____ ➡ _____

(3) It is an excited adventure movie.

_____ ➡ _____

(4) He approached the barked dog.

_____ ➡ _____

The World of Cartoons

Boat! Land!

Did you laugh when you saw the cartoon above? If so, the cartoonist
= If you laughed when you saw the cartoon above
was successful. Cartoonists are the people who make cartoons. They
주격 관계대명사
want to catch your interest, and usually, make you laugh with simple
사역동사+목적어+동사원형   ~으로(도구, 수단)
language and creative drawings.

People have made cartoons for hundreds of years. There are many
현재완료-계속   수 백의
types of cartoons, and they play different roles. One form of cartoon is
a picture with a few words. It is sometimes called a "gag cartoon." The
~이 있는   ~라고 불린다
cartoonist makes a funny character, and the character makes you laugh
사역동사
by doing or saying silly things.
전치사 by의 목적어로 doing과 saying
Another type of cartoon is called a caricature. In a caricature, some
남아 있는 것 중 또 다른 하나를 가리킬 때
parts of a character are different or bigger than usual. Look at the
big의 비교급
picture on the right. Which parts of the man's face jump out at you?
        S   V
Artists have used this type of cartoon to make fun of well-known
현재완료 - 계속   ~하기 위해서(to부정사의 부사적 용법 중 목적)
people.

cartoonist: 만화가
successful: 성공한, 성공적인
catch one's interest: ~의 관심을 끌다
creative: 창의적인, 독창적인
type: 형태
play a role: 역할을 하다
silly: 어리석은
caricature: 캐리커처
usual: 평소의, 보통의
jump out at: ~에게 금방 눈에 띄다, ~에게 분명히 보이다
make fun of: ~을 놀리다
well-known: 잘 알려진, 유명한

📎 **확인문제**

● 다음 문장이 본문의 내용과 일치하면 T, 일치하지 않으면 F를 쓰시오.

1 We can say that a cartoonist was successful when he made us think about something seriously. ☐

2 A few words are used in a gag cartoon. ☐

3 A funny character in a gag cartoon makes you laugh by doing or saying silly things. ☐

4 A gag cartoon is used to make fun of famous people. ☐

5 A caricature describes people as they are. ☐

When several cartoon pictures come together and tell a story, we
몇몇의(셀 수 있는 명사 수식)
have a comic strip. Comic strips have been in newspapers for many
현재완료(계속)
years. They are often just amusing stories. People have also used comic
strips for education. Comics can make information clearer and easier
5형식 동사(make+목적어+목적격보어)
to learn. You have probably seen comic history or science books.
to부정사의 부사적 용법 (형용사 수식)　현재완료(경험)

You have surely seen many cartoon movies, or animated movies,
too. These are very popular among people of all ages. Movement and
sounds are added to pictures, so they come alive. Artists and writers
수동태　　　　　　　　　　　　　서술적 용법으로 쓰이는 형용사
can develop fascinating characters and tell interesting stories through
└, 매력을 유발하고 흥미를 유발하는 것이므로 현재분사 ,┘
animation.

In the 1990s, a new type of cartoon was developed. It is called
개발되는 것이므로 수동태
a webtoon. Webtoons are published online, so you can read them
webtoons 지칭
anytime, anywhere on your phone or computer. They are very popular,
and some of them are even made into TV dramas or movies.
～으로 만들어지다

New forms of cartoons may appear in the future. They could be
new forms of cartoons 지칭
different and even more exciting than now, but one thing will remain
the same: they will help us laugh, relax, and learn.
준사역동사(help+목적어+(to) V)

come together: 합쳐지다

comic strip: 신문의 연재만화

amusing: 재미있는, 즐거운

education: 교육

probably: 아마도

surely: 분명히, 확실히

among: ～ 중에

of all ages: 모든 연령의

movement: 움직임

develop: 개발하다, 만들다

fascinating: 매력적인

animation: 만화영화 제작

publish: 출판하다

be made into: ～로 만들어지다

appear: 나타나다, 등장하다

remain: 계속 ～이다

 확인문제

● 다음 문장이 본문의 내용과 일치하면 T, 일치하지 <u>않으면</u> F를 쓰시오.

1　A comic strip doesn't tell a story. ☐

2　We can't see comic strips in newspapers. ☐

3　Newspapers can make information clearer. ☐

4　There are comic history books. ☐

5　Webtoons were developed in the 1990s. ☐

6　All of the webtoons were made into TV dramas or movies. ☐

● 우리말을 참고하여 빈칸에 알맞은 말을 쓰시오.

1 Boat! _____!

2 Did you _____ when you _____ the cartoon _____?

3 If _____, the cartoonist was _____.

4 Cartoonists are the people _____ _____ _____.

5 They want _____ _____ your interest, and usually, _____ _____ _____ with simple language and _____ _____.

6 People _____ _____ cartoons _____ hundreds of years.

7 There are _____ _____ _____ _____, and they play different roles.

8 One form of cartoon _____ a picture with _____ _____ _____.

9 It _____ sometimes _____ a "gag cartoon."

10 The cartoonist _____ _____ _____ _____, and the character makes you _____ by _____ or _____ silly things.

11 _____ type of cartoon _____ _____ a caricature.

12 In a caricature, _____ _____ of a character _____ _____ or _____ _____ _____.

13 Look at the picture _____ the right.

14 _____ _____ of the man's face _____ out at you?

15 Artists _____ _____ this type of cartoon _____ _____ _____ well-known people.

16 When _____ cartoon pictures _____ _____ and tell a story, we have _____ _____ _____.

17 Comic strips _____ _____ in newspapers _____ many years.

18 They are often _____ _____ _____.

19 People _____ _____ _____ comic strips _____ _____.

20 Comics can _____ information _____ and _____ _____ _____.

21 You _____ _____ _____ comic history or science books.

22 You _____ _____ _____ many cartoon movies, or _____ _____, too.

23 These are very _____ _____ _____ _____ _____ _____.

24 Movement and sounds _____ _____ _____ pictures, so they _____ _____.

25 Artists and writers can _____ _____ characters and tell _____ stories _____ animation.

26 In the 1990s, a new type of cartoon _____ _____.

27 It _____ _____ a webtoon.

28 Webtoons _____ _____ online, so you can _____ _____ anytime, anywhere _____ your phone or computer.

29 They are very _____, and some of _____ _____ even made _____ TV dramas or movies.

30 New forms of cartoons _____ _____ in the future.

31 They could be _____ and even more _____ _____ now, but one thing will _____ the same: they will help us _____, _____, and _____.

17 연재만화는 여러 해 동안 신문에 실려 왔다.

18 그것들은 종종 그저 재미있는 이야기이다.

19 사람들은 연재만화를 교육용으로 사용해 오기도 했다.

20 만화는 정보를 더 명료하고 더 배우기 쉽게 만들 수 있다.

21 여러분은 아마 만화 역사책이나 과학책을 본 적이 있을 것이다.

22 여러분은 많은 만화영화도 당연히 봤을 것이다.

23 이것들은 모든 연령대의 사람들에게 매우 인기가 많다.

24 동작이나 소리가 그림에 더해져서 그림들이 생생하게 살아난다.

25 미술가들과 작가들은 매력적인 캐릭터를 개발하고 만화영화 제작을 통해 재미있는 이야기를 들려준다.

26 1990년대에 새로운 형식의 만화가 개발되었다.

27 그건 웹툰이라고 불린다.

28 웹툰은 온라인으로 출판되기 때문에 여러분이 휴대 전화나 컴퓨터로 언제 어디서나 볼 수 있다.

29 그것은 매우 인기가 있고, 그들 가운데 일부는 심지어 텔레비전 드라마나 영화로 만들어지기도 한다.

30 미래에는 새로운 형태의 만화가 나타날지도 모른다.

31 그것은 지금과는 다르고 한층 더 재미있겠지만, 한 가지는 같을 것이다. 그것은 우리가 웃고, 쉬고, 배우도록 도와줄 것이다.

● 우리말을 참고하여 본문을 영작하시오.

1 배다! 육지다!

➡ _____

2 위의 만화를 보고 웃었는가?

➡ _____

3 그랬다면 그 만화가는 성공했다.

➡ _____

4 만화가들은 만화를 만드는 사람들이다.

➡ _____

5 그들은 여러분의 관심을 끌고, 대개는 간단한 말과 독창적인 그림으로 여러분을 웃게 하고 싶어 한다.

➡ _____

6 사람들은 수백 년 동안 만화를 만들어 왔다.

➡ _____

7 만화에는 많은 종류가 있으며, 그것들은 다양한 역할을 한다.

➡ _____

8 만화의 한 형태로 몇 마디 말을 쓴 그림이 있다.

➡ _____

9 간혹 그것은 '개그 만화'라고 불린다.

➡ _____

10 만화가는 웃긴 캐릭터를 만들고, 그 캐릭터는 우스꽝스러운 행동이나 말을 함으로써 여러분을 웃게 만든다.

➡ _____

11 다른 종류의 만화는 캐리커처라고 불린다.

➡ _____

12 캐리커처에서 캐릭터의 어떤 부분은 평소와 다르거나 더 크다.

➡ _____

13 오른쪽의 그림을 보아라.

➡ _____

14 남자 얼굴의 어떤 부분이 여러분에게 분명히 보이는가?

➡ _____

15 미술가들은 유명한 사람들을 풍자하기 위해 이런 종류의 만화를 그려 왔다.

➡ _____

16 몇 가지 만화 그림이 모여서 이야기를 들려주게 되면, 그것이 연재만화가 된다.

➡ _____

17 연재만화는 여러 해 동안 신문에 실려 왔다.

➡ _____

18 그것들은 종종 그저 재미있는 이야기이다.

➡ _____

19 사람들은 연재만화를 교육용으로 사용해 오기도 했다.

➡ _____

20 만화는 정보를 더 명료하고 더 배우기 쉽게 만들 수 있다.

➡ _____

21 여러분은 아마 만화 역사책이나 과학책을 본 적이 있을 것이다.

➡ _____

22 여러분은 많은 만화영화도 당연히 봤을 것이다.

➡ _____

23 이것들은 모든 연령대의 사람들에게 매우 인기가 많다.

➡ _____

24 동작이나 소리가 그림에 더해져서 그림들이 생생하게 살아난다.

➡ _____

25 미술가들과 작가들은 매력적인 캐릭터를 개발하고 만화영화 제작을 통해 재미있는 이야기를 들려준다.

➡ _____

26 1990년대에 새로운 형식의 만화가 개발되었다.

➡ _____

27 그건 웹툰이라고 불린다.

➡ _____

28 웹툰은 온라인으로 출판되기 때문에 여러분이 휴대 전화나 컴퓨터로 언제 어디서나 볼 수 있다.

➡ _____

29 그것은 매우 인기가 있고, 그들 가운데 일부는 심지어 텔레비전 드라마나 영화로 만들어지기도 한다.

➡ _____

30 미래에는 새로운 형태의 만화가 나타날지도 모른다.

➡ _____

31 그것은 지금과는 다르고 한층 더 재미있겠지만, 한 가지는 같을 것이다. 그것은 우리가 웃고, 쉬고, 배우도록 도와줄 것이다.

➡ _____

_____

[01~07] 다음 글을 읽고 물음에 답하시오.

Boat!

Land!

Did you ①laugh when you saw the cartoon above? If so, the cartoonist was ②successful. Cartoonists are the people who make cartoons. They want to catch your interest, and usually, make you laugh with simple language and creative drawings.

People have made cartoons for hundreds of years. There are many types of cartoons, and they play ③the same roles. One form of cartoon is a picture with a few words. It is sometimes called a "gag cartoon." The cartoonist makes a funny character, and the character makes you laugh ___(A)___ doing or saying ④silly things.

Another type of cartoon is called a caricature. In a caricature, some parts of a character are different or bigger than ⑤usual. Look at the picture on the right. Which parts of the man's face jump out at you? Artists have used this type of cartoon to make fun of well-known people.

01 ①~⑤ 중 글의 흐름상 어색한 것은?

①   ②   ③   ④   ⑤

중요

02 다음 중 빈칸 (A)에 들어갈 말과 같은 말이 들어가는 것은?

① Are you interested _____ the movie?

② Don't give _____ your dream.

③ Please turn _____ the light when you go out.

④ I feel very proud _____ you.

⑤ Let's check them one _____ one.

서답형

03 What is the second type of cartoon called? Answer in five words.

➡ _____

서답형

04 What does a cartoonist make in a gag cartoon? Answer in English with a full sentence.

➡ _____

중요

05 Which is TRUE about a caricature?

① There are many types of caricatures.

② It makes fun of famous people.

③ Cartoonists don't have an interest in it.

④ It doesn't make people laugh.

⑤ It describes people as they are.

중요

06 다음 중 위 글을 읽고 답할 수 없는 것은?

① What do cartoonists want to do?

② What do cartoonists use to make people laugh?

③ How long have people made cartoons?

④ What is the third type of cartoon?

⑤ What is a gag cartoon?

서답형

07 What do cartoonists do? Answer in English with a full sentence.

➡ _____

[08~10] 다음 글을 읽고 물음에 답하시오.

When several cartoon pictures come together and tell a story, we have a comic strip. Comic strips have been in newspapers __(A)__ many years.

[A] You have probably seen comic history or science books. You have surely seen many cartoon movies, or animated movies, too.

[B] They are often just amusing stories. People have also used comic strips for education. Comics can make information clearer and easier to learn.

[C] These are very popular among people of all ages. Movement and sounds are added to pictures, so they come alive.

Artists and writers can develop fascinating characters and tell interesting stories through animation.

08 다음 중 빈칸 (A)에 들어갈 말과 다른 말이 들어가는 것은?

① I haven't seen her _____ a while.
② Carrie has met him _____ a long time.
③ They have lived here _____ last year.
④ She has known him _____ ten years.
⑤ Jina has danced _____ an hour.

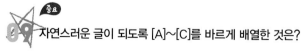

09 자연스러운 글이 되도록 [A]~[C]를 바르게 배열한 것은?

① [A] – [C] – [B]
② [B] – [A] – [C]
③ [B] – [C] – [A]
④ [C] – [B] – [A]
⑤ [C] – [A] – [B]

10 Which is NOT true about comic strips?

① It has a story.
② It is also used as an educational purpose.
③ It has one picture.
④ We can see it in newspapers.
⑤ Its stories are amusing.

[11~13] 다음 글을 읽고 물음에 답하시오.

In the 1990s, a new type of cartoon was developed. It is (A)[calling / called] a webtoon. Webtoons are published online, so you can read (B)[it / them] anytime, anywhere on your phone or computer. They are very popular, and some of them are even made into TV dramas or movies.

New forms of cartoons may (C)[appear / be appeared] in the future. They could be different and even more exciting than now, but one thing will remain the same: they will help us laugh, relax, and learn.

11 (A)~(C)에서 어법상 옳은 것을 바르게 짝지은 것은?

① calling – it – appear
② calling – it – be appeared
③ calling – them – be appeared
④ called – them – appear
⑤ called – it – appear

서답형

12 Write the reason why we can read webtoons anytime, anywhere on our phone or computer. Use the phrase 'it's because'.

➡ _____

13 다음 중 위 글을 읽고 답할 수 <u>없는</u> 것은?

① When was a new type of cartoon developed?

② Where are webtoons published?

③ What do we call a new type of cartoon?

④ Who usually sees webtoons?

⑤ What do cartoons help us to do?

[14~16] 다음 글을 읽고 물음에 답하시오.

> Boat!
> Land!
> Did you laugh when you saw the cartoon above? If so, the cartoonist was successful. Cartoonists are the people ___(A)___ make cartoons. They want to catch your interest, and usually, make you laugh with simple language and creative drawings.
> People have made cartoons for hundreds of years. There are many types of cartoons, and they play different roles.

14 빈칸 (A)에 들어갈 말로 적절한 것을 <u>모두</u> 고르시오.

① which   ② that   ③ whom
④ who   ⑤ what

15 다음 중 위 글에 이어질 내용으로 가장 적절한 것은?

① the reason why people see cartoons

② the number of cartoonists

③ various types of cartoons

④ how cartoons have survived for hundreds of years

⑤ what cartoonists want to draw

서답형

16 다음과 같이 풀이되는 말을 위 글에서 찾아 쓰시오.

> achieving results you wanted or hoped for

➡ _____

[17~20] 다음 글을 읽고 물음에 답하시오.

> One form of cartoon is a picture with a few words. It is sometimes called a "gag cartoon." The cartoonist makes a funny character, and the character makes you laugh by doing or saying silly things.
> Another type of cartoon is called a caricature. In a caricature, some parts of a character are different or bigger than usual. Look at the picture on the right. Which parts of the man's face jump out at you? Artists have used this type of cartoon to make fun of well-known people.

서답형

17 How do the characters in a gag cartoon make people laugh? Answer in English with a full sentence.

➡ _____

_____

18 다음 중 위 글을 바르게 이해한 사람은?

① 은지: Cartoonists don't want to draw gag cartoons.

② 준석: There are more than two types of cartoons.

③ 지민: It is unnatural to laugh when we see a character in a gag cartoon.

④ 태형: Cartoonists who draw caricatures aren't interested in famous people.

⑤ 정국: Artists draw a caricature to make someone feel good.

19 다음 중 개그 만화에서 볼 수 있는 것은?

① A man's eyes jumping out at readers

② Two characters talking too much

③ A picture with no words

④ A character saying stupid things

⑤ A character's arms bigger than usual

서답형

20 What do we call a picture with a few words? Answer in English with six words.

➡ _____

[21~26] 다음 글을 읽고 물음에 답하시오.

When several cartoon pictures come together and tell a story, we have a comic strip. Comic strips have been in newspapers for many years. They are often just (A) [amusing / amused] stories. People have also used comic strips for education. Comics can make information clearer and easier to learn. You have probably seen comic history or science books.

You have surely seen many cartoon movies, or animated movies, (B)[too / either]. These are very popular among people of all ages. Movement and sounds are added to pictures, so they come (C)[live / alive]. Artists and writers can develop fascinating characters and tell interesting stories through animation.

① In the 1990s, a new type of cartoon was developed. ② Webtoons are published online, so you can read them anytime, anywhere on your phone or computer. ③ They are very popular, and some of them are even made into TV dramas or movies. ④

New forms of cartoons may appear in the future. ⑤ They could be different and even more exciting than now, but (D)one thing will remain the same: they will help us laugh, relax, and learn.

21 다음 중 주어진 문장이 들어가기에 가장 적절한 곳은?

It is called a webtoon.

①   ②   ③   ④   ⑤

22 (A)~(C)에서 어법상 옳은 것을 바르게 짝지은 것은?

① amused – either – alive
② amused – too – live
③ amusing – too – alive
④ amusing – too – live
⑤ amusing – either – alive

서답형

23 다음 물음에 완전한 문장의 영어로 답하시오.

Q: What is a comic strip made of and what does it tell?

➡ _____

_____

서답형

24 Write the reason why people have used comic strips for education. Use the phrase 'It's because'.

➡ _____

_____

중요

25 다음 중 위 글을 읽고 답할 수 있는 것은?

① How many cartoon pictures do we need to make a comic strip?
② Who makes the animated movies?
③ Where can we read webtoons?
④ How many webtoons were made into TV dramas or movies?
⑤ How do cartoons make people laugh?

서답형

26 밑줄 친 (D)가 의미하는 것을 위 글에서 찾아 우리말로 쓰시오.

➡ _____

[01~07] 다음 글을 읽고 물음에 답하시오.

Boat!

Land!

Did you laugh when you saw the cartoon above? (A)If so, the cartoonist was successful. Cartoonists are the people who make cartoons. They want to catch your interest, and usually, make you laugh with simple language and creative drawings.

_____(a)_____

There are many types of cartoons, and (B) they play different roles. One form of cartoon is a picture with a few words. It is sometimes called a "gag cartoon." The cartoonist makes a funny character, and the character makes you laugh by doing or saying silly things.

Another type of cartoon is called a caricature. In a caricature, some parts of a character are different or bigger than usual. Look at the picture on the right. Which parts of the man's face jump out at you? Artists have used this type of cartoon to make fun of well-known people.

01 다음 두 문장을 하나의 문장으로 빈칸 (a)에 쓰시오. 주어진 단어를 활용하시오.

> People started to make cartoons hundreds of years ago. They still make cartoons now. (for)

➡ _____

02 What do cartoonists use to make people laugh? Answer in English with a full sentence.

➡ _____

03 밑줄 친 (A)가 의미하는 것을 구체적으로 쓰시오.

➡ _____

04 밑줄 친 (B)가 가리키는 것을 위 글에서 찾아 쓰시오.

➡ _____

05 According to the passage, what does a gag cartoon make us do? Answer in English with a full sentence.

➡ _____

06 Which type of cartoon is this picture? Answer in English with a full sentence.

Take a look. We are famous.

➡ _____

07 다음 중 위 글의 내용과 일치하지 <u>않는</u> 것을 두 군데 찾아 바르게 고치시오.

> Cartoonists make cartoons. They make you laugh with simple language and creative drawings. There are various types of cartoons. One form of cartoon is a picture with many words. There is a funny character which makes you laugh by doing wise things. Caricature is another type of cartoon. In a caricature, some parts of a character are bigger than usual.

_____ ➡ _____

_____ ➡ _____

[08~13] 다음 글을 읽고 물음에 답하시오.

When several cartoon pictures come together and tell a story, we have a comic strip. Comic strips have been in newspapers for many years. They are often just amusing stories. People have also used comic strips for education. Comics can make information clearer and easier to learn. You have probably seen comic history or science books.

You have surely seen many cartoon movies, or animated movies, too. These are very popular among people of all ages. Movement and sounds are added to pictures, so they come alive. Artists and writers can develop fascinating characters and tell interesting stories through animation.

In the 1990s, a new type of cartoon was developed. It is called a webtoon. Webtoons are published online, so you can read them anytime, anywhere on your phone or computer. They are very popular, and some of them are even made into TV dramas or movies.

New forms of cartoons may appear in the future. They could be different and even more exciting than now, but one thing will remain the same: they will help us laugh, relax, and learn.

08 If you want to deliver information more clearly, what type of cartoon can you use?

➡ _____

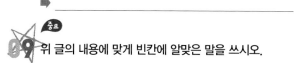

09 위 글의 내용에 맞게 빈칸에 알맞은 말을 쓰시오.

In the way that _____,
pictures come alive.

➡ _____

10 What can artists and writers do through animation? Answer in English with eleven words.

➡ _____
_____

11 When were webtoons developed? Answer in English with a full sentence.

➡ _____

12 위 글의 내용에 맞게 대화의 빈칸을 채우시오.

A: Look! There are some cartoon pictures and they tell a story. What is it?
B: It is called _____.
A: How is the story?
B: It is usually _____. It is also used for _____.

13 위 글의 내용에 맞게 빈칸에 알맞은 말을 쓰시오.

Although new forms of cartoons may appear in the future, they _____ just like now.

➡ _____

해석

My Speaking Portfolio – Step 3

Here is a useful tip for you. I've washed my sneakers this way many times.
= 현재완료 (경험)

First, put the sneakers, warm water, and washing powder in a plastic bag.
동명사

Then close the bag and leave it for seven minutes. Lastly, take the sneakers
= Next. And that

out of the bag and wash them. They'll look like new sneakers.
= the sneakers   look like+명사: ~처럼 보이다

구문해설 ・useful: 유용한 ・sneakers: 운동화 ・washing powder: 세제 ・plastic bag: 비닐봉지

여기 당신을 위한 유용한 조언이 있어요. 나는 내 운동화를 여러 번 이런 방식으로 세탁했어요. 첫째, 운동화, 온수, 그리고 세제를 비닐봉지에 넣으세요. 그리고 비닐봉지를 묶어 7분 동안 두세요. 마지막으로 운동화를 비닐봉지에서 꺼내 씻으세요. 그들은 새 운동화처럼 보일 거예요.

My Writing Portfolio

Giyeong, My Favorite Cartoon Character

My favorite cartoon character is Giyeong of *Black Rubber Shoes*. He is an elementary school student. He is humorous and kind. However, he is not very
그러나

smart and sometimes causes trouble. I like him because he looks on the bright
주어 he에 수의 일치   이유를 이끄는 접속사

side of everything and always tries to help others.
다른 사람들

구문해설 ・favorite: 가장 좋아하는 ・elementary school: 초등학교 ・cause: 유발하다
・look on: ~을 바라보다

기영, 내가 가장 좋아하는 만화 캐릭터

내가 가장 좋아하는 만화 캐릭터는 〈검정 고무신〉의 기영이다. 그는 초등학교 학생이다. 그는 재미있고 친절하다. 하지만, 그는 별로 똑똑하지 않고, 때때로 말썽을 피운다. 그는 모든 것의 긍정적인 면을 보고 항상 다른 이들을 도우려 하기 때문에 나는 그를 좋아한다.

Words in Action B

The Best Animated Movie for Children's Education

Animals welcome the city's plan to build an amusement park in the forest.
to부정사의 형용사적 용법(the city's plan 수식)

However, they soon suffer from serious pollution. An old elephant makes a
곧

suggestion. The animals and the city reach an agreement to create a better world for everyone.

구문해설 ・amusement park: 놀이공원 ・suffer from: ~으로 고통 받다 ・suggestion: 제안
・reach an agreement: 합의점에 도달하다

아이들의 교육을 위한 최고의 만화영화

동물들은 숲속에 놀이공원을 지으려는 도시의 계획을 환영한다. 하지만, 그들은 곧 심각한 오염에 시달린다. 나이 든 코끼리가 한 가지 제안을 한다. 동물들과 도시는 모든 이들을 위한 더 좋은 세상을 만들기 위한 합의에 이른다.

영역별 핵심문제

Words & Expressions

01 다음 영영풀이가 가리키는 것을 고르시오.

> a type of lotion that you put on your skin to protect it from being damaged by the sun

① sunscreen   ② raincoat
③ sauce   ④ sneaker
⑤ plate

02 다음 중 밑줄 친 부분의 뜻풀이가 바르지 <u>않은</u> 것은?

① He made a <u>silly</u> mistake. 어리석은
② Why don't you <u>boil</u> water first? 끓이다
③ <u>Spread</u> butter on the bread with the knife. 번지다
④ <u>Cartoons</u> are often fun for people of all ages. 만화
⑤ It's hard to <u>choose</u> just one flavor of ice cream. 고르다

03 다음 우리말을 주어진 단어를 이용하여 영작하시오.

(1) Emma는 오렌지 주스를 유리잔에 부어 그것을 마셨다. (glass, drank)

  ➡ _____

_____

(2) 우리는 설거지해야 할 많은 접시가 있다. (wash, of)

  ➡ _____

(3) 나는 달걀과 많은 채소를 볶는 것을 좋아한다. (eggs, lots)

  ➡ _____

04 다음 문장의 빈칸에 들어갈 말을 〈보기〉에서 골라 쓰시오. (필요한 경우 형태를 바꿀 것.)

> ┤ 보기 ├
> of all ages / watch out / comic strip / jump out at me / come together

(1) When technology and imagination _____, amazing inventions can be created.
(2) His first _____ was published in 1972.
(3) _____ for cars when you ride a bike.
(4) The singer is loved by people _____.
(5) The red balloon really _____.

05 다음 주어진 문장의 밑줄 친 down과 같은 의미로 쓰인 것은?

> You look <u>down</u>. What's wrong with you?

① He bent <u>down</u> to pick up the paper.
② She jumped <u>down</u> off the table.
③ Today, I feel a little <u>down</u>.
④ The stone rolled <u>down</u> the hill.
⑤ Listening to the music, tears ran <u>down</u> on my face.

Conversation

06 다음 대화가 자연스럽게 이어지도록 순서대로 배열하시오.

> (A) Yes, I've climbed to the top of the mountain twice.
> (B) Have you ever been to Sokcho?
> (C) Really? Then, you've climbed Mt. Seorak, haven't you?
> (D) Yes, I have. Actually my uncle lives there, so I visit him every year.

➡ _____

[07~08] 다음 대화를 읽고 물음에 답하시오.

Emily: Oh, look at the long line at the box office.

Tony: Yeah, there's a ticket machine over there.

_____ (A) _____

Emily: All right. Do you know how to use the machine?

Tony: Sure. It's easy. First, select a movie and a showtime.

Emily: Okay. We can watch the seven o'clock show. Then what?

Tony: Well, select the number of tickets and choose our seats.

Emily: Okay. Two tickets, and I want to sit in the back.

Tony: No problem. Lastly, pay for the tickets.

Emily: It's very simple.

07 위 대화의 빈칸 (A)에 들어갈 말로 어색한 것은?

① Let's buy the tickets from the machine.

② How about buying the tickets from the machine?

③ Why don't we buy the tickets from the machine?

④ I think we can buy the tickets from the machine.

⑤ Have you bought the tickets from the machine?

08 위 대화의 내용과 일치하도록 표를 완성하시오.

<How to Use a Ticket Machine>

Step	What to do
1	select (A)_____ and (B)_____
2	select the number of tickets and (C)_____
3	(D)_____

[09~11] 다음 대화를 읽고 물음에 답하시오.

Suji: Good morning, Chef Garcia!

Garcia: Hello, Suji. (A)나초 피자를 만들어 본 적 있나요?

Suji: Nacho pizza? No, I haven't.

Garcia: Kids will love it, and I'll tell you how to make @it.

Suji: Sounds good!

Garcia: It's easy to make. First, put nacho chips on a plate and spread pizza sauce on ⓑ them.

Suji: Okay. Let me help you with the pizza sauce.

Garcia: Thanks. Next, put some ham, onions, and peppers on top.

Suji: Okay. Then?

Garcia: Add cheese and bake for about 12 minutes in the oven.

Suji: I can't wait to taste it!

09 위 대화의 밑줄 친 (A)의 우리말을 6단어로 영작하시오.

➡ _____

10 위 대화의 밑줄 친 @와 ⓑ가 가리키는 것을 각각 찾아 쓰시오.

➡ @ _____ ⓑ _____

11 위 대화의 내용과 일치하지 않는 것은?

① 수지는 나초 피자를 만들어 본 적이 없다.

② 나초 피자를 만들기는 쉽다.

③ 나초 피자를 만들기 위해 접시 위에 나초 칩을 올려놓고 그 위에 피자 소스를 바른다.

④ 햄, 양파, 피망으로 피자 소스를 만든다.

⑤ 치즈를 올리고 약 12분 동안 오븐에서 굽는다.

12 다음 대화의 내용과 일치하지 <u>않는</u> 것은?

> Anna: Do you know how to make fried rice?
>
> Jinsu: Sure. It's easy. First, cut the vegetables into small pieces.
>
> Anna: Okay. What do you do next?
>
> Jinsu: Put some oil in the pan. Then, fry the vegetables with rice.
>
> Anna: Wow, it's really simple.

① Jinsu knows how to make fried rice.

② To make fried rice, Anna and Jinsu need vegetables, oil, and rice.

③ Before putting some oil in the pan, Anna needs to cut the vegetables into small pieces.

④ Anna needs to fry the small pieces of vegetables with rice after putting some oil in the pan.

⑤ Anna helps Jinsu cut the vegetables into small pieces.

13 다음 대화의 빈칸 (A)~(C)에 들어갈 알맞은 말을 고르시오

> Jane: Kevin, you look (A)[up / down].
>
> Kevin: Nothing (B)[seriously / serious]. Sometimes my feelings change a lot.
>
> Jane: I understand. Many teens have ups and downs in their feelings.
>
> Kevin: Oh, really?
>
> Jane: Have you watched the animated movie "Shining Days"?
>
> Kevin: No, I haven't. Why do you ask?
>
> Jane: It is about a teenager's feelings. It will help you (C)[understand / understanding] your feelings better.
>
> Kevin: That sounds good! I'll watch it.

➡ (A)_____ (B)_____ (C)_____

Grammar

14 다음 중 동사의 과거분사형으로 바르지 <u>않은</u> 것은?

① put – put　　　② read – read

③ do – done　　　④ cut – cut

⑤ drive – driven

15 다음 우리말을 영어로 바르게 옮긴 것은?

> 나의 아버지는 전에 미국에 가 본 적이 없다.

① My father didn't go to America.

② My father doesn't have been to America before.

③ My father has gone to America now.

④ My father has not visited America once.

⑤ My father hasn't been to America before.

16 다음 빈칸에 들어갈 말이 바르게 짝지어진 것은?

> • Kevin has been in U.K. _____.
> • Kevin has been in U.K. _____ this Monday.
> • Kevin has been in U.K. _____ a week.

① for – since – yet

② once – since – for

③ yet – for – since

④ yet – since – for

⑤ ago – for – since

17 주어진 어구를 바르게 배열하여 다음 우리말을 영어로 쓰시오. 필요하다면 어형을 바꾸시오.

> 무대 위에서 뛰고 있는 소년을 아니?
> (know / jump / you / on / the boy / the stage / do)

➡ _____

18 다음 중 어법상 올바른 문장은?

① When have you seen the singer?
② I have called him two hours ago.
③ I didn't have talked with her for a while.
④ Ryan has been to Spain with his family.
⑤ She has lived in New York when she was young.

19 다음 두 문장을 하나의 문장으로 바르게 쓴 것은?

> I forgot her address. I still can't remember it.

① I have remembered her address.
② I want to remember her address.
③ I forgot her address.
④ I have forgotten her address.
⑤ I haven't forgotten her address.

20 다음 중 빈칸에 들어갈 동사 bake의 형태가 다른 하나는?

① I know the girl _____ some bread.
② They ate _____ potatoes for lunch.
③ What is she _____?
④ We saw her _____ many cookies.
⑤ She needed _____ soda.

21 주어진 단어를 활용하여 다음 우리말을 영어로 쓰시오.

> 나는 작년부터 이 문제를 가지고 있었어.
> (have / problem)

➡ _____

22 주어진 문장의 밑줄 친 부분과 쓰임이 같은 것은?

> I have never seen an elephant.

① Paul has lost his laptop computer.
② Julian has gone to his home.
③ They have been married for 15 years.
④ How long have you stayed here?
⑤ She has used the chair once.

23 다음 중 밑줄 친 부분을 바르게 고치지 않은 것은?

> ⓐ Korea has been in a war in 1952.
> ⓑ Cynthia played tennis since 2011.
> ⓒ I saw my favorite singer once until now.
> ⓓ My cousin has lost his cellphone a week ago.
> ⓔ Who has put this paper on the table the other day?

① ⓐ: was
② ⓑ: has played
③ ⓒ: have seen
④ ⓓ: lost
⑤ ⓔ: putted

24 다음 빈칸에 알맞은 말을 쓰시오.

> 그 도난당한 차는 옆 블록에서 발견되었어.
> The _____ car was _____ on the next block.

25 다음 두 문장을 하나의 문장으로 표현하시오.

> They went to the library at noon. They are still in the library.

➡ _____

Reading

[26~28] 다음 글을 읽고 물음에 답하시오.

Boat!

Land!

Did you laugh when you saw the cartoon above? ① If so, the cartoonist was successful. ② They want to catch your interest, and usually, make you laugh with simple language and creative drawings. ③ People (A)have made cartoons for hundreds of years. ④ There are many types of cartoons, and they play different roles. ⑤ One form of cartoon is a picture with a few words. It is sometimes called a "gag cartoon." The cartoonist makes a funny character, and the character makes you laugh by doing or saying silly things.

26 다음 중 주어진 문장이 들어가기에 가장 적절한 곳은?

> Cartoonists are the people who make cartoons.

①   ②   ③   ④   ⑤

27 다음 중 밑줄 친 (A)와 쓰임이 같은 것은?

① I have been to Paris twice.

② They have gone out.

③ He has read the book for an hour.

④ We haven't met each other before.

⑤ She has lost her key.

28 다음 중 위 글의 내용과 일치하는 것은?

① A cartoonist is successful when he or she makes us sad.

② Cartoonists use language which is not simple.

③ Cartoons were made recently.

④ Cartoonists make us laugh with creative drawings.

⑤ We can find lots of words in a gag cartoon.

[29~30] 다음 글을 읽고 물음에 답하시오.

Another type of cartoon is called a caricature. In a caricature, some parts of a character are different or bigger than   (A) . Look at the picture on the right. Which parts of the man's face jump out at you? Artists have used this type of cartoon to make fun of well-known people.

When several cartoon pictures come together and tell a story, we have a comic strip. Comic strips have been in newspapers for many years. They are often just amusing stories. People have also used comic strips for education. Comics can make information clearer and easier to learn. You have probably seen comic history or science books.

29 다음과 같이 풀이되는 말을 빈칸 (A)에 쓰시오.

> normal; happening most often

➡ _____

30 다음 중 위 글의 앞에 나올 내용으로 가장 적절한 것은?

① lives of many cartoonists

② a type of cartoon made into movies

③ types of cartoon

④ how to make cartoons

⑤ reasons why cartoons are popular

[01~02] 다음 대화를 읽고 물음에 답하시오.

Jane: Kevin, you look down.

Kevin: Nothing ⓐserious. Sometimes my feelings change a lot.

Jane: I understand. Many teens have ⓑups and downs in their feelings.

Kevin: Oh, really?

Jane: Have you ⓒwatching the animated movie "Shining Days"?

Kevin: No, I ⓓhaven't. Why do you ask?

Jane: It is about a teenager's feelings. It will help you ⓔunderstand your feelings better.

Kevin: That sounds good! I'll watch it.

✎ 출제율 90%

01 위 대화의 밑줄 친 ⓐ~ⓔ 중 어법상 어색한 것을 찾아 바르게 고치시오.

_____ ➡ _____

✎ 출제율 100%

02 위 대화를 읽고 대답할 수 없는 것은?

① What does Kevin look like?

② According to Jane, what do teenagers have in their feelings?

③ What does Jane suggest to Kevin?

④ What kind of movie is "Shining Days"?

⑤ How can watching "Shining Days" help Kevin?

[03~05] 다음 대화를 읽고 물음에 답하시오.

Emily: Oh, look at the long line at the box office.

Tony: Yeah, there's a ticket machine over there. Let's buy the tickets from the machine.

Emily: All right. Do you know how to use the machine?

Tony: Sure. It's easy. First, select a movie and a showtime.

Emily: Okay. We can watch the seven o'clock show. Then what?

Tony: Well, select the number of tickets and choose our seats.

Emily: Okay. Two tickets, and I want to sit in the back.

Tony: No problem. Lastly, pay for the tickets.

Emily: It's very simple.

✎ 출제율 90%

03 From what do Tony and Emily want to buy the tickets?

➡ _____

✎ 출제율 95%

04 When will Tony and Emily watch the movie?

➡ _____

✎ 출제율 85%

05 Where does Emily want to sit?

➡ _____

✎ 출제율 95%

06 다음 대화에서 (A)~(E)가 자연스럽게 이어지도록 순서대로 배열하시오.

Suji: Good morning, Chef Garcia!

Garcia: Hello, Suji. Have you ever made nacho pizza?

Suji: Nacho pizza? No, I haven't.

Garcia: Kids will love it, and I'll tell you how to make it.

Suji: Sounds good!

(A) Okay. Let me help you with the pizza sauce.

(B) Lastly, add cheese and bake for about 12 minutes in the oven.

(C) It's easy to make. First, put nacho chips on a plate and spread pizza sauce on them.

(D) Okay. Then?

(E) Thanks. Next, put some ham, onions, and peppers on top.

➡ _____

[07~09] 다음 대화를 읽고 물음에 답하시오.

Anna: Do you know how to make fried rice?

Jinsu: Sure. It's easy. First, (A)[cut / put] the vegetables into small pieces.

Anna: Okay. What do you do next?

Jinsu: (B)[Bake / Put] some oil in the pan. Then, (C)[fry / spread] the vegetables with rice.

Anna: Wow, it's really simple.

07 위 대화의 빈칸 (A)~(C)에 들어갈 말로 바르게 짝지어진 것은?

	(A)	(B)	(C)
①	cut	Bake	fry
②	cut	Put	spread
③	cut	Put	fry
④	put	Put	spread
⑤	put	Bake	fry

08 What should Anna and Jinsu do after putting some oil in the pan?

➡ _____

09 What ingredients should Anna and Jinsu prepare to make fried rice?

➡ _____

10 다음 짝지어진 대화가 <u>어색한</u> 것은?

① A: Have you ever cooked fried rice?
   B: Yes, I have cooked it many times.

② A: I have never been to Beijing. How about you?
   B: I went there last summer.

③ A: Have you ever touched a snake?
   B: Yes, I did. I was so scared.

④ A: You have been to Canada. Haven't you?
   B: No, I haven't.

⑤ A: Have you been to Busan?
   B: Busan? No, I've never been there.

11 다음 문장에서 쓰인 현재완료의 용법이 나머지와 <u>다른</u> 하나는?

① We have just eaten dinner.

② Has the concert already started?

③ They haven't met each other yet.

④ I have had a headache for an hour.

⑤ She has just found the ticket.

12 다음 중 어법상 올바른 것은?

① The man has made a big mistake at work yesterday.

② Mr. Jones is practicing the flute for three years.

③ I don't want to eat freezing food.

④ The walking boy with his friends is my brother.

⑤ Cindy has been interested in painting for many years.

13 출제율95%

다음 빈칸에 들어갈 말이 바르게 짝지어진 것은?

> • The _____ chicken will be served.
> • Do you know the _____ boy?

① cook – shout
② cooking – shouted
③ cooking – shouting
④ cooked – shouted
⑤ cooked – shouting

14 출제율100%

다음 빈칸에 들어갈 시제가 다른 하나는?

① Kelly _____ her laptop computer yesterday. She was relieved.
② Tom _____ the book ten times until now. He really likes reading it.
③ Brad wants to know when Angela _____ home last night.
④ Molly _____ some pictures of Zach when they traveled together.
⑤ When I was young, I _____ a lamb.

15 출제율95%

주어진 동사를 어법에 맞게 빈칸에 쓰시오.

(1) I met a boy _____ Chris last week. (name)
(2) When are you going to fix the _____ refrigerator? (break)
(3) The _____ news made her say nothing. (surprise)

16 출제율90%

주어진 단어를 활용하여 다음 우리말을 영어로 쓰시오. 필요하다면 어형을 바꾸시오.

> 나는 추천된 책을 살 거야.
> (the / I / book / will / recommend / buy)

➡ _____

17 출제율95%

현재완료 시제를 이용하여 다음 우리말을 영어로 쓰시오.

> Smith씨는 작년부터 내게 영어를 가르쳐 주고 있다.

➡ _____

[18~24] 다음 글을 읽고 물음에 답하시오.

When several cartoon pictures come together and tell a story, we have a comic strip. Comic strips have been in newspapers for many years. They are often just amusing stories. People have also used comic strips for education. Comics can make information clearer and easier ⓐto learn. You have probably seen comic history or science books.

You have surely seen many cartoon movies, or animated movies, too. These are very popular among people of all ages. Movement and sounds are added to pictures, so they come alive. Artists and writers can develop fascinating characters and tell ____(A)____ stories through animation.

In the 1990s, a new type of cartoon was developed. It is called a webtoon. Webtoons are published online, so you can read them anytime, anywhere on your phone or computer. They are very popular, and some of them are even made into TV dramas or movies.

New forms of cartoons may appear in the future. (B)They could be different and even more exciting than now, but one thing will remain the same: they will help us laugh, relax, and learn.

18 출제율90%

주어진 단어를 어법에 맞게 빈칸 (A)에 쓰시오.

> interest

➡ _____

19 출제율90%

밑줄 친 (B)가 가리키는 것을 위 글에서 찾아 쓰시오.

➡ _____

20 출제율90%

다음 중 밑줄 친 ⓐ와 쓰임이 같은 것은?

① We want you to visit your uncle.
② It is difficult to learn a foreign language.
③ He went to the market to buy milk.
④ The problem is easy to solve.
⑤ You need something warm to wear.

21 출제율90%

Choose one that is NOT true about a comic strip.

① There are history books using it.
② It has been used for education.
③ The stories are amusing.
④ It is published online.
⑤ It is made of several cartoon pictures.

22 출제율90%

According to the passage, what makes pictures come alive? Answer in English with a full sentence.

➡ _____

_____

23 출제율100%

다음 중 위 글의 내용을 잘못 이해한 사람은?

① Sam: In order to make a comic strip, I need some cartoon pictures and a story.
② Tom: I will look into newspapers to find a comic strip.
③ Jim: There are many science books using comic strips.
④ June: Only children like animated movies.
⑤ Paul: Sometimes comics are used to teach history easily.

24 출제율95%

다음 중 위 글을 읽고 답할 수 없는 것은?

① What does a comic strip have?
② How do pictures come alive?
③ What do writers tell through animation?
④ How long does it take to make a comic strip?
⑤ What is very popular among people of all ages?

[25~26] 다음 글을 읽고 물음에 답하시오.

My favorite cartoon character is Giyeong of *Black Rubber Shoes*. He is an elementary school student. He is humorous and kind. ___(A)___, he is not very smart and sometimes causes trouble. I like him because he looks on the bright side of everything and always tries to help others.

25 출제율95%

다음 중 빈칸 (A)에 들어갈 말로 가장 적절한 것은?

① In addition   ② However
③ For example   ④ Moreover
⑤ Fortunately

26 출제율90%

Write the reason why the writer likes the cartoon character. Answer in English with a full sentence.

➡ _____

_____

서술형 실전문제

Jane: Kevin, you look down.

Kevin: Nothing serious. Sometimes my feelings change a lot.

Jane: I understand. Many teens have ups and downs in their feelings.

Kevin: Oh, really?

Jane: Have you watched the animated movie "Shining Days"?

Kevin: No, I haven't. Why do you ask?

Jane: It is about a teenager's feelings. It will help you understand your feelings better.

Kevin: That sounds good! I'll watch it.

01 Has Kevin seen "Shining Days"?

➡ _____

02 What kind of Movie is "Shining Days"?

➡ _____

03 How can watching "Shining Days" help Kevin?

➡ _____

04 다음 두 문장의 차이를 서술하시오.

(1) Amelia has been to Canada.
(2) Amelia has gone to Canada.

➡ _____
_____
_____

05 다음 두 문장을 하나의 문장으로 쓰시오.

I lost my favorite book. I don't have it now.

➡ _____

06 주어진 단어를 활용하여 다음 우리말을 영어로 쓰시오.

그 울고 있는 소년은 삶은 달걀을 다섯 개 먹었어요. (cry / boil)

➡ _____

07 다음은 한국을 방문한 Steve의 일기 중 일부이다. Steve의 경험을 말하는 문장을 완성하시오.

I _____ a lot of Korean food, but _____ sannakji yet. I want to eat it someday.

08 다음 빈칸에 알맞은 말을 쓰시오.

그녀는 떨리는 목소리로 "부끄러운 줄 아세요." 라고 그에게 말했다.
She told in _____, "Shame on you."

[09~10] 다음 글을 읽고 물음에 답하시오.

My favorite cartoon character is Giyeong of *Black Rubber Shoes*. He is an elementary school student. He is humorous and kind.

However, he is not very smart and sometimes causes trouble. I like him because he looks on the bright side of everything and always tries to help others.

09 What cartoon is the writer's favorite character from? Answer in English with a full sentence.

➡ _____

10 What's the character like? Answer in English with a full sentence.

➡ _____

_____

[11~13] 다음 글을 읽고 물음에 답하시오.

People have made cartoons for hundreds of years. There are many types of cartoons, and they play different roles. One form of cartoon is a picture with a few words. It is sometimes called a "gag cartoon." The cartoonist makes a funny character, and the character makes you laugh by doing or saying silly things.

Another type of cartoon is called a caricature. In a caricature, some parts of a character are different or bigger than usual. Look at the picture on the right. Which parts of the man's face jump out at you?
_____(A)_____
When several cartoon pictures come together and tell a story, we have a comic strip. Comic strips have been in newspapers for many years. They are often just amusing stories. People have also used comic strips for education.

11 주어진 글을 하나의 문장으로 빈칸 (A)에 쓰시오.

Artists used this type of cartoon to make fun of well-known people. They still use it.

➡ _____

_____

12 주어진 단어를 바르게 배열하여 위 글의 제목을 쓰시오.

(roles / types / their / various / of / and / cartoons)

➡ _____

_____

13 위 글의 내용에 맞게 빈칸에 알맞은 말을 쓰시오.

There are three types of cartoons in the passage. One is _____. A funny character in the cartoon _____ by doing and saying silly things. Another is _____. It is used to make fun of famous people. The other is _____. They have _____ stories.

14 Read the following paragraph and write the reason why artists have drawn a caricature. Answer in English with a full sentence.

Another type of cartoon is called a caricature. In a caricature, some parts of a character are different or bigger than usual. Look at the picture on the right. Which parts of the man's face jump out at you? Artists have used this type of cartoon to make fun of well-known people.

➡ _____

_____

01 다음 대화의 내용과 일치하도록 Kevin의 일기를 완성하시오.

Jane: Kevin, you look down.

Kevin: Nothing serious. Sometimes my feelings change a lot.

Jane: I understand. Many teens have ups and downs in their feelings.

Kevin: Oh, really?

Jane: Have you watched the animated movie "Shining Days"?

Kevin: No, I haven't. Why do you ask?

Jane: It is about a teenager's feelings. It will help you understand your feelings better.

Kevin: That sounds good! I'll watch it.

Mon, Nov 4th, 2019

Today, I was (A)_____ with nothing serious. These days, my feelings changed a lot. At that time, Jane came to me and understood my feeling, saying that many teens have (B)_____ in their feelings. To understand my feelings better, she suggested (C)_____. She explained that it is about (D)_____. It sounded good, so I decided to see this movie soon.

---

02 다음 만화 캐릭터에 관한 정보를 보며 글을 완성하시오.

- 캐릭터: Iron Man
  - from Tales of Suspense
  - a genius scientist
- 특징: - owns a weapon company
  - invented a suit of armor to save his life

- 좋아하는 이유:
  - is very rich
  - is the leader of the superhero team, the Avengers

My favorite cartoon character is _____ of _____. He is _____. He _____ and _____. I like _____ because _____.

단원별 모의고사

01 다음 영영풀이가 가리키는 것을 고르시오.

> a process of teaching and learning

① teacher   ② learner
③ classroom   ④ education
⑤ educator

02 다음 우리말에 맞게 주어진 어휘를 사용하여 영작하시오.

(1) Jake는 연극에서 산타 클로스 역할을 했다. (Santa Clause, role)

➡ _____

(2) 사람들이 나를 놀릴 때 화가 난다. (fun, angry)

➡ _____

(3) 채소를 작은 조각으로 자르세요. (cut, pieces)

➡ _____

03 다음 우리말을 주어진 단어를 이용하여 영작하시오.

(1) 축구 팀원들은 공통의 목표를 갖고 있다. (goal)

➡ _____

(2) 만화영화로 영어를 배우는 것은 재미있다. (it, animated)

➡ _____

(3) 삶에는 기복이 있다. (there, ups)

➡ _____

04 다음 문장의 빈칸에 들어갈 말을 〈보기〉에서 골라 쓰시오.

> ┤ 보기 ├
> movement / amusing / publish / probably

(1) I like to listen to _____ stories on the radio.

(2) The old lady _____ knows more about the building than anyone.

(3) The cat made a sudden _____ and caught a mouse.

(4) They agreed to _____ the new novel next year.

[05~07] 다음 대화를 읽고 물음에 답하시오.

Suji: Good morning, Chef Garcia!

Garcia: Hello, Suji. Have you ever made nacho pizza?

Suji: Nacho pizza? No, I haven't.

Garcia: Kids will love it, and I'll tell you how to make it.

Suji: Sounds good!

Garcia: It's easy to make. First, put nacho chips on a plate and spread pizza sauce on them.

Suji: Okay. (A)Let me help you with the pizza sauce.

Garcia: Thanks. Next, put some ham, onions, and peppers on top.

Suji: Okay. Then?

Garcia: Add cheese and bake for about 12 minutes in the oven.

Suji: (B)I can't wait to taste it!

05 위 대화의 밑줄 친 (A)와 바꾸어 쓸 수 있는 것은?

① I'll give you a hand with the pizza sauce.
② I want you to help me with the pizza sauce.
③ Would you help me with the pizza sauce?
④ I need your help with the pizza sauce.
⑤ Can you give me your hand with the pizza sauce?

06 위 대화의 밑줄 친 (B)와 바꾸어 쓸 수 있는 것은?

① I don't want to wait to taste it.
② I don't like to taste it.
③ I'm not good at tasting it.
④ I'm looking forward to tasting it.
⑤ I haven't tasted it.

07 위 대화의 내용과 일치하도록 빈칸을 완성하시오.

<How to make nacho pizza>

Step	Procedure
1	put _____ on a plate
2	_____ pizza sauce on the nacho chips
3	put _____ on top
4	add _____ and bake for _____ in the oven

[08~10] 다음 대화를 읽고 물음에 답하시오.

Jane: Kevin, you look down.
Kevin: Nothing serious. Sometimes my feelings change a lot.
Jane: ⓐ I understand. Many teens have _____(A)_____ in their feelings.
Kevin: ⓑ Oh, really?
Jane: ⓒ Have you watched the animated movie "Shining Days"?
Kevin: ⓓ No, I haven't. Why do you ask?
Jane: ⓔ It will help you understand your feelings better.
Kevin: That sounds good! I'll watch it.

08 위 대화의 빈칸 (A)에 '기복'을 나타내는 표현을 3단어로 완성하시오.

➡ _____

09 위 대화의 ⓐ~ⓔ 중 주어진 문장이 들어가기에 적절한 곳은?

It is about a teenager's feelings.

① ⓐ ② ⓑ ③ ⓒ ④ ⓓ ⑤ ⓔ

10 위 대화의 내용과 일치하지 <u>않는</u> 것은?

① Kevin은 기분이 안 좋아 보인다.
② Kevin은 때때로 감정이 많이 바뀌는 심각한 문제를 갖고 있다.
③ 많은 십대들이 감정의 기복이 있다.
④ Shining Days라는 만화영화는 십 대의 감정에 관한 것이다.
⑤ Jane은 Shining Days라는 영화가 Kevin의 감정을 더 잘 이해하도록 도와줄 것이라고 생각한다.

[11~12] 다음 대화를 읽고 물음에 답하시오.

Emily: Oh, look at the long line at the box office.
Tony: Yeah, there's a ticket machine over there. Let's buy the tickets from the machine.
Emily: All right. (A)그 기계를 어떻게 쓰는지 아니?
Tony: Sure. It's easy. First, select a movie and a showtime.
Emily: Okay. We can watch the seven o'clock show. Then what?
Tony: Well, select the number of tickets and choose our seats.
Emily: Okay. Two tickets, and I want to sit in the back.
Tony: No problem. Lastly, pay for the tickets.
Emily: It's very simple.

11 위 대화의 밑줄 친 (A)의 우리말을 <보기>에 주어진 단어를 모두 사용하여 영작하시오.

┌─ 보기 ┐
know / to / you / machine / the / do / how / use
└────────┘

➡ _____

12 위 대화의 내용과 일치하는 것은?

① Emily and Tony are going to buy their tickets at the ticket counter.

② Emily and Tony are going to sit in the middle.

③ Emily and Tony have to choose seats before they select the showtime.

④ Emily already knows how to buy tickets using the ticket machine.

⑤ Emily and Tony have to pay for the tickets after choosing their seats.

13 다음 빈칸에 들어갈 말로 가장 적절한 것은?

Linda hasn't found her car key _____.

① just   ② already   ③ ago
④ yet   ⑤ before

14 다음 중 주어진 문장의 밑줄 친 부분과 쓰임이 같은 것은?

Where can I find a recycling bin?

① Can you see the crying baby?

② I heard someone calling my name.

③ Who shot the flying bird?

④ There are boys flying kites.

⑤ Diana couldn't find her sleeping bag.

15 다음 중 어법상 바르지 않은 것은?

① Look at the man playing the violin.

② Patrick has just finished the project.

③ Someone called you when you went out.

④ There was an unexpecting danger around us.

⑤ Susan has used this coffee machine for ten years.

16 주어진 단어를 활용하여 다음 우리말을 여덟 단어로 이루어진 한 문장으로 쓰시오.

이러한 표현들은 종종 구어체 영어에서 사용된다. (expression / use / speak)

➡ _____

[17~20] 다음 글을 읽고 물음에 답하시오.

Boat! Land!

Did you laugh when you saw the cartoon above? If so, the cartoonist was successful. Cartoonists are the people who make cartoons. They want to catch ①your interest, and usually, make you (A)[laugh / to laugh] with simple language and creative drawings.

People have made cartoons for hundreds of years. There are ②many types of cartoons, and they play different roles. One form of cartoon is a picture with a few words. It is sometimes called a "gag cartoon." The cartoonist makes a funny character, and the character makes you laugh by doing or (B)[say / saying] silly things.

Another type of cartoon is called a caricature. In a caricature, some parts of a character (C)[is / are] different or bigger than usual. Look at the picture on the right. Which parts of the man's face jump out at you? Artists have used this type of cartoon to make fun of well-known people.

When several cartoon pictures ③come together and tell a story, we have a comic strip. Comic strips have been in newspapers for many years. They are often just amusing stories. People ④have also used comic strips for education. Comics can make information clearer and ⑤more difficult to learn. You have probably seen comic history or science books.

17 ①~⑤ 중 글의 흐름상 어색한 것은?

①   ②   ③   ④   ⑤

18 (A)~(C)에서 어법상 알맞은 것을 쓰시오.

➡ (A) _____ (B) _____ (C) _____

19 How long have people made cartoons? Answer in English with a full sentence.

➡ _____

20 다음 중 위 글의 내용과 일치하는 것은?

① Cartoonists aren't interested in drawing creative things.
② People who draw a gag cartoon use as many words as possible.
③ There is only one picture in a comic strip.
④ We can't find a comic strip in newspapers now.
⑤ Comics help us understand history or science clearly.

[21~22] 다음 글을 읽고 물음에 답하시오.

You have surely seen many cartoon movies, or animated movies, too. These are very popular among people of all ages. Movement and sounds are added to pictures, so they come alive. Artists and writers can develop fascinating characters and tell interesting stories through animation.

In the 1990s, a new type of cartoon was developed. It is called a webtoon. Webtoons are published online, so you can read them anytime, anywhere on your phone or computer. They are very popular, and some of them are even made into TV dramas or movies.

New forms of cartoons may appear in the future. They could be different and even more exciting than now, but one thing will remain the same: they will help us laugh, relax, and learn.

21 위 글의 내용과 일치하지 <u>않는</u> 것은?

① Many cartoon movies are loved by people of all ages.
② Artists develop fascinating characters through animation.
③ Webtoons are read online.
④ Some TV dramas are based on webtoons.
⑤ The writer doesn't think a new type of cartoon will appear.

22 웹툰의 강점으로 가장 적절한 것은?

① They have funny characters.
② They are easy to read whenever you want.
③ They have the latest information.
④ They are loved by people of all ages.
⑤ They have sounds and movement.

Viva, South America!

 의사소통 기능

- 어떤 사실을 알고 있는지 묻고 답하기

  A: Do you know what the capital of Peru is?

  B: Yes. It's Lima.

- 놀람 표현하기

  A: You know what? Dogs can smile.

  B: Really? That's surprising.

언어 형식

- 최상급

  Suji is **the tallest** student in our school.

- 간접의문문

  Do you know **how old the building is**?

Words & Expressions

Key Words

- □ **across** [əkrɔ́:s] 튀 건너서, 가로질러
- □ **area** [έəriə] 뗑 지역
- □ **benefit** [bénəfit] 뗑 이익, 혜택
- □ **bridge** [bridʒ] 뗑 다리
- □ **capital** [kǽpətl] 뗑 수도
- □ **contain** [kəntéin] 띵 포함하다
- □ **continent** [kántənənt] 뗑 대륙
- □ **desert** [dézərt] 뗑 사막
- □ **especially** [ispéʃəli] 튀 특히
- □ **fantastic** [fæntǽstik] 톙 환상적인, 엄청난
- □ **flow** [flou] 띵 흐르다
- □ **Mars** [ma:rz] 뗑 화성
- □ **mountain range** 산맥
- □ **natural** [nǽtʃərəl] 톙 자연의, 천연의
- □ **ocean** [óuʃən] 뗑 대양
- □ **origin** [ɔ́:rədʒin] 뗑 기원, 원산
- □ **outer space** 우주, 외계
- □ **patience** [péiʃəns] 뗑 인내심
- □ **pepper** [pépər] 뗑 고추
- □ **per** [pər] 쩐 ~당, ~마다
- □ **pilot** [páilət] 뗑 조종사
- □ **prepare** [pripέər] 띵 준비하다
- □ **probably** [prábəbli] 튀 아마도
- □ **rainforest** [réinfɔ̀:rist] 뗑 열대 우림
- □ **ride** [raid] 띵 타다
- □ **roller coaster** 롤러코스터
- □ **salt flat** 솔트 플랫 (바닷물이 증발하고 남은 염분으로 이루어진 평원)
- □ **scared** [skɛərd] 톙 겁먹은, 무서워하는
- □ **sea level** 해수면
- □ **shy** [ʃai] 톙 수줍은, 부끄럼 타는
- □ **similar** [símələr] 톙 비슷한, 유사한
- □ **social studies** 사회(과목)
- □ **soil** [sɔil] 뗑 흙, 토양
- □ **sunrise** [sʌ́nraiz] 뗑 해돋이, 일출
- □ **sunscreen** [sʌ́nskrì:n] 뗑 자외선 차단제
- □ **through** [θru:] 쩐 ~을 통하여
- □ **tourist** [túərist] 뗑 관광객
- □ **unique** [ju:ní:k] 톙 독특한
- □ **view** [vju:] 뗑 전망
- □ **waterfall** [wɔ́tərfɔ̀l] 뗑 폭포
- □ **wide** [waid] 톙 넓은
- □ **wonder** [wʌ́ndər] 뗑 경이, 놀라움
- □ **work of art** 예술품, 미술품

Key Expressions

- □ **all year round** 일 년 내내, 연중
- □ **at first** 처음에는
- □ **be full of** ~으로 가득하다
- □ **be similar to** ~와 비슷하다
- □ **by oneself** 혼자서, 홀로
- □ **by the way** 그건 그렇고
- □ **go away** 없어지다
- □ **name after** ~을 따라 이름 짓다
- □ **throw a party** 파티를 열다
- □ **to be honest** 솔직히 말하면

Word Power

※ 서로 반대되는 뜻을 가진 어휘

□ **wide** (넓은) ↔ **narrow** (좁은)

□ **similar** (비슷한, 유사한) ↔ **different** (다른)

□ **benefit** (이익) ↔ **loss** (손실, 손해)

□ **sunrise** (해돋이, 일출) ↔ **sunset** (일몰)

□ **natural** (자연의) ↔ **artificial** (인공적인)

□ **unique** (독특한) ↔ **usual** (평범한)

□ **patient** (인내심 있는) ↔ **impatient** (성급한, 조급한)

□ **dry** (마른) ↔ **wet** (젖은)

※ 복합어

rain	snow	back	hand
rainbow (무지개)	**snowball** (눈뭉치)	**backache** (요통)	**handbag** (핸드백)
raincoat (우비)	**snowboard** (스노보드)	**background** (배경)	**handball** (핸드볼)
raindrop (빗방울)	**snowman** (눈사람)	**backpack** (배낭)	**handbook** (안내서)
rainfall (강우)	**snow storm** (눈보라)	**backseat** (뒷자리)	**handcart** (손수레)

English Dictionary

□ **across** 건너서, 가로질러
→ from one side of something to the other
어떤 것의 한쪽에서 다른 쪽으로

□ **benefit** 이익
→ an advantage that something gives you
무언가가 당신에게 주는 이점

□ **continent** 대륙
→ a large mass of land surrounded by sea
바다에 의해 둘러싸인 거대한 땅

□ **natural** 천연의, 자연의
→ existing in nature; not made or caused by humans
자연에 존재하는; 인간에 의해 만들어지거나 야기되지 않은

□ **origin** 기원
→ the point from which something starts; the cause of something
무언가가 시작되는 기점; 무언가의 원인

□ **patience** 인내심
→ the ability to stay calm without becoming angry
화내지 않고 침착함을 유지하는 능력

□ **pilot** 조종사
→ a person who operates the controls of an aircraft, especially as a job
특히 직업으로 항공기 조종장치를 작동하는 사람

□ **prepare** 준비하다
→ to make a plan for something that will happen
일어날 무언가에 대한 계획을 세우다

□ **rainforest** 열대 우림
→ a forest in a tropical area that receives a lot of rain
많은 비가 오는 열대 지역의 숲

□ **soil** 토양, 흙
→ the top layer of the earth in which plants and trees grow
식물들과 나무들이 자라는 땅의 표층

□ **waterfall** 폭포
→ a place where a stream or river falls from a high place, for example over a cliff or rock
예를 들어 절벽이나 바위와 같은 높은 장소로부터 냇물 또는 강이 떨어지는 장소

□ **wide** 넓은
→ measuring a large distance from one side to the other
한쪽에서 다른 쪽까지 멀리 떨어진 거리를 나타내는

□ **wonder** 경이, 놀라움
→ a thing that causes a feeling of great surprise or admiration
엄청난 놀라움 또는 예찬의 감정을 야기하는 것

서답형

01 다음 짝지어진 단어의 관계가 같도록 빈칸에 알맞은 말을 쓰시오.

> similar : different = _____ : narrow

중요

02 다음 중 밑줄 친 부분의 뜻풀이가 바르지 <u>않은</u> 것은?

① Asia is the largest <u>continent</u> in the world. 대륙
② My father usually <u>prepares</u> my dinner for me. 준비한다
③ He and his mother have very <u>similar</u> interests. 비슷한
④ The waterfall is a natural <u>wonder</u> which attracts lots of tourists. 호기심을 갖다
⑤ The planet gets a lot of oxygen from the <u>rainforest</u>. 열대 우림

서답형

03 다음 우리말에 맞게 빈칸에 알맞은 말을 쓰시오.

(1) 우리는 폭포를 볼 때까지 강 옆을 걸었다.
➡ We walked next to the river until we could see the _____.
(2) 이 지역의 사람들은 마실 물을 충분히 갖고 있지 않다.
➡ People in this _____ do not have enough water to drink.
(3) 내 동생은 강아지들에게 참을성이 없다.
➡ My sister has no _____ with the puppies.

04 다음 영영풀이가 가리키는 것을 고르시오.

> the ability to stay calm without becoming angry

① patience   ② view
③ wonder   ④ desert
⑤ capital

서답형

05 다음 문장의 빈칸에 들어갈 말을 〈보기〉에서 골라 쓰시오.

> ┤ 보기 ├
> similar / unique / probably / wide / across

(1) I will _____ be home by midnight.
(2) The river is so wide that we cannot swim _____.
(3) You can imagine how _____ the ocean is.
(4) Spanish is _____ to Portuguese in many ways.
(5) Jack has a _____ hair color, so anyone can easily find him.

중요

06 다음 문장에 공통으로 들어갈 말을 고르시오.

> • Coffee, tea and soft drinks usually _____ caffeine.
> • Each pack _____s twenty apple pies.
> • Actually, the gold medal _____s only 1.34 percent of gold.

① contain   ② flow
③ spend   ④ prepare
⑤ view

01 다음 짝지어진 단어의 관계가 같도록 빈칸에 알맞은 말을 쓰시오.

> teach : teacher = tour : _____

02 다음 우리말에 맞게 빈칸에 알맞은 말을 쓰시오.

(1) 그들은 우주 공간에 어떤 생명체들이 있다고 믿는다.
➡ They believe there are some creatures in _____ _____.

(2) 나는 폭포의 크기에 놀랐다.
➡ I was surprised at the size of the _____.

(3) 고추는 많은 비타민 C를 함유하고 있다.
➡ Peppers _____ a lot of vitamin C.

03 다음 문장의 빈칸에 들어갈 말을 〈보기〉에서 골라 알맞은 형태로 쓰시오.

┌── 보기 ├──
go away / all year round / be full of / by oneself / social studies / throw a party
└───────

(1) A lot of tourists visit Europe _____.
(2) I felt like all my stress _____.
(3) I don't want to stay here _____.
(4) At first, I didn't have any interest in _____.
(5) The park _____ children and their parents.
(6) Kathy decided to _____ this weekend.

04 다음 우리말에 맞게 주어진 단어를 사용하여 영작하시오.

(1) 감자 가격은 100 그램당 250원이다.
➡ _____
_____

(2) 사하라 사막의 기후는 매우 뜨겁고 건조하다.
➡ _____
_____

(3) 당신은 이 대륙에서 코알라들과 캥거루들을 찾을 수 있다.
➡ _____
_____

05 다음 우리말과 일치하도록 주어진 단어를 모두 배열하여 영작하시오.

(1) 이 지역은 일 년 내내 습하다.
(is / year / this / humid / all / region / round)
➡ _____
_____

(2) 한국의 동쪽에 큰 산맥이 있다.
(side / Korea / there / of / is / on / the / eastern / a / mountain / big / range)
➡ _____
_____

(3) 경기장은 흥분한 축구팬들로 가득했다.
(was / full / the / of / fans / soccer / stadium / excited)
➡ _____
_____

(4) 그건 그렇고 누가 이 영화를 감독했는지 알고 있니?
(know / by / do / way / who / the / directed / movie / the / you)
➡ _____
_____

Conversation

1 어떤 사실을 알고 있는지 묻고 답하기

> **A** Do you know what the capital of Peru is? 페루의 수도가 무엇인지 알고 있니?
> **B** Yes. It's Lima. 응. 리마야.

■ 어떤 것에 관해 알고 있는지 물을 때는 'Do you know ~?'를 이용해 표현한다. 특정 인물에 관해 알고 있는지 물을 때는 'Do you know who ~ is?'로 표현하고, 사물에 관해 알고 있는지 물을 때는 'Do you know what ~ is?'로 표현한다.

알고 있는지 묻기

- Do you know who wrote the book? 누가 그 책을 썼는지 알고 있니?
- Do you know where Fred put the bread? Fred가 어디에 빵을 두었는지 알고 있니?
- Guess who she is. 그녀가 누군지 맞혀 봐.
- Can you guess what it is? 이게 무엇인지 추측할 수 있겠니?

핵심 Check

1. 다음 우리말과 일치하도록 빈칸에 알맞은 말을 쓰시오.

(1) **A:** _____ _____ _____ that December 10 is Ray's birthday?

(너는 12월 10일이 Ray의 생일인 거 알고 있니?)

B: Yes. I'm going to _____ a surprise party for him.

(응. 나는 그를 위해 깜짝 파티를 열어 주려고 해.)

(2) **A:** Do you know _____ _____ _____ _____ is?

(너는 이 건물이 얼마나 오래되었는지 아니?)

B: No, I have no idea. (아니, 나는 몰라.)

2 놀람 표현하기

> **A** You know what? Dogs can smile. 그거 알아? 개들이 웃을 수 있대.
>
> **B** Really? That's surprising. 정말? 놀랍구나.

■ 상대방이 놀라운 사실이나 잘 몰랐던 사실을 설명할 때 That's surprising.(정말 놀랍구나.), 'What a surprise!' 또는 'I can't believe it.'을 통해 놀라움을 표현할 수 있다.

놀람 표현하기

- What a surprise! 정말 놀랍다!
- That's incredible. 굉장하다.
- I can't believe it. 믿을 수가 없어.
- You're kidding. 농담이겠죠.
- You're joking. 농담이겠죠.
- (It's) Unbelievable. 믿을 수 없어.
- That's amazing. 굉장하다.

핵심 Check

2. 다음 우리말과 일치하도록 빈칸에 알맞은 말을 쓰시오.

(1) **A:** _____ _____ _____? Koalas only spend 15 minutes a day on social activity.

(그거 알아? 코알라들은 하루에 15분만 사회활동에 쓴데.)

B: Really? That's _____. (정말? 놀랍구나.)

(2) **A:** I _____ that elephants use sand as sunscreen.

(나는 코끼리들이 모래를 자외선 차단제로 사용한다고 들었어.)

B: I _____ believe it. (정말 놀랍구나.)

Communication: Listen –Dialog 1

Sujin: Dad, I like this tomato soup.

Dad: I'm happy you like ❶it.

Sujin: ❷By the way, do you know ❸where the tomato was first grown?

Dad: Italy or somewhere in Europe?

Sujin: No, the tomato came from South America.

Dad: Really? How did you know ❹that?

Sujin: I learned it from Ms. Song, my ❺social studies teacher.

Dad: That's good.

Sujin: 아빠, 저는 이 토마토 수프가 마음에 들어요.

Dad: 네가 좋아하니 기쁘구나.

Sujin: 그런데 아빠는 토마토가 처음에 어디에서 재배되었는지 아세요?

Dad: 이탈리아나 유럽 어딘가가 아닐까?

Sujin: 아니에요, 토마토는 남아메리카에서 왔어요.

Dad: 정말? 너는 그걸 어떻게 알았니?

Sujin: 저는 그걸 사회 선생님이신 송 선생님께 배웠어요.

Dad: 훌륭하구나.

❶ it은 tomato soup을 가리킨다.
❷ By the way: 그런데
❸ 간접의문문 형태로 '의문사+주어+동사' 어순으로 이어진다.
❹ that은 토마토가 남아메리카에서 왔다는 것을 가리킨다.
❺ social studies: 사회(과목)

Check(√) True or False

(1) Sujin's doesn't know where the tomato came from.   T ☐ F ☐

(2) The tomato was first grown in South America.   T ☐ F ☐

Wrap Up – Listening ❻

Mike: Do you know Sumin ❶won first prize at the speech contest?

Sue: ❷I can't believe it. She was very quiet and ❸shy last year.

Mike: Yeah. She ❹joined the drama club this year, and she has changed a lot.

Sue: I see. I want to join the club, too.

Mike: 너는 수민이가 말하기 대회에서 우승한 걸 알고 있니?

Sue: 그것 참 놀랍다. 작년에 그 애는 정말 조용하고 수줍음이 많았는데.

Mike: 맞아. 그 애가 올해 연극 동아리에 가입했는데, 많이 바뀌었대.

Sue: 그렇구나. 나도 그 동아리에 가입하고 싶다.

❶ win (the) first prize: 일등상을 타다, 일등으로 입상하다
❷ 놀라움을 표현하며 'What a surprise!' 또는 'That's amazing.'으로 바꾸어 쓸 수 있다.
❸ shy: 수줍음이 많은
❹ join: 가입하다

Check(√) True or False

(3) It was Sumin who won first prize at the speech contest.   T ☐ F ☐

(4) Sumin changed a lot before joining the drama club.   T ☐ F ☐

Communication: Listen – Dialog 2

Jenny: Did you see the pictures ❶Ms. Song took?

Brian: What pictures?

Jenny: She traveled around South America ❷by herself last summer.

Brian: Really? ❸What a surprise!

Jenny: She showed us pictures of beautiful places. I ❹especially liked the pictures of pyramids.

Brian: Are there pyramids in South America?

Jenny: Yes. She said some pyramids are about 3,800 meters above ❺sea level.

Brian: I can't believe it.

❶ the pictures (that/which) Ms. Song took. 목적격 관계대명사가 생략되었다.
❷ by oneself: 혼자서
❸ 놀라움을 표현하며 'That's surprising!' 또는 'I can't believe it.' 등으로 바꾸어 표현할 수 있다.
❹ especially: 특히
❺ sea level: 해수면

Communication – Listen More

Hana: How was the roller coaster ride, Jongha?

Jongha: It was ❶fantastic. I really enjoyed ❷it.

Hana: Ha ha. You closed your eyes ❸while riding.

Jongha: Did you see? ❹To be honest, I was really scared at first.

Hana: Do you know ❺how fast this roller coaster is?

Jongha: I have no idea.

Hana: It goes ❻as fast as 140 km per hour.

Jongha: Wow! That's surprising!

Hana: Let's ride ❼it one more time!

Jongha: Look at the sign. We can't ride ❼it after 8 p.m.

Hana: Oh, maybe next time.

❶ fantastic: 환상적인
❷ it은 the roller coaster ride를 가리킨다.
❸ while ~ing: ~하는 동안
❹ To be honest: 솔직히 말하면
❺ 간접의문문으로 '의문사+주어+동사' 어순으로 이어진다.
❻ 'as 원급 as' 형태로 원급 비교를 나타낸다.
❼ it은 the roller coaster를 가리킨다.

Communicate: Speak

Amy: Do you know what the ❶capital of Peru is?

Jinsu: I have no idea. What is ❷it?

Amy: It's Lima.

Jinsu: I didn't know that.

❶ capital: 수도
❷ it은 페루의 수도를 가리킨다.

Wrap Up – Listening ❺

Jack: Do you know Junha got a puppy?

Minji: No. Where did he get it? From a ❶pet shop?

Jack: No. ❷I heard he got the puppy from his uncle.

Minji: I want ❸one, too.

❶ pet shop: 애완 동물 가게
❷ I heard (that) ~ = I was told (that) ~
❸ one은 a puppy를 가리킨다.

● 다음 우리말과 일치하도록 빈칸에 알맞은 말을 쓰시오.

Communication: Listen – Dialog 1

Sujin: Dad, I like this _____ _____.

Dad: I'm _____ you like it.

Sujin: _____ _____ _____, do you know _____ the tomato

was first _____?

Dad: Italy or _____ in Europe?

Sujin: No, the tomato came from _____ _____.

Dad: Really? _____ did you know that?

Sujin: I learned it from Ms. Song, my _____ _____ teacher.

Dad: That's good.

Communication: Listen – Dialog 2

Jenny: Did you see the pictures Ms. Song _____?

Brian: What pictures?

Jenny: She _____ around South America _____ _____ last

summer.

Brian: Really? What a _____!

Jenny: She showed us pictures of beautiful places. I _____ liked the

pictures of _____.

Brian: _____ _____ pyramids in South America?

Jenny: Yes. She said some pyramids are about 3,800 meters _____

_____ _____.

Brian: I _____ _____ _____.

Communication: Listen More

Hana: _____ _____ the roller coaster ride, Jongha?

Jongha: It was _____. I really enjoyed it.

Hana: Ha ha. You _____ your eyes while _____.

Jongha: Did you see? _____ _____ _____, I was really _____ at first.

Hana: Do you know _____ _____ this roller coaster _____?

Jongha: I have _____ _____.

Hana: It goes _____ _____ _____ 140 km per hour.

Jongha: Wow! That's _____!

Hana: Let's _____ it one more time!

Jongha: Look at the _____. We can't ride it _____ 8 p.m.

Hana: Oh, _____ next time.

Communicate: Speak

Amy: Do you know _____ _____ _____ _____ _____ _____?

Jinsu: I have _____ _____. What is it?

Amy: It's Lima.

Jinsu: I didn't _____ that.

Wrap Up – Listening ❺

Jack: Do you know Junha got a _____?

Minji: No. _____ did he get it? From a pet shop?

Jack: No. I _____ he got the puppy from his _____.

Minji: I want one, too.

Wrap Up – Listening ❻

Mike: Do you know Sumin _____ _____ _____ at the speech contest?

Sue: I can't believe it. She was very _____ and _____ last year.

Mike: Yeah. She _____ the drama club this year, and she _____ _____ a lot.

Sue: I see. I want to _____ the club, _____.

해석

Hana: 롤러코스터 어땠어, 종하야?
Jongha: 신나더라. 난 정말 재미있었어.
Hana: 하하. 너는 타는 동안에 눈을 감고 있던걸.
Jongha: 봤어? 솔직히 말하면 처음에는 정말 무서웠어.
Hana: 너 이 롤러코스터가 얼마나 빠른지 알고 있니?
Jongha: 모르겠어.
Hana: 이건 시속 140km로 달린대.
Jongha: 와! 정말 놀랍다!
Hana: 우리 한 번 더 타자!
Jongha: 표지판을 봐. 저녁 8시 이후에는 그것을 탈 수 없어.
Hana: 아, 다음에 타지 뭐.

Amy: 너는 페루의 수도가 어디인지 알고 있니?
Jinsu: 아니 모르겠어. 어디야?
Amy: 리마야.
Jinsu: 그건 몰랐네.

Jack: 너는 준하에게 강아지가 생긴 걸 알고 있니?
Minji: 아니. 어디에서 났대? 애완동물 가게에서?
Jack: 아니. 나는 그가 강아지를 삼촌 댁에서 얻었다고 들었어.
Minji: 나도 강아지를 키우고 싶다.

Mike: 너는 수민이가 말하기 대회에서 우승한 걸 알고 있니?
Sue: 그것 참 놀랍다. 작년에 그 애는 정말 조용하고 수줍음이 많았는데.
Mike: 맞아. 그 애가 올해 연극 동아리에 가입했는데, 많이 바뀌었대.
Sue: 그렇구나. 나도 그 동아리에 가입하고 싶다.

[01~02] 다음 대화를 읽고 물음에 답하시오.

Jack: (A)Do you know Junha got a puppy?
Minji: No. Where did he get it? From a pet shop?
Jack: No. (B)I heard he got the puppy from his uncle. (that, told)
Minji: I want one, too.

01 위 대화의 밑줄 친 (A)와 의도가 같은 것을 <u>모두</u> 고르시오.

① Do you wonder if Junha got a puppy?
② Have you heard Junha got a puppy?
③ Is Junha likely to get a puppy?
④ You know Junha got a puppy, don't you?
⑤ Is it possible for Junha to get a puppy?

02 위 대화의 밑줄 친 (B)와 의미가 같도록 주어진 단어를 사용하여 다시 쓰시오.

➡ _____

[03~04] 다음 대화를 읽고 물음에 답하시오.

Mike: Do you know Sumin won first prize at the speech contest?
Sue: (A)정말 놀랍구나. (can't) She was very quiet and shy last year.
Mike: Yeah. She joined the drama club this year, and she has changed a lot.
Sue: I see. I want to join the club, too.

03 위 대화의 밑줄 친 (A)의 우리말을 주어진 단어를 사용하여 영작하시오.

➡ _____

04 위 대화의 내용과 일치하지 <u>않는</u> 것은?

① 말하기 대회에서 수민이가 우승하였다.
② 수민이는 작년에 정말 조용하고 수줍음이 많았다.
③ 수민이는 올해 연극 동아리에 가입했다.
④ Sue도 연극 동아리에 가입하고 싶어 한다.
⑤ 연극 동아리는 작년과 올해 많이 바뀌었다.

[01~03] 다음 대화를 읽고 물음에 답하시오.

Sujin: Dad, I like this tomato soup.

Dad: I'm happy you like it.

Sujin: By the way, (A)토마토가 처음에 어디에서 재배되었는지 아세요?

Dad: Italy or somewhere in Europe?

Sujin: No, the tomato came from South America.

Dad: Really? _____(B)_____

Sujin: I learned it from Ms. Song, my social studies teacher.

Dad: That's good.

서답형

01 위 대화의 밑줄 친 (A)의 우리말을 <보기>에 주어진 단어를 모두 배열하여 완성하시오.

┌─── 보기 ├───
where / grown / first / was / know / you
/ do / tomato / the
└──────────────

➡ _____

02 위 대화의 빈칸 (B)에 들어갈 말로 적절한 것을 모두 고르시오.

① How do you like it?
② How did you know that?
③ What did you know about that?
④ Where did you learn?
⑤ What did you learn about that?

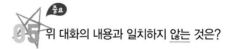

위 대화를 읽고 대답할 수 없는 것은?

① Does Sujin like the tomato soup?
② Where is the origin of the tomato?
③ What did Sujin learn from Ms. Song?
④ What subject does Ms. Song teach?
⑤ What was first grown in Italy?

[04~05] 다음 대화를 읽고 물음에 답하시오.

Jenny: Did you see the pictures Ms. Song took?

Brian: What pictures?

Jenny: She traveled around South America by herself last summer.

Brian: Really? (A)What a surprise!

Jenny: She showed us pictures of beautiful places. I especially liked the pictures of pyramids.

Brian: Are there pyramids in South America?

Jenny: Yes. She said some pyramids are about 3,800 meters above sea level.

Brian: I can't believe it.

04 위 대화의 밑줄 친 (A)와 바꾸어 쓰기 어색한 것은?

① Unbelievable!
② That's amazing!
③ That's surprising!
④ I can't believe it.
⑤ What a relief!

05 위 대화의 내용과 일치하지 않는 것은?

① Ms. Song took a trip to South America by herself last summer.
② Jenny saw Ms. Song's pictures of beautiful places in South America.
③ Ms. Song took some pictures of pyramids in South America.
④ Jenny heard that some pyramids were about 3,800 meters above sea level.
⑤ Brian didn't believe that there were some pyramids about 3,800 meters above sea level.

[06~07] 다음 대화를 읽고 물음에 답하시오.

> Hana: How was the roller coaster ride, Jongha?
>
> Jongha: It was fantastic. I really enjoyed it.
>
> Hana: Ha ha. You closed your eyes while (A)[ridden / riding].
>
> Jongha: Did you see? To be honest, I was really (B)[scared / scaring] at first.
>
> Hana: (D)Do you know how fast is fast this roller coaster?
>
> Jongha: I have no idea.
>
> Hana: It goes as fast as 140 km per hour.
>
> Jongha: Wow! That's (C)[surprised / surprising]!
>
> Hana: Let's ride it one more time!
>
> Jongha: Look at the sign. We can't ride it after 8 p.m.
>
> Hana: Oh, maybe next time.

06 위 대화의 (A)~(C)에 들어갈 말로 바르게 짝지어진 것은?

	(A)	(B)	(C)
①	ridden	scared	surprised
②	ridden	scaring	surprising
③	riding	scared	surprising
④	riding	scaring	surprising
⑤	riding	scared	surprised

서답형

07 위 대화의 밑줄 친 (D)를 어법상 바르게 고치시오.

➡ _____

08 다음 짝지어진 대화가 어색한 것은?

① A: You know what? Tom and Junho are cousins.

　 B: That's surprising.

② A: Did you hear Jason won first prize?

　 B: At the national contest? What a surprise!

③ A: Look. A seven-year-old boy's cartoon is a big hit.

　 B: The drawings are great. I can't believe it.

④ A: Do you know what the capital of Peru is?

　 B: Yes, I have. Can you tell me what it is?

⑤ A: Do you know who wrote this book?

　 B: I have no idea.

09 다음 대화에서 (A)~(E)가 자연스럽게 이어지도록 순서대로 배열하시오.

> Jenny: Did you see the pictures Ms. Song took?
>
> Brian: What pictures?
>
> Jenny: She traveled around South America by herself last summer.
>
> Brian: Really? What a surprise!
>
> (A) I can't believe it.
>
> (B) Are there pyramids in South America?
>
> (C) Yes. She said some pyramids are about 3,800 meters above sea level.
>
> (D) She showed us pictures of beautiful places. I especially liked the pictures of pyramids.

➡ _____

[01~02] 다음 대화를 읽고 물음에 답하시오.

Jenny: Did you see the pictures Ms. Song took?

Brian: What pictures?

Jenny: She traveled around South America by ___(A)___ last summer.

Brian: Really? What a surprise!

Jenny: She showed us pictures of beautiful places. I especially liked the pictures of pyramids.

Brian: Are there pyramids in South America?

Jenny: Yes. She said some pyramids are about 3,800 meters above sea level.

Brian: I can't believe it.

01 위 대화의 빈칸 (A)에 '혼자서, 홀로'의 의미가 되도록 빈칸을 완성하시오.

➡ _____

02 What are Jenny and Brian talking about?

➡ _____

_____

[03~04] 다음 대화를 읽고 물음에 답하시오.

Jack: Do you know Junha got a puppy?

Minji: No. Where did he get it? From a pet shop?

Jack: No. I heard he got the puppy from his uncle.

Minji: I want one, too.

03 What did Junha get from his uncle?

➡ _____

04 What does Minji want to get?

➡ _____

05 다음 대화의 내용과 일치하도록 빈칸을 완성하시오.

Mike: Do you know Sumin won first prize at the speech contest?

Sue: I can't believe it. She was very quiet and shy last year.

Mike: Yeah. She joined the drama club this year, and she has changed a lot.

Sue: I see. I want to join the club, too.

⬇

Today, I heard the winner of the speech contest was (A)_____. I was surprised a lot. She is not what she used to be last year. Last year, she was very (B)_____. But she has changed a lot after (C)_____ this year. I want to be a more active and confident person like Sumin.

06 다음 대화에서 (A)~(E)가 자연스럽게 이어지도록 배열하시오.

Sujin: Dad, I like this tomato soup.

Dad: I'm happy you like it.

(A) Really? How did you know that?

(B) Italy or somewhere in Europe?

(C) By the way, do you know where the tomato was first grown?

(D) No, the tomato came from South America.

(E) I learned it from Ms. Song, my social studies teacher.

➡ _____

Grammar

① 최상급

> • He is **the tallest** boy of them. 그는 그들 중에서 가장 키가 큰 소년이다.
>
> • You are **the kindest** person that I have ever known. 너는 내가 아는 사람 중 가장 친절해.

■ 셋 이상을 비교하여 정도가 가장 높은 것을 나타낼 때 최상급을 사용한다. 형용사의 최상급은 정관사 the를 사용하지만, 부사의 최상급에서는 정관사 the를 생략하는 것이 일반적이다.

구분	최상급	예
대부분의 형용사/부사	+-(e)st	tallest, shortest
'자음+y'로 끝나는 경우	-y → -iest	happiest, earliest
'단모음+단자음'으로 끝나는 경우	마지막 자음 추가 + -est	biggest, hottest
-ous, -ful 등으로 끝나는 2음절어 / 3음절 이상인 경우	most +	mous famous most exciting
불규칙 변화	best, worst, most, least	

• Today is **the hottest** day of the year. 오늘은 연중 가장 더운 날이다.

• The rose is **the most beautiful** flower in my garden. 장미는 내 정원에서 가장 아름다운 꽃이야.

• This is **the brightest** color of all. 이것은 모든 색 중에서 가장 밝은 색이야.

■ 비교급과 원급을 이용하여 최상급의 의미를 표현할 수 있다.

• Julia is **the prettiest** in her class. Julia는 그녀의 반에서 가장 예쁘다.

= Julia is **prettier than any other** girl in her class. (비교급+than any other+단수 명사)
　　Julia는 반에 있는 다른 어떤 소녀보다 더 예쁘다.

= Julia is **prettier than all the other** girls in her class. (비교급+than all the other+복수 명사)
　　Julia는 반에 있는 다른 모든 소녀들보다 더 예쁘다.

= **No other** girl in her class is **as pretty as** Julia. (부정 주어+so[as] 원급 as)
　　그녀의 반에 있는 다른 어떤 소녀도 Julia만큼 예쁘지 않다.

= **No other** girl in her class is **prettier than** Julia. (부정 주어+비교급+than)
　　그녀의 반에 있는 다른 어떤 소녀도 Julia보다 더 예쁘지 않다.

핵심 Check

1. 다음 우리말과 일치하도록 주어진 말을 이용하여 빈칸에 알맞은 말을 쓰시오.

(1) Alex는 셋 중에서 가장 재미있는 소년이야. (funny)

➡ Alex is _____ _____ _____ of the three.

(2) 에베레스트산은 세계에서 가장 높은 산이다. (high)

➡ Mt. Everest is _____ _____ _____ in the world.

② 간접의문문

> • I wonder **why** she is upset. 나는 그녀가 왜 화가 났는지 궁금해.
>
> • Do you want to know **when** you should go? 언제 가야 하는지 알고 싶니?

■ 간접의문문은 명사절을 이끌며 주어, 목적어, 보어 역할을 한다. 의문사가 있는 간접의문문은 '의문사+주어+동사' 어순으로 쓰인다. 직접의문문인 '의문사+동사+주어 ~?'의 어순과 혼동하지 않도록 유의한다.

  • **Who** are you going to meet? 〈직접의문문〉 누구를 만날 예정이니?

  Can you tell me **who** you are going to meet? 〈간접의문문〉 네가 누구를 만날 건지 말해 줄래?

  • I wonder **when** he bought the car. 나는 언제 그가 그 차를 샀는지 궁금해.

  • I forgot **where** I put my key. 나는 열쇠를 어디에 뒀는지 잊어버렸어.

■ 다음과 같이 의문사가 주어 역할을 하는 경우가 있다. 이때에는 '의문사+동사'의 어순이 된다.

  • He asked me **who** called him. 그는 누가 그에게 전화했는지 내게 물었다.

■ 의문사가 없는 경우 간접의문문의 어순은 'if/whether+주어+동사'로 쓴다.

  • Can you tell me? + Do you like her?
  → Can you tell me **if[whether]** you like her? 그녀를 좋아하는지 말해 줄래?

  • Let me know **if[whether]** the letter arrived safely. 그 편지가 안전하게 도착했는지 내게 알려줘.

  • I wonder **if[whether]** the girl came alone. 그 소녀가 혼자 왔는지 궁금해.

■ 주절에 think, believe, imagine 등과 같은 동사가 있을 경우 간접의문문을 만들 때에는 의문사를 문두로 배치한다.

  • **How old** do you think she is? 그녀가 몇 살이라고 생각해?

  • **Who** do you believe stole the money? 누가 그 돈을 훔쳤다고 믿는 거야?

핵심 Check

2. 다음 우리말과 일치하도록 빈칸에 알맞은 말을 쓰시오.

  (1) 나는 그들이 제때에 그 파티에 왔는지 궁금해.

   ➡ I wonder _____ they came to the party in time.

  (2) 그가 언제 떠났는지 말해 줘.

   ➡ Tell me _____ _____ _____.

  (3) 그가 얼마나 키가 큰지 아니?

   ➡ Do you know _____ _____ _____ _____?

01 다음 문장에서 어법상 <u>어색한</u> 부분을 바르게 고쳐 쓰시오.

(1) I don't know what is she doing.

_____ ➡ _____

(2) Ted didn't know how did she break in his house.

_____ ➡ _____

(3) He is the famousest movie star of the five.

_____ ➡ _____

(4) James is busiest man in the company.

_____ ➡ _____

02 주어진 형용사의 최상급을 빈칸에 쓰시오.

(1) This is _____ pen of all. (cheap)

(2) This is _____ book of the seven. (interesting)

(3) It is _____ museum in the world. (big)

(4) It is _____ problem. (difficult)

(5) It is _____ snowfall in ten years. (heavy)

03 주어진 어구를 바르게 배열하여 다음 우리말을 영어로 쓰시오.

(3) go out: 나가다

(1) 그가 왜 늦게 왔는지 말해 줘. (late / tell / came / why / me / he)

➡ _____

(2) 그녀가 어디로 가고 있는지 말해 줄래? (going / tell / you / she / can / me / where / is)

➡ _____

(3) 그 소년이 언제 나갔는지 기억하니? (out / do / the boy / you / when / remember / went)

➡ _____

(4) June은 누가 그 집을 지었는지 모른다. (the house / doesn't / June / who / know / built)

➡ _____

(5) 누가 들어왔는지 아니? (in / know / came / who / do / you)

➡ _____

01 다음 중 최상급의 형태가 <u>다른</u> 하나는?

① popular
② interesting
③ likely
④ simple
⑤ amazing

02 다음 빈칸에 들어갈 말로 가장 적절한 것은?

> Do you remember ＿＿＿＿＿＿＿＿ ?

① who the ball kicked
② when was she going home
③ what did happen last night
④ when my birthday is
⑤ how can you get here

03 다음 중 주어진 문장과 같은 의미의 문장은?

> Jessica is the smartest girl of all.

① Jessica is as smart as all the other girls.
② Jessica is not smarter than all.
③ No other girl is as smart as Jessica.
④ Anyone is smarter than Jessica.
⑤ Jessica is not as smart as all.

서답형
04 주어진 단어를 활용하여 다음 우리말을 영어로 쓰시오.

> Branda는 그들이 그녀의 도움을 필요로 하는지 추측하려고 애썼다.
> (try to guess)

➡ ＿＿＿＿＿＿＿＿＿＿＿＿＿＿＿＿

05 다음 우리말을 영어로 바르게 옮긴 것은?

> 그 시계가 얼마인지 아니?

① Do you know how the watch is much?
② Do you know how much is the watch?
③ Do you know how long you have to watch it?
④ Do you know how much the watch is?
⑤ Do you know how expensive the watch is?

서답형
06 주어진 단어를 활용하여 다음 우리말을 영어로 쓰시오.

> 그것은 세상에서 가장 쉬운 일이 아니다.
> (that / job)

➡ ＿＿＿＿＿＿＿＿＿＿＿＿＿＿＿＿

07 다음 빈칸에 들어갈 말로 적절하지 <u>않은</u> 것은?

> I want to know ＿＿＿＿ she will throw a party for him. Can I ask her?

① why
② when
③ if
④ whether
⑤ that

서답형
08 다음 빈칸에 알맞은 말을 각각 쓰시오.

> No other animal in the world is bigger than this whale.
> = This whale is ＿＿＿＿ than any other animal in the world.
> = No other animal is as ＿＿＿＿ as this whale.
> = This whale is ＿＿＿＿ animal in the world.

09 다음 중 주어진 문장의 밑줄 친 부분과 쓰임이 같은 것은?

> We don't know <u>if</u> he will help us.

① <u>If</u> you want to take part in the race, let us know.

② You can go to the party <u>if</u> you want to.

③ I will call you back <u>if</u> I find your book.

④ Can you give her this message <u>if</u> you see her?

⑤ Can you tell me <u>if</u> you bought the bag?

10 다음 중 문장의 전환이 바르지 <u>않은</u> 것은?

① I wonder. Are you a student?
→ I wonder whether you are a student.

② Can you tell me? When is your birthday?
→ Can you tell me when your birthday is?

③ I want to know. How did he finish his homework?
→ I want to know how he finished his homework.

④ I am not certain. Is she clever?
→ I am not certain if she is clever.

⑤ Do you believe? Who made the cookies yesterday?
→ Do you believe who made the cookies yesterday?

11 8 단어로 이루어진 문장으로 다음 우리말을 영어로 쓸 때 세 번째와 다섯 번째 오는 단어를 바르게 짝지은 것은?

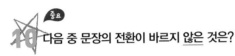

> 그 영화에서 가장 재미있는 캐릭터는 누구니?

① the – in
② funniest – in
③ the – character
④ funniest – the
⑤ is – character

12 다음 중 의미가 <u>다른</u> 하나는?

① Her voice is the most beautiful in our class.

② Her voice is more beautiful than any other voice in our class.

③ No other voice in our class is more beautiful than her voice.

④ Her voice is as beautiful as all the other voices in our class.

⑤ No other voice in our class is as beautiful as her voice.

서답형

13 빈칸에 알맞은 말을 쓰시오.

> 영국 사람들은 건강이 가장 중요한 것이라고 생각한다.

➡ The British think _____ _____.

서답형

14 같은 의미가 되도록 빈칸에 알맞은 말을 쓰시오.

> Tom is the most diligent man in the office.
> = No other man in the office is _____ _____ than Tom.

15 다음 중 빈칸에 들어갈 말이 바르게 짝지어진 것은?

> • Do you know _____?
> • It is _____ hotel that I've ever visited.

① what time it is – more comfortable

② how he is old – more comfortable

③ who did the laundry – the most comfortable

④ what time is it – the most comfortable

⑤ who broke it – more comfortable

16 주어진 단어를 어법에 맞게 활용하여 다음 우리말을 영어로 쓰시오.

> David는 우리 학교에서 최고의 학생이다.
> (good)

➡ _____

17 다음 중 어법상 바르지 <u>않은</u> 것은?

① Do you know what he is eating?

② Can you tell me who the leader is?

③ Which one is the prettyest dress?

④ I want the cutest doll in this store.

⑤ I remember when she gave me the card.

18 다음 중 주어진 문장과 같은 의미의 문장은?

> This train is the fastest train in the world.

① This train is not as fast as all the other trains in the world.

② No other train in the world is faster than this train.

③ This train is as fast as the other train in the world.

④ This train is faster than the other train.

⑤ This train is not faster than any other train in the world.

19 다음 빈칸에 알맞은 말을 쓰시오.

> 나무늘보는 지구상에서 가장 게으른 동물이다.
> Sloths are _____ on earth.

20 다음 대화의 빈칸에 알맞은 말을 세 단어로 쓰시오.

> A: I want to know _____.
> B: He works at a bank.

➡ _____

21 다음 빈칸에 들어갈 말로 가장 적절한 것은?

> I would like to know. Are you safe?
> = I would like to know _____ you are safe.

① that   ② when

③ how   ④ when

⑤ if

22 다음 우리말을 영어로 <u>잘못</u> 옮긴 것은?

① 이것은 세상에서 가장 위험한 직업입니다.
   → This is the most dangerous job in the world.

② 그녀가 언제 나갈 건지 알려줘.
   → Let me know when she will go out.

③ 바이칼 호수는 지구상에서 가장 깊은 호수로 알려져 있습니다.
   → Lake Baikal is known as the deepest lake on the earth.

④ 누가 이 꽃병을 깨트렸는지는 중요하지 않아.
   → Who broke this vase doesn't matter.

⑤ 이 물은 내가 본 것 중 가장 깨끗한 물이야.
   → This water is the most clean water that I've ever seen.

23 주어진 단어를 활용하여 다음 우리말을 영어로 쓰시오.

> 누가 그 결정을 내렸는지 궁금해요.
> (wonder / make)

➡ _____

24 다음 두 문장을 하나의 문장으로 쓰시오.

> Do you think? How can we get to the park?

➡ _____

01 단어 long을 활용하여 다음 빈칸에 알맞은 말을 어법에 맞게 쓰시오.

> The Amazon River is _____ river in the world. It is _____ than any other river in the world.

02 다음 두 문장을 하나의 문장으로 쓰시오.

(1) Can I ask? Are you mad at me?

➡ _____

(2) Do you know? Where does Tom live?

➡ _____

(3) Can you tell me? Who is she?

➡ _____

(4) I wonder. What happened to you?

➡ _____

(5) Please tell me. Why did he break the promise?

➡ _____

(6) Do you think? When will the book be published?

➡ _____

(7) Let me know. Is she going to tell him the truth?

➡ _____

_____

03 다음 빈칸에 알맞은 말을 쓰시오.

> No other boy in our gym is as brave as John.
> = John is _____ in our gym.

04 다음은 네 개 식당의 평점이다. good과 bad를 활용하여 빈칸에 알맞은 말을 쓰시오.

> Restaurant A: ★★★
> Restaurant B: ★★★★☆
> Restaurant C: ★☆
> Restaurant D: ★★☆

(1) Restaurant C is _____ restaurant of the four.

(2) Restaurant B is _____ restaurant of the four.

(3) No other restaurant of the four is _____ than restaurant C.

05 다음 대화의 빈칸에 알맞은 말을 쓰시오.

> A: Where is he going?
> B: I don't know _____, but I think he will tell us later.

06 주어진 단어를 활용하여 다음 우리말을 영어로 쓰시오.

> 2월은 1년 중 가장 짧은 달이다.
> (of the year)

➡ _____

07 다음 빈칸에 알맞은 말을 쓰시오.

> Jason은 우리 반에서 가장 인기 있는 소년이야.
> Jason is _____ boy in our class.

08 주어진 단어를 바르게 배열하여 다음 우리말을 영어로 쓰시오. 필요하다면 단어를 추가하시오.

> 한국에서 가장 유명한 장소들을 소개할게.
> (in / me / introduce / let / famous / places / Korea)

➡ _____

09 주어진 단어를 바르게 배열하여 대화를 완성하시오.

> A: I wonder (thinks / who / a thief / him)
> B: Mary and Jocelyn.

➡ _____

10 다음 우리말과 일치하도록 주어진 단어를 이용하여 빈칸에 알맞은 말을 쓰시오.

> 그는 내가 아는 사람 중 가장 창의적인 사람이야.
> (creative)
> He is _____ that I've ever known.

11 다음 대화의 빈칸에 알맞은 말을 쓰시오.

> A: Do you know _____?
> B: He is seventeen years old.

12 주어진 단어를 활용하여 다음 우리말을 영어로 쓰시오.

> 지구상에서 가장 추운 도시는 어디야?
> (on earth)

➡ _____

13 다음 문장과 같은 뜻의 문장을 완성하시오.

> Education is the most important thing in the world.

➡ No other thing in the world _____
_____.

➡ No other thing in the world _____
_____.

➡ Education is _____
_____ in the world.

➡ Education is _____
_____ in the world.

14 주어진 단어를 활용하여 다음 우리말을 영어로 쓰시오.

> 그녀가 누구라고 생각해? (think / who)

➡ _____

15 다음 대화를 읽고 빈칸에 알맞은 말을 쓰시오.

> Alex: Where are you going?
> Emily: I am going to a theater.
> Alex: Are you going there to see a movie?
> Emily: No. I do a part-time job there.

➡ Alex wants to know _____.
So Emily tells him that she is going to a theater. Alex wonders _____
_____. Emily says that she is going there to do a part-time job.

Home of Natural Wonders

Do you know where the driest desert on Earth is? How about the highest waterfall? Yes, they are both in South America. This continent is full of natural wonders that will surprise you.

Atacama Desert

The Atacama is the driest desert on Earth. In some parts, it gets almost no rain at all — only 1–3 millimeters per year! The ground in some areas is so dry that no plants can grow. Do you know what scientists do in such a dry place? The soil in this desert is very similar to the soil on Mars, so they prepare for trips to outer space. The Atacama is also one of the best places on Earth to watch stars.

Angel Falls

If you go to Venezuela, you can see the world's highest waterfall. It is 979 meters high. Clouds often cover the top, so you need patience and a little luck to get a good view.

natural: 자연의, 천연의
wonder: 경이, 놀라움
desert: 사막
waterfall: 폭포
continent: 대륙
be full of: ~으로 가득하다
both: 둘 다
area: 지역
soil: 토양, 흙
similar: 비슷한
prepare for: ~을 준비하다
outer space: 우주 공간
patience: 인내심
luck: 운

📎 **확인문제**

● 다음 문장이 본문의 내용과 일치하면 T, 일치하지 <u>않으면</u> F를 쓰시오.

1 The world's highest waterfall is in South America. ☐

2 It is impossible to see a drop of rain in the Atacama Desert. ☐

3 In the Atacama, plants can't grow because of hot weather. ☐

4 Angel Falls is more than a thousand meters high. ☐

5 Getting a good view of Angel Falls is easy. ☐

Actually, the waterfall is named after Jimmie Angel, a pilot from the
United States who first flew over the waterfall in 1933. You can still
get to the top of the beautiful waterfall only by plane.

The Amazon

The Amazon runs across the continent through seven countries. It
travels from Peru in the west and flows into the Atlantic Ocean. The
Amazon River is interesting in many ways. For the most part, it has
no bridges. That is because it usually runs through rainforests and wet
areas, not cities or towns. Also, in many places the river is very wide,
so you cannot see the other side! You probably do not want to swim in
this river. It is home to some very big snakes and fish that eat meat.

The Andes

The Andes are the world's longest mountain range. Do you know
how long the mountain range is? It is about 7,000 kilometers long! It
also contains the highest mountains outside of Asia. About a third of
the people in South America live in the Andes. Many unique animals
also live there.

name after: ~을 따라 이름 짓다
across: ~을 건너서, ~을 가로질러
rainforest: (열대) 우림
wide: 넓은
probably: 아마도
mountain range: 산맥
contain: 들어 있다, 포함하다
unique: 독특한

확인문제

● 다음 문장이 본문의 내용과 일치하면 T, 일치하지 않으면 F를 쓰시오.

1 You need to get on a plane if you want to get to the top of Angel Falls.
2 The Amazon River has many bridges.
3 The Amazon River is narrow enough to see the other side.
4 It is not a good idea to swim in the Amazon River.
5 No other mountain range is longer than the Andes.
6 Many ordinary animals can be found in the Andes.

• 우리말을 참고하여 빈칸에 알맞은 말을 쓰시오.

1 Do you know _____ _____ _____ _____ on Earth is?

2 How about _____ _____ waterfall?

3 Yes, _____ _____ _____ in South America.

4 This continent _____ _____ _____ natural wonders _____ will surprise you.

5 The Atacama is _____ _____ _____ on Earth.

6 In some parts, _____ _____ almost no rain _____ _____ — only 1–3 millimeters per year!

7 The ground in some areas _____ _____ _____ no plants can grow.

8 Do you know _____ _____ _____ in such a dry place?

9 The soil in this desert is very _____ _____ the soil on Mars, so _____ _____ _____ _____ to outer space.

10 The Atacama is also _____ _____ _____ on Earth to watch stars.

11 If you go to Venezuela, you can _____ _____ _____ waterfall.

12 _____ is 979 meters _____.

13 Clouds often _____ the top, so you need _____ and a little _____ to get a good view.

14 Actually, the waterfall is _____ _____ Jimmie Angel, a pilot from the United States _____ first _____ over the waterfall in 1933.

1	여러분은 지구에서 가장 건조한 사막이 어디인지 알고 있나요?
2	가장 높은 폭포는 어떠한가요?
3	그렇습니다. 그것들은 둘 다 남 아메리카에 있습니다.
4	이 대륙은 여러분을 놀라게 할 자연 경관으로 가득하답니다.
5	아타카마 사막은 지구에서 가장 건조한 사막입니다.
6	몇몇 지역은 비가 전혀 오지 않아서, 연간 강수량이 1~3mm에 그칩니다!
7	어떤 지역의 토양은 너무 건조해서 어떤 식물도 자랄 수가 없습니다.
8	이처럼 건조한 곳에서 과학자들이 무슨 일을 하는지 알고 있나요?
9	이 사막의 토양은 화성의 토양과 아주 비슷해서, 그들은 우주로의 여행을 준비합니다.
10	또한 아타카마 사막은 지구에서 별을 관측하기에 가장 좋은 장소 가운데 하나이기도 합니다.
11	여러분이 베네수엘라에 간다면, 세계에서 가장 높은 폭포를 볼 수 있을 것입니다.
12	그것은 높이가 979m입니다.
13	구름이 꼭대기 부분을 자주 에워싸기 때문에, 멋진 경치를 보려면 인내심과 약간의 운이 필요합니다.
14	사실 그 폭포는 1933년에 처음으로 폭포 너머 비행을 한 미국의 비행사 Jimmie Angel에게서 이름을 따왔습니다.

15 You can _____ _____ _____ the top of the beautiful waterfall only _____ plane.

16 The Amazon _____ _____ the continent _____ seven countries.

17 It _____ _____ Peru in the west and _____ _____ the Atlantic Ocean.

18 The Amazon River _____ _____ in many ways.

19 For the most part, it has _____ _____ .

20 That is _____ _____ _____ _____ _____ rainforests and wet areas, not cities or towns.

21 Also, in many places the river is very wide, so you cannot _____ _____ _____ _____ !

22 You probably do not want to _____ _____ this river.

23 It is _____ to some very big snakes and fish _____ eat meat.

24 The Andes are _____ _____ _____ mountain _____ .

25 Do you know _____ _____ _____ _____ _____ is?

26 It is _____ 7,000 kilometers _____ !

27 It also _____ the highest _____ outside of Asia.

28 About _____ _____ _____ _____ _____ in South America live in the Andes.

29 Many _____ _____ also live there.

15 여전히 비행기로만 그 아름다운 폭포의 꼭대기에 갈 수 있습니다.

16 아마존강은 일곱 개의 나라를 거쳐 대륙을 가로질러 흐릅니다.

17 그것은 서쪽의 페루에서 시작하여 대서양으로 흘러갑니다.

18 아마존강은 많은 점에서 흥미롭습니다.

19 강의 대부분에는 다리가 없습니다.

20 그것은 강이 대개 도시나 마을이 아닌, 열대 우림과 습지를 지나 흐르기 때문입니다.

21 또한 많은 곳에서 강이 너무 넓어서 그 건너편을 볼 수조차 없습니다!

22 여러분은 아마도 이 강에서 헤엄치고 싶지 않을 것입니다.

23 이곳은 몇몇 아주 큰 뱀과 고기를 먹는 물고기들의 서식지입니다.

24 안데스 산맥은 세계에서 가장 긴 산맥입니다.

25 여러분은 그 산맥의 길이가 얼마인지 아시나요?

26 그것은 약 7,000km입니다.

27 또한 그곳에는 아시아 외의 지역에서 가장 높은 산이 있습니다.

28 남아메리카 인구의 3분의 1 정도가 안데스 산맥에 살고 있습니다.

29 그리고 독특한 동물들이 많이 서식하고 있기도 합니다.

● 우리말을 참고하여 본문을 영작하시오.

1 여러분은 지구에서 가장 건조한 사막이 어디인지 알고 있나요?

➡ _____

2 가장 높은 폭포는 어떠한가요?

➡ _____

3 그렇습니다, 그것들은 둘 다 남아메리카에 있습니다.

➡ _____

4 이 대륙은 여러분을 놀라게 할 자연 경관으로 가득하답니다.

➡ _____

5 아타카마 사막은 지구에서 가장 건조한 사막입니다.

➡ _____

6 몇몇 지역은 비가 전혀 오지 않아서, 연간 강수량이 1~3mm에 그칩니다!

➡ _____

7 어떤 지역의 토양은 너무 건조해서 어떤 식물도 자랄 수가 없습니다.

➡ _____

8 이처럼 건조한 곳에서 과학자들이 무슨 일을 하는지 알고 있나요?

➡ _____

9 이 사막의 토양은 화성의 토양과 아주 비슷해서, 그들은 우주로의 여행을 준비합니다.

➡ _____

10 또한 아타카마 사막은 지구에서 별을 관측하기에 가장 좋은 장소 가운데 하나이기도 합니다.

➡ _____

11 여러분이 베네수엘라에 간다면, 세계에서 가장 높은 폭포를 볼 수 있을 것입니다.

➡ _____

12 그것은 높이가 979m입니다.

➡ _____

13 구름이 꼭대기 부분을 자주 에워싸기 때문에, 멋진 경치를 보려면 인내심과 약간의 운이 필요합니다.

➡ _____

14 사실 그 폭포는 1933년에 처음으로 폭포 너머 비행을 한 미국의 비행사 Jimmie Angel에게서 이름을 따왔습니다.

➡ _____

_____

15 여전히 비행기로만 그 아름다운 폭포의 꼭대기에 갈 수 있습니다.

➡ _____

16 아마존강은 일곱 개의 나라를 거쳐 대륙을 가로질러 흐릅니다.

➡ _____

17 그것은 서쪽의 페루에서 시작하여 대서양으로 흘러갑니다.

➡ _____

18 아마존강은 많은 점에서 흥미롭습니다.

➡ _____

19 강의 대부분에는 다리가 없습니다.

➡ _____

20 그것은 강이 대개 도시나 마을이 아닌, 열대 우림과 습지를 지나 흐르기 때문입니다.

➡ _____

21 또한 많은 곳에서 강이 너무 넓어서 그 건너편을 볼 수조차 없습니다!

➡ _____

22 여러분은 아마도 이 강에서 헤엄치고 싶지 않을 것입니다.

➡ _____

23 이곳은 몇몇 아주 큰 뱀과 고기를 먹는 물고기들의 서식지입니다.

➡ _____

24 안데스 산맥은 세계에서 가장 긴 산맥입니다.

➡ _____

25 여러분은 그 산맥의 길이가 얼마인지 아시나요?

➡ _____

26 그것은 약 7,000km입니다.

➡ _____

27 또한 그곳에는 아시아 외의 지역에서 가장 높은 산이 있습니다.

➡ _____

28 남아메리카 인구의 3분의 1 정도가 안데스 산맥에 살고 있습니다.

➡ _____

29 그리고 독특한 동물들이 많이 서식하고 있기도 합니다.

➡ _____

[01~05] 다음 글을 읽고 물음에 답하시오.

Do you know ①where the driest desert on Earth is? How about ②the highest waterfall? Yes, they are both in South America. This continent ③is full of natural wonders that will surprise you.

Atacama Desert

The Atacama is the driest desert on Earth. In some parts, it gets almost no rain at all — only 1–3 millimeters per year! The ground in some areas is so dry _____(A)_____ no plants can grow. Do you know what scientists do in such a dry place? The soil in this desert is very ④similar to the soil on Mars, so they prepare for trips to outer space. The Atacama is also one of the best ⑤place on Earth to watch stars.

01 빈칸 (A)에 들어갈 말로 가장 적절한 것은?

① who   ② when   ③ what
④ that   ⑤ which

서답형

02 다음과 같이 풀이되는 말을 위 글에서 찾아 쓰시오.

> a large mass of land surrounded by sea

➡ _____

03 다음 중 위 글의 내용과 일치하는 것은?

① The Atacama has the highest waterfall in the world.
② The ground of the Atacama is always wet.
③ Scientists aren't interested in the Atacama.
④ It is hard to see stars in the Atacama.
⑤ Thanks to the Atacama, scientists can prepare for trips to outer space.

04 ①~⑤ 중 어법상 바르지 않은 것은?

①   ②   ③   ④   ⑤

서답형

05 According to the passage, where is the Atacama? Answer in English with a full sentence.

➡ _____

[06~08] 다음 글을 읽고 물음에 답하시오.

Angel Falls

If you go to Venezuela, you can see the world's highest waterfall. It is 979 meters high. Clouds often cover the top, so you need patience and a little luck to get a good view. Actually, the waterfall is named _____(A)_____ Jimmie Angel, a pilot from the United States who first flew over the waterfall in 1933. You can still get to the top of the beautiful waterfall only by plane.

06 다음 중 빈칸 (A)에 들어갈 말과 같은 말이 들어가는 것은?

① Did you turn _____ the light when you went out of the room?
② My dad is always busy _____ playing golf.
③ The glass is full _____ orange juice.
④ My sister is good _____ speaking English and Chinese.
⑤ Jamie has looked _____ the injured dog since yesterday.

서답형

07 When did Jimmie Angel first fly over Angel Falls? Answer in English with a full sentence.

➡ _____

08 다음 중 위 글을 읽고 답할 수 있는 것은?

① Where is Venezuela?

② How wide is Angel falls?

③ When did Jimmie Angel start his flying?

④ Why do you need a little luck to get a good view of Angel Falls?

⑤ Why is it impossible to get to the top of Angel Falls?

[09~13] 다음 글을 읽고 물음에 답하시오.

The Amazon

The Amazon runs across the continent through seven countries. It travels from Peru in the west and flows into the Atlantic Ocean. The Amazon River is ___(A)___ in many ways. For the most part, it has no bridges. That is because it usually runs through rainforests and wet areas, not cities or towns. Also, in many places the river is very wide, so you cannot see the other side! You probably do not want to swim in this river. It is home to some very big snakes and fish that eat meat.

The Andes

The Andes are the world's longest mountain range. Do you know how long the mountain range is? It is about 7,000 kilometers long! It also contains the highest mountains outside of Asia. About a third of the people in South America live in the Andes. Many (B)unique animals also live there.

서답형

09 단어 interest를 어법에 맞게 빈칸 (A)에 쓰시오.

➡ _____

10 밑줄 친 (B)를 대신하여 쓰일 수 있는 것은?

① common   ② ordinary

③ unusual   ④ regular

⑤ familiar

중요

11 다음 중 위 글의 내용을 바르게 이해한 학생은?

① 주하: 아마존강이 남미 대륙 전체를 거쳐 흐른다니, 정말 대단해.

② 경수: 아마존강은 결국 태평양으로 흘러가는 거군.

③ 예지: 강이 너무 넓어서 건너편을 볼 수 없을 정도라니, 대단히 넓은 강임에 분명해.

④ 성재: 아마존강이 세계에서 가장 긴 강이라는 것은 몰랐어.

⑤ 진하: 아마존강에서 수영하는 것이 내 소망이야.

서답형

12 Where does the Amazon River start from? Answer in English with a full sentence.

➡ _____

중요

13 다음 중 위 글을 읽고 안데스 산맥에 관하여 알 수 있는 정보는?

① the length of the Andes

② the lives of people who live in the Andes

③ the kinds of the animals

④ the height of the Andes

⑤ the number of people who live in South America

[14~17] 다음 글을 읽고 물음에 답하시오.

Do you know where the driest desert on Earth is? How about the highest waterfall? Yes, they are both in South America. This continent is full of natural wonders ___(A)___ will surprise you.

Atacama Desert

The Atacama is the driest desert on Earth. ① In some parts, it gets almost no rain at all — only 1–3 millimeters per year! ② The ground in some areas is so dry that no plants can grow. ③ The soil in this desert is very similar to the soil on Mars, so they prepare for trips to outer space. ④ The Atacama is also one of the best places on Earth to watch stars. ⑤

14 빈칸 (A)에 들어갈 말로 가장 적절한 것은?

① which   ② what   ③ who
④ when   ⑤ why

15 ①~⑤ 중 주어진 문장이 들어가기에 가장 적절한 곳은?

Do you know what scientists do in such a dry place?

①   ②   ③   ④   ⑤

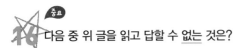

다음 중 위 글을 읽고 답할 수 없는 것은?

① Where is the Atacama located?
② Where is the highest waterfall?
③ How much does it rain in some parts of the Atacama?
④ What continent is full of natural wonders?
⑤ How many stars can be watched in the Atacama?

서답형

17 Write the reason why it is impossible that plants can grow in some parts of the Atacama. Use the phrase 'It's because.'

➡ _____

[18~20] 다음 글을 읽고 물음에 답하시오.

Angel Falls

If you go to Venezuela, you can see the world's highest waterfall. It is 979 meters high. Clouds often cover the top, so you need patience and a little luck to get a good (A) view. Actually, the waterfall is named after Jimmie Angel, a pilot from the United States who first flew over the waterfall in 1933. You can still get to the top of the beautiful waterfall only by plane.

18 다음 중 밑줄 친 (A)와 같은 의미로 사용된 것은?

① Jason and I have different views.
② His views on the subject were well known.
③ The view from the hotel room was fantastic.
④ He has a positive view on the issue.
⑤ What is needed is exchanging views.

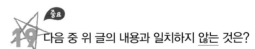

다음 중 위 글의 내용과 일치하지 <u>않는</u> 것은?

① Angel Falls lies in Venezuela.
② No other waterfall in the world is as high as Angel Falls.
③ You can see a clear view of the waterfall anytime you want.
④ The waterfall is named after a pilot from the United States.
⑤ You can't get to the top of Angel Falls without a plane.

서답형

20 Who was Jimmie Angel? Answer in English with a full sentence.

➡ _____

_____

[21~22] 다음 글을 읽고 물음에 답하시오.

The Amazon

The Amazon runs (A)[into / across] the continent through seven countries. It travels from Peru in the west and flows into the Atlantic Ocean. The Amazon River is interesting in many ways. For the most part, it has no bridges. (B)[That is because / That is why] it usually runs through rainforests and wet areas, not cities or towns. Also, in many places the river is very wide, so you cannot see (C)[another / the other] side! You probably do not want to swim in this river. It is home to some very big snakes and fish that eat meat.

중요

21 (A)~(C) 중 어법상 옳은 것끼리 바르게 짝지은 것은?

① into – That is because – another
② into – That is why – the other
③ into – That is because – the other
④ across – That is because – the other
⑤ across – That is why – another

서답형

22 Write the reason why it is dangerous to swim in the Amazon River. Use the word below.

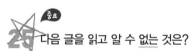

(because)

➡ _____

_____

[23~24] 다음 글을 읽고 물음에 답하시오.

The Andes

The Andes are the world's longest mountain range. (A)Do you know how the mountain range is long? It is about 7,000 kilometers long! It also contains the highest mountains outside of Asia. (B)About a third of the people in South America live in the Andes. Many unique animals also live there.

서답형

23 위 글의 밑줄 친 (A)를 어법에 맞게 고쳐 쓰시오.

➡ _____

24 다음 중 밑줄 친 (B)를 대신하여 쓰일 수 있는 것은?

① Roughly   ② Closely
③ Fairly   ④ Almost
⑤ Mostly

중요

25 다음 글을 읽고 알 수 없는 것은?

I went to Kaieteur Falls with my family. The waterfall sits in the Amazon Rainforest in Guyana, and it is 226 meters high. I was surprised at the size of the waterfall. I could see the brown rocks and green trees there. My trip to Kaieteur Falls made me feel good. I felt like all my stress went away.

① where the waterfall is
② how high the waterfall is
③ how the writer felt when he first saw the waterfall
④ what the writer saw there
⑤ how the writer got to the waterfall

[01~05] 다음 글을 읽고 물음에 답하시오.

Do you know where the driest desert on Earth is? How about the highest waterfall? Yes, they are both in South America. This continent is full of natural wonders that will surprise you.

Atacama Desert

(a)The Atacama is the driest desert on Earth. In some parts, it gets almost no rain at all — only 1–3 millimeters per year! The ground in some areas is so ___(A)___ that no plants can grow. Do you know what scientists do in such a dry place? The soil in this desert is very similar to the soil on Mars, so they prepare for trips to outer space. The Atacama is also one of the best places on Earth to watch stars.

01 빈칸 (A)에 들어갈 알맞은 말을 위 글에서 찾아 어법에 맞게 쓰시오.

➡ _____

02 Write the reason why the Atacama is the driest desert on Earth. Use the phrase 'Because.'

➡ _____
_____

03 다음 빈칸에 알맞은 말을 써서 밑줄 친 (a)를 대신하여 쓸 수 있는 문장을 완성하시오.

No other desert on earth _____ _____ _____ the Atacama.

04 위 글의 내용에 맞게 빈칸에 알맞은 말을 쓰시오.

Atacama Desert is _____ desert on Earth. Its soil is very _____ the soil on _____. It is one of the best places _____.

05 What can you see in South America? Answer in English with a full sentence.

➡ _____
_____

[06~09] 다음 글을 읽고 물음에 답하시오.

Angel Falls

If you go to Venezuela, you can see the world's highest waterfall. It is 979 meters high. Clouds often cover the top, so you need patience and a little luck to get a good view. Actually, the waterfall is named after Jimmie Angel, a pilot from the United States who first flew over the waterfall in 1933. You can still get to the top of the beautiful waterfall only by plane.

06 How did the world's highest waterfall get its name?

➡ _____
_____
_____

07 Write the reason why you need patience and a little luck to get a good view when you want to see Angel Falls. Use the phrase 'It's because.'

➡ _____

08 다음은 위 글의 내용을 요약한 것이다. 글의 내용에 맞게 빈칸에 알맞은 말을 쓰시오.

> Angel Falls is the _____ waterfall on Earth. It is named after an American _____. You can reach the top only by _____.

09 According to the passage, how high is the waterfall? Answer in English with a full sentence.

➡ _____

[10~14] 다음 글을 읽고 물음에 답하시오.

The Amazon

The Amazon runs across the continent through seven countries.

[A] That is because it usually runs through rainforests and wet areas, not cities or towns.
[B] The Amazon River is interesting in many ways. For the most part, it has no bridges.
[C] It travels from Peru in the west and flows into the Atlantic Ocean.

Also, in many places the river is very wide, so you cannot see the other side! You probably do not want to swim in this river. It is home to some very big snakes and fish that eat meat.

The Andes

The Andes are the world's longest mountain range. (D)여러분은 그 산맥의 길이가 얼마인지 아시나요? It is about 7,000 kilometers long! It also contains the highest mountains outside of Asia. About a third of the people in South America live in the Andes. Many unique animals also live there.

10 자연스러운 글이 되도록 [A]~[C]를 바르게 나열하시오.

➡ _____

11 위 글의 내용에 맞게 다음 빈칸에 알맞은 말을 쓰시오.

> A: Do you know _____ _____ _____ _____ _____ in the world is?
>
> B: Yes, I do. They are the Andes. The Andes are _____ _____ any other mountain range in the world.

12 밑줄 친 우리말 (D)를 영어로 쓰시오.

➡ _____

13 아마존강에 대한 두 사람의 대화를 완성하시오.

> A: I wonder _____ _____ _____ _____ _____ _____.
>
> B: In many places, it is too _____ to _____ the other side.

14 According to the passage, where does the Amazon River flow into? Answer in English with a full sentence.

➡ _____

My Speaking Portfolio

A: Which country do you want to visit?

B: Brazil. Do you know where Brazil is?
의문사+주어+동사

A: Yes, I do. It's in South America. Do you know that Brazil is the biggest
= the+최상급
country in South America?

B: What a surprise! I didn't know that. So, what's the first thing you want to
what으로 시작하는 감탄문   = thing that(= which) you
see in Brazil?

A: I want to see Iguazu Falls from the sky.

구문해설 · country: 나라, 국가 · sky: 하늘

A: 너는 어느 나라를 가 보고 싶니?

B: 브라질. 너는 브라질이 어디에 있는지 알고 있니?

A: 응, 알아. 그건 남아메리카에 있어. 너는 남아메리카에서 브라질이 가장 큰 나라라는 거 알고 있니?

B: 정말 놀랍다! 그건 몰랐네. 그러면 너는 브라질에서 가장 처음으로 보고 싶은 게 뭐야?

A: 나는 하늘에서 이구아수 폭포를 보고 싶어.

My Writing Portfolio

A Day in Nature

I went to Kaieteur Falls with my family. The waterfall sits in the Amazon
(어떤 곳에) 있다
Rainforest in Guyana, and it is 226 meters high. I was surprised at the size
= Kaieteur Falls   ~에 놀랐다
of the waterfall. I could see the brown rocks and green trees there. My trip to
Kaieteur Falls made me feel good. I felt like all my stress went away.
사역동사+목적어+동사원형   ~한 느낌이 들었다

구문해설 · sit in: ~에 위치해 있다 · surprised: 놀란

자연에서의 하루

나는 가족과 함께 카이에투 폭포에 갔다. 그 폭포는 가이아나에 있는 아마존 열대 우림에 위치하고 있고, 높이는 226m이다. 나는 폭포의 크기에 놀랐다. 나는 그곳에서 갈색 바위와 초록색 나무를 볼 수 있었다. 카이에투 폭포로의 여행은 나를 기분 좋게 만들어 주었다. 내 모든 스트레스가 사라진 것 같았다.

Wrap Up – Reading

Salar de Uyuni in Bolivia is the world's largest salt flat. Thousands of years
세계에서 가장 큰   수천의
ago, there was water, but it all dried up. Now, a large salt desert is left about
뒤의 명사에 수의 일치   수동태
3,656 meters above sea level. Salar de Uyuni is one of the most visited natural
one of the 최상급+복수 명사
wonders of South America, too. All year round a lot of people visit this place
= many
to take pictures of its unique natural beauty. In fact, the salt flat makes any
to부정사의 부사적 용법 중 목적 (~하기 위해서)   사실
tourist a great photographer. Every picture you take in Salar de Uyuni will be
앞에 관계대명사 that 생략
a beautiful work of art!

구문해설 · dry up: 마르다 · above sea level: 해발 · all year round: 일 년 내내
· unique: 독특한 · flat: 평원

볼리비아에 있는 살라르 데 우유니는 세계에서 가장 큰 솔트 플랫(소금 평원)이다. 수천 년 전에는 그곳에 물이 있었지만, 모두 말라버렸다. 지금은 해발 약 3,656미터에 큰 소금 사막이 남겨져 있다. 살라르 데 우유니는 또한 방문객이 가장 많은 남아메리카의 자연 경관 중의 하나이다. 일 년 내내 많은 사람들이 독특한 자연의 아름다움을 사진으로 찍기 위해 이 장소를 방문한다. 사실, 그 솔트 플랫은 어떤 방문객도 훌륭한 사진작가로 만든다. 살라르 데 우유니에서 당신이 찍은 모든 사진은 아름다운 예술 작품이 될 것이다!

01 다음 짝지어진 단어의 관계가 같도록 빈칸에 알맞은 말을 쓰시오.

possible : impossible = patient : _____

02 다음 영영풀이가 가리키는 것을 고르시오.

a person who operates the controls of an aircraft, especially as a job

① tourist   ② pilot

③ guide   ④ steward

⑤ crew

03 다음 중 밑줄 친 부분의 뜻풀이가 바르지 않은 것은?

① I want to know the origin of the civilization. 기원

② My favorite subject is social studies. 사회

③ The band is especially popular in Japan. 특히

④ Josh has always been scared of dogs. 수줍음 많은

⑤ The casting for the movie was fantastic. 엄청난, 환상적인

04 다음 주어진 문장의 밑줄 친 flow와 다른 의미로 쓰인 것은?

As I was listening to the music, tears began to flow from my eyes.

① The river flows northward to the sea.

② Rivers flow to the ocean.

③ I can't find where the water is flowing out.

④ The spring has a flow of 300 gallons a minute.

⑤ The Han River flows through Seoul from east to west.

05 다음 문장에 공통으로 들어갈 말을 고르시오.

• Are you able to _____ a horse?

• My children _____ the bus to school every day.

• Jimmy and I went out to _____ a bike.

① view   ② ride

③ fly   ④ contain

⑤ wonder

06 다음 우리말에 맞게 빈칸에 알맞은 말을 쓰시오.

(1) 그 마을은 Monsanto 산을 따라 이름 지어졌다.

➡ The village is _____ the mountain, Monsanto.

(2) 우리는 선생님을 위해 깜작 파티를 열 계획 중이다.

➡ We are planning to _____ a surprise _____ for my teacher.

(3) 솔직히 말하면, 나는 연극 동아리에 가입하고 싶지 않아.

➡ _____, I don't want to join the drama club.

Conversation

[07~09] 다음 대화를 읽고 물음에 답하시오.

Sujin: Dad, I like this tomato soup.

Dad: I'm happy you like (A)it.

Sujin: By the way, (B)do you know where was the tomato first grown?

Dad: Italy or somewhere in Europe?

Sujin: No, the tomato came from South America.

Dad: Really? How did you know that?

Sujin: I learned (C)it from Ms. Song, my social studies teacher.

Dad: That's good.

07 위 대화의 (A)와 (C)의 it이 각각 가리키는 것을 찾아 쓰시오.

➡ (A) _____

   (C) _____

08 위 대화의 밑줄 친 (B)를 어법상 바르게 고치시오.

➡ _____

09 위 대화의 내용과 일치하지 <u>않는</u> 것은?

① 수진은 토마토 수프가 마음에 든다.

② 아빠는 수진이가 토마토 수프를 좋아해서 기분이 좋다.

③ 토마토는 남아메리카에서 왔다.

④ 수진은 송 선생님에게서 사회를 배운다.

⑤ 토마토 수프는 이탈리아에서 전해졌다.

[10~12] 다음 대화를 읽고 물음에 답하시오.

Hana: How was the roller coaster ride, Jongha?

Jongha: It was fantastic. I really enjoyed it.

Hana: Ha ha. You closed your eyes while riding.

Jongha: Did you see? To be honest, I was really scared at first.

Hana: Do you know how fast this roller coaster is?

Jongha: I have no idea.

Hana: _____(A)_____

Jongha: Wow! That's surprising!

Hana: Let's ride it one more time!

Jongha: Look at the sign. We can't ride it after 8 p.m.

Hana: Oh, maybe next time.

10 위 대화의 빈칸 (A)에 들어갈 말을 〈보기〉에 주어진 어구를 모두 사용하여 영작하시오.

┌─ 보기 ┐

fast / as / per / it / as / goes / 140 km / hour

➡ _____

11 위 대화의 내용과 일치하도록 롤러코스터 안내문을 완성하시오.

<Enjoy the roller coaster!>

1) Must be at least 120 cm tall to ride.

2) Runs as fast as (A)_____.

3) Can enjoy from 10 a.m to (B)_____.

12 위 대화에서 롤러코스터를 타는 동안 종하의 기분 변화로 적절한 것은?

① joyful → nervous

② fantastic → worried

③ worried → disappointed

④ scared → pleased

⑤ fantastic → fearful

[13~14] 다음 대화를 읽고 물음에 답하시오.

> Jenny: Did you see the pictures Ms. Song took?
>
> Brian: What pictures?
>
> Jenny: She traveled around South America (A)[by / of] herself last summer.
>
> Brian: Really? (B)[How / What] a surprise!
>
> Jenny: She showed us pictures of beautiful places. I especially liked the pictures of pyramids.
>
> Brian: Are there pyramids in South America?
>
> Jenny: Yes. She said some pyramids are about 3,800 meters above sea level.
>
> Brian: I (C)[can / can't] believe it.

13 위 대화의 괄호 (A)~(C)에 들어갈 알맞은 말을 고르시오.

➡ (A) _____ (B) _____ (C) _____

14 위 대화의 내용과 일치하도록 Jenny의 일기를 완성하시오.

> I was impressed that Ms. Song traveled around South America by herself last summer. I thought she was really brave. She showed me (A)_____
> _____. Among them, I love (B)_____. She explained that (C)_____
> _____. It sounded very interesting, so I decided to visit there someday.

Grammar

15 11단어를 이용하여 다음 문장을 영어로 쓸 때, 다섯 번째로 오는 단어는?

> 그는 내가 만나 본 사람 중 가장 지루한 사람이야.

① the   ② most   ③ boring
④ person   ⑤ that

16 다음 중 주어진 문장의 밑줄 친 부분과 쓰임이 같은 것은?

> Tell me who broke into your house.

① That is the man who told me how to get to the post office.
② Where is the boy who was wearing a cap?
③ I don't remember who you were talking about.
④ The boy who Jessica likes is my cousin.
⑤ Did you find the man who bought you coffee?

17 다음 중 주어진 문장과 같은 의미의 문장을 모두 고르시오.

> Nothing is more valuable than honesty.

① Honesty is not as valuable as everything.
② No other thing is less valuable than honesty.
③ Honesty is not as valuable as nothing.
④ Honesty is the most valuable thing.
⑤ Honesty is more valuable than anything else.

18 다음 우리말을 영어로 바르게 옮긴 것은?

> 누가 너를 파티에 초대했는지 말해 줄래?

① Can you tell me who you invited to the party?

② Can you tell me who you want to invite to the party?

③ Can you tell me who was invited to the party?

④ Can you tell me who wanted to invite you to the party?

⑤ Can you tell me who invited you to the party?

19 주어진 어구를 활용하여 다음 우리말을 영어로 쓰시오.

> 너는 네 삶에서 가장 행복한 순간을 기억하고 있니? (remember, of your life)

➡ _____

20 다음 중 어법상 바르지 <u>않은</u> 것은?

① I want to know when you bought this lamp.

② I am fastest runner on our team.

③ Do you know who wrote this book?

④ What is the tallest building in this city?

⑤ Tell me where you are going to meet Jackson tomorrow.

21 다음 빈칸에 들어갈 말로 가장 적절한 것은?

> No other planet in our solar system is as bright as Venus.
> = Venus is _____ in our solar system.

① not as bright as the other planet

② the least bright planet

③ brighter than all the other planet

④ the brightest planet

⑤ less bright than other planet

22 다음 중 어법상 바르지 <u>않은</u> 것은?

> A: I ①<u>wonder</u> how ②<u>you think</u> about the cake.
> B: ③<u>It was</u> very good. Actually it was ④<u>the deliciousest</u> cake that ⑤<u>I've ever</u> eaten.

23 다음 빈칸에 알맞은 말을 일곱 단어로 쓰시오.

> A: Who is the wisest man in the town?
> B: No other man _____ Patrick.

24 다음 대화를 읽고 빈칸에 알맞은 말을 쓰시오.

> Jack: Are you free?
> Paul: Not really.

➡ Jack wants to know _____ .

25 다음 두 문장을 하나의 문장으로 쓰시오.

> I wonder. Did you find what you were looking for?

➡ _____
_____

26 최상급과 주어진 단어를 활용하여 다음 우리말을 영어로 쓰시오.

> 내게 목요일은 그 주 중 최악의 날이었어. (bad, for)

➡ _____

Reading

[27~29] 다음 글을 읽고 물음에 답하시오.

(A)Do you know where is the driest desert on Earth? How about the highest waterfall? Yes, they are ①both in South America. This continent is full of natural wonders that will ②surprise you.

Atacama Desert

The Atacama is the driest desert on Earth. In some parts, it gets almost ③no rain at all — only 1–3 millimeters per year! The ground in some areas is so dry that no plants can grow. Do you know what scientists do in such a ④dry place? The soil in this desert is very ⑤different from the soil on Mars, so they prepare for trips to outer space. The Atacama is also one of the best places on Earth to watch stars.

27 밑줄 친 (A)에서 어법상 틀린 것을 찾아 바르게 고쳐 쓰시오.

➡ _____

28 ①~⑤ 중 글의 흐름상 어색한 것은?

① ② ③ ④ ⑤

29 다음 중 위 글의 내용과 일치하는 것은?

① We find natural wonders in South America.
② The Atacama is not as dry as all the other deserts in the world.
③ Scientists want to explore the Atacama Desert to study the desert.
④ It is impossible to watch stars in the Atacama because of sand.
⑤ Some areas of the Atacama aren't very dry.

[30~33] 다음 글을 읽고 물음에 답하시오.

Salar de Uyuni in Bolivia is the world's largest salt flat. Thousands of years ago, there was water, but it all dried up. Now, a large salt desert is left about 3,656 meters above sea level. Salar de Uyuni is one of the most visited natural wonders of South America, too. (A) All year round a lot of people visit this place (B)to take pictures of its unique natural beauty. In fact, the salt flat makes any tourist a great ⓐ . Every picture you take in Salar de Uyuni will be a beautiful work of art!

30 빈칸 ⓐ에 들어갈 말로 가장 적절한 것은?

① scientist ② painter
③ dentist ④ photographer
⑤ pianist

31 밑줄 친 (A)의 의미로 가장 적절한 것은?

① round and round
② throughout the year
③ all your efforts
④ over and over
⑤ time after time

32 다음 중 밑줄 친 (B)와 쓰임이 같은 것은?

① They decided to break the promise.
② It is my job to protect you.
③ Is there anything to wear?
④ He went out to buy some fruit.
⑤ Polly felt sad to see the bird die.

33 Where is the world's largest salt flat? Answer in English with a full sentence.

➡ _____

[01~02] 다음 대화를 읽고 물음에 답하시오.

Jenny: Did you see the pictures Ms. Song took?

Brian: What pictures?

Jenny: She traveled around South America by herself last summer.

Brian: (A) Really? What a surprise!

Jenny: (B) I especially liked the pictures of pyramids.

Brian: (C) Are there pyramids in South America?

Jenny: (D) Yes. She said some pyramids are about 3,800 meters above sea level.

Brian: (E) I can't believe it.

01 위 대화의 (A)~(E) 중 주어진 문장이 들어가기에 적절한 곳은?

> She showed us pictures of beautiful places.

① (A)　② (B)　③ (C)　④ (D)　⑤ (E)

02 위 대화를 읽고 대답할 수 없는 것은?

① Where did Ms. Song travel last summer?
② With whom did Ms. Song take a trip around South America?
③ What did Ms. Song show Jenny?
④ What pictures did Jenny especially like?
⑤ How long did Ms. Song stay in South America?

[03~05] 다음 대화를 읽고 물음에 답하시오.

Hana: How was the roller coaster ride, Jongha?

Jongha: It was fantastic. I really enjoyed it.

Hana: Ha ha. You closed your eyes while riding.

Jongha: Did you see? _____(A)_____, I was really scared at first.

Hana: Do you know how fast this roller coaster is?

Jongha: I have no idea.

Hana: It goes as fast as 140 km per hour.

Jongha: Wow! _____(B)_____

Hana: Let's ride it one more time!

Jongha: Look at the sign. We can't ride it after 8 p.m.

Hana: Oh, maybe next time.

03 위 대화의 빈칸 (A)에 '솔직히 말하자면'을 뜻하는 표현을 주어진 단어를 사용하여 쓰시오. (be)

➡ _____

04 위 대화의 빈칸 (B)에 들어가기에 알맞은 것은?

① I'm sorry for that.
② I can't believe it.
③ Thank you for your help.
④ I'm curious about it.
⑤ I'm not happy with it.

05 위 대화의 내용과 일치하지 않는 것은?

① 종하는 롤러코스터가 정말 재미있었다.
② 종하는 롤러코스터를 타는 동안 눈을 감고 있었다.
③ 롤러코스터는 시속 140 km로 달린다.
④ 롤러코스터는 저녁 8시 이후에는 탈 수 없다.
⑤ 종하는 무서워서 롤러코스터를 한 번 더 타지 않았다.

[06~08] 다음 대화를 읽고 물음에 답하시오.

Sujin: Dad, I like this tomato soup.

Dad: I'm happy you like it.

Sujin: _____(A)_____, do you know where the tomato was first grown?

Dad: Italy or somewhere in Europe?

Sujin: No, the tomato came from South America.

Dad: Really? How did you know that?

Sujin: I learned it from Ms. Song, my social studies teacher.

Dad: That's good.

06 위 대화의 빈칸 (A)에 '그건 그렇고'를 뜻하는 말을 3 단어로 쓰시오.

➡ _____

07 Where did the tomato come from?

➡ _____

08 Who taught the origin of the tomato to Sujin?

➡ _____

[09~10] 다음 대화를 읽고 물음에 답하시오.

Jane: _____(A)_____

Brian: Brazil. Do you know where Brazil is?

Jane: Yes, I do. It's in South America. Do you know that Brazil is the biggest country in South America?

Brian: What a surprise! I didn't know that. So, what's the first thing you want to see in Brazil?

Jane: I want to see Iguazu Falls from the sky.

09 위 대화의 빈칸에 들어갈 질문을 〈보기〉에 있는 단어를 모두 배열하여 영작하시오.

┌─ 보기 ┐

you / country / visit / to / do / want / which

➡ _____

10 위 대화의 내용과 일치하지 <u>않는</u> 것은?

① Brian은 브라질을 방문하고 싶어 한다.

② 브라질은 남아메리카에 위치해 있다.

③ 브라질은 남아메리카에서 가장 큰 국가이다.

④ Jane은 브라질에 가면 이구아수 폭포를 보고 싶어 한다.

⑤ Brian은 브라질이 남아메리카에 위치해 있다는 것에 놀랐다.

11 다음 중 최상급의 형태가 <u>다른</u> 하나는?

① dark   ② thick

③ long   ④ helpful

⑤ fast

12 다음 중 빈칸에 들어갈 말로 가장 적절한 것은?

I'd like to know. Did she push you first?
= I'd like to know _____ you first.

① why she pushed

② whether did she push

③ when she pushed

④ if she pushed

⑤ how did she pushed

13 다음 중 의미가 <u>다른</u> 하나는? (출제율 95%)

① Your advice is the most helpful advice.
② Your advice is more helpful than any other advice.
③ No other advice is as good as your advice.
④ No other advice is more helpful than your advice.
⑤ Your advice is not more helpful than any other advice.

14 주어진 단어를 활용하여 다음 우리말을 영어로 쓰시오. (출제율 90%)

> 그녀가 무엇을 하고 있다고 생각해?
> (think / do)

➡ _____

15 다음 중 어법상 바르지 <u>않은</u> 것은? (출제율 100%)

① Jack is one of the most thoughtful student in the class.
② I forgot where I put my umbrella.
③ No other car is as fast as my car.
④ How we talk to people is important.
⑤ The dress is more beautiful than any other dress in this room.

16 다음 두 문장을 하나의 문장으로 쓰시오. (출제율 95%)

> Please tell me. Did she tell you her number?

➡ _____

17 다음 빈칸에 들어갈 말로 가장 적절한 것은? (출제율 90%)

> No other clock in this store is as cheap as this clock.
> = This clock is _____ in this store.

① cheaper than other clocks
② not as cheap as that clock
③ the most cheap clock
④ cheaper than any other clock
⑤ not the cheapest clock

[18~21] 다음 글을 읽고 물음에 답하시오.

Do you know where the driest desert on Earth is? How about the highest waterfall? Yes, they are both in South America. This continent is full of natural wonders that will surprise you.

Atacama Desert
The Atacama is the driest desert on Earth. In some parts, it gets almost no rain at all — only 1–3 millimeters per year! The ground in some areas is so dry that no plants can grow. Do you know what scientists do in (A)such a dry place? The soil in this desert is very similar to the soil on Mars, so they prepare for trips to outer space. The Atacama is also one of the best places on Earth (B)to watch stars.

18 밑줄 친 (A)가 의미하는 것을 위 글에서 찾아 쓰시오. (출제율 90%)

➡ _____

19 다음 중 밑줄 친 (B)와 쓰임이 같은 것은? (출제율 95%)

① I hope to see you again.
② It is good to have dinner with her.
③ He went out to find his watch.
④ She felt sad to hear the news.
⑤ I need something to write about.

20 다음 중 위 글의 내용과 일치하지 <u>않는</u> 것은?

① The highest waterfall is in South America.
② Natural wonders of South America will surprise you.
③ Scientists enjoy their trip to the Atacama.
④ Only 1–3mm of rain falls per year in some parts of the Atacama.
⑤ Scientists prepare for trips to outer space in the Atacama.

21 다음은 위 글을 요약한 것이다. 빈칸에 알맞은 말을 쓰시오.

> The Atacama is _____ _____ _____ in the world. It is a good place to _____ _____ _____ and _____ _____.

[22~25] 다음 글을 읽고 물음에 답하시오.

Angel Falls

If you go to Venezuela, you can see the world's highest waterfall. It is 979 meters high. Clouds often cover the top, so you need patience and a little luck to get a good view. Actually, the waterfall is named after Jimmie Angel, a pilot from the United States who first flew over the waterfall in 1933. You can still get to the top of the beautiful waterfall only by plane.

The Amazon

The Amazon runs across the continent through seven countries. It travels from Peru in the west and flows into the Atlantic Ocean. The Amazon River is interesting in many ways. For the most part, it has no bridges. That

is because it usually runs through rainforests and wet areas, not cities or towns. Also, in many places the river is very wide, ___(A)___ you cannot see the other side! You probably do not want to swim in this river. It is home to some very big snakes and fish that eat meat.

22 다음 중 (A)에 들어갈 말로 가장 적절한 것은?

① although   ② so   ③ when
④ because   ⑤ however

23 다음과 같이 풀이되는 말을 위 글에서 찾아 쓰시오.

> the ability to stay calm without becoming angry

➡ _____

24 다음 중 위 글의 내용과 일치하는 것은?

① The world's highest waterfall is in Peru.
② You can climb to the top of the waterfall.
③ You cannot easily see the top of the waterfall because of clouds.
④ It is safe to swim in the Amazon River.
⑤ Fish that live in the Amazon only eat meat.

25 According to the passage, how many countries does the Amazon run through? Answer in English with a full sentence.

➡ _____

[01~03] 다음 대화를 읽고 물음에 답하시오.

Mike: Do you know Sumin won first prize at the speech contest?

Sue: I can't believe it. She was very quiet and shy last year.

Mike: Yeah. She joined the drama club this year, and she has changed a lot.

Sue: I see. I want to join the club, too.

01 Who won the speech contest?

➡ _____

02 What was Sumin's characteristic last year?

➡ _____

03 What club did Sumin join this year?

➡ _____

04 주어진 단어를 활용하여 다음 대화의 빈칸에 알맞은 말을 쓰시오.

A: You drink a lot. I wonder _____ (how / water) a day.

B: I drink ten cups of water a day.

➡ _____

05 다음 두 문장을 하나의 문장으로 쓰시오.

(1) I'd like to know. Are you comfortable?

➡ _____

(2) I wonder. When did you come home?

➡ _____

06 다음 그림을 보고 빈칸에 알맞은 말을 쓰시오.

(1) Stuart is _____ student in the class. (smart)

(2) Carl is _____ student in the class. (noisy)

07 다음 우리말을 조건에 맞게 문장을 완성하시오.

내게는 다른 어떤 스포츠도 테니스를 치는 것만큼 신나지 않아.

(1) 최상급을 이용하여

➡ _____
to me.

(2) 부정 주어와 원급을 이용하여

➡ _____
to me.

[08~09] 다음 글을 읽고 물음에 답하시오.

Do you know where the driest desert on Earth is? How about the highest waterfall? Yes, (A)they are both in South America. This continent is full of natural wonders that will surprise you.

Atacama Desert

The Atacama is the driest desert on Earth. In some parts, it gets almost no rain at all — only 1–3 millimeters per year! The ground in some areas is so dry that no plants can grow.

Do you know what scientists do in such a dry place? The soil in this desert is very similar to the soil on Mars, so they prepare for trips to outer space. The Atacama is also one of the best places on Earth to watch stars.

08 밑줄 친 (A)가 가리키는 것을 위 글에서 찾아 쓰시오.

➡ _____

09 위 글의 내용에 맞게 빈칸에 알맞은 말을 쓰시오.

> A: I wonder what scientists do in the Atacama.
> B: _____(A)_____
> A: Why do they do that in the desert?
> B: It's because _____(B)_____ .

➡ (A) _____
  (B) _____

[10~12] 다음 글을 읽고 물음에 답하시오.

Salar de Uyuni in Bolivia is the world's largest salt flat. Thousands of years ago, there was water, but it all dried up. Now, a large salt desert is left about 3,656 meters above sea level. Salar de Uyuni is one of the most visited natural wonders of South America, too. All year round a lot of people visit this place to take pictures of its unique natural beauty. In fact, the salt flat makes any tourist a great photographer. (A)Every picture you take in Salar de Uyuni will be a beautiful work of art!

10 According to the passage, how was Salar de Uyuni made? Answer in Korean.

➡ _____

11 Write the reason why the writer says like the underlined (A). Use the phrase 'It's because.'

➡ _____
  _____

12 다음 문장에서 위 글의 내용과 일치하지 <u>않는</u> 부분을 바르게 고쳐 쓰시오.

> (1) Salar de Uyuni is located about 3,656 meters under sea level.
> (2) People visit Salar de Uyuni during a certain period.
> (3) Salar de Uyuni is the most visited natural wonder of South America.

➡ (1) _____
    ➡ _____
  (2) _____
    ➡ _____
  (3) _____
    ➡ _____

01 다음 대화의 내용과 일치하도록 Sujin의 일기를 완성하시오.

Sujin: Dad, I like this tomato soup.

Dad: I'm happy you like it.

Sujin: By the way, do you know where the tomato was first grown?

Dad: Italy or somewhere in Europe?

Sujin: No, the tomato came from South America.

Dad: Really? How did you know that?

Sujin: I learned it from Ms. Song, my social studies teacher.

Dad: That's good.

Mon, Dec 2th, 2019

I was happy when I tasted my father's tomato soup. It was so delicious. When I tasted the soup, I remembered what I learned from Ms. Song, my (A)_____ teacher. She let me know (B)_____ the tomato was first grown. I asked my father if he knew about it or not. At first, he guessed the tomato was from (C)_____. I told him that (D)_____. I was proud of myself when I shared what I learned from the teacher with my father.

02 다음 질문과 답변을 읽고 Jason이 가 본 장소에 관한 글을 완성하시오.

Q: Where did you go?　A: I went to Gwanak Mountain.

Q: Who were you with?　A: I was with my family.

Q: What did you learn about the place?　A: It is 632 meters high and is in the south of Seoul.

Q: What did you see?　A: I saw the bridges over the Han River.

Q: How did you feel?　A: I felt like all my stress went away.

I went to _____ with _____. The mountain is _____. It is in _____. I saw _____. My trip to Gwanak Mountain made me feel good. I felt like _____.

단원별 모의고사

01 다음 영영풀이가 가리키는 것을 고르시오.

> a place where a stream or river falls from a high place, for example over a cliff or rock

① rainforest ② waterfall
③ snowstorm ④ rainfall
⑤ ocean

02 다음 문장의 빈칸에 들어갈 말을 〈보기〉에서 골라 쓰시오.

> ┌─ 보기 ─┐
> wonders / sunrise / scared / Mars / view

(1) Have you ever watched _____ ?
(2) I would like a room with a nice _____.
(3) NASA found the new evidence about water on _____.
(4) My sister looked _____ when she saw the bear.
(5) The Grand Canyon is one of the natural _____ of the world.

03 다음 주어진 문장의 밑줄 친 wonder와 같은 의미로 쓰인 것은?

> There is no one who can find out all the wonders of the sea.

① I think AI is one of the wonders of modern science.
② I wonder if I can ask you a favor.
③ I wonder what happened to you.
④ I always wondered why he didn't want to marry.
⑤ I wonder whether my brother is at home or not.

04 다음 우리말과 일치하도록 주어진 단어를 모두 배열하여 영작하시오.

(1) 수많은 예술품들이 도난당했다.
(art / a / of / works / stolen / were / number / of)
➡ _____

(2) 암스테르담은 해수면보다 4미터 아래에 있다.
(sea / is / 4 meters / Amsterdam / level / below)
➡ _____

05 다음 대화가 자연스럽게 이어지도록 순서대로 배열하시오.

> (A) I want one, too.
> (B) No. Where did he get it? From a pet shop?
> (C) Do you know Junha got a puppy?
> (D) No. I heard he got the puppy from his uncle.

➡ _____

[06~08] 다음 대화를 읽고 물음에 답하시오.

Hana: How was the roller coaster ride, Jongha?
Jongha: It was fantastic. I really enjoyed it.
Hana: Ha ha. You closed your eyes while riding.
Jongha: Did you see? (A)To be honest, I was really scared at first.
Hana: Do you know how fast this roller coaster is?
Jongha: I have no idea.
ⓐ Wow! That's surprising!
ⓑ Oh, maybe next time.
ⓒ Let's ride it one more time!
ⓓ It goes as fast as 140 km per hour.
ⓔ Look at the sign. We can't ride it after 8 p.m.

06 위 대화에서 ⓐ~ⓔ가 자연스럽게 이어지도록 순서대로 배열하시오.

➡ _____

07 위 대화에서 밑줄 친 (A)와 바꾸어 쓸 수 있는 것은?

① Generally speaking
② Frankly speaking
③ Strictly speaking
④ Broadly speaking
⑤ Personally speaking

08 위 대화의 내용과 일치하는 것은?

① Hana was scared when she rode the roller coaster.
② While riding the roller coaster, Jongha felt fantastic first but he was scared later.
③ Jongha couldn't open his eyes because of strong winds.
④ The roller coaster is much faster than 140 km per hour.
⑤ The roller coaster runs until 8 p.m.

[09~10] 다음 대화를 읽고 물음에 답하시오.

Sujin: Dad, I like this tomato soup.
Dad: I'm happy you like it.
Sujin: (A)[By / On] the way, do you know where the tomato was first grown?
Dad: Italy or somewhere in Europe?
Sujin: No, the tomato came from South America.
Dad: Really? (B)[What / How] did you know that?
Sujin: I (C)[taught / learned] it from Ms. Song, my social studies teacher.
Dad: That's good.

09 위 대화의 빈칸 (A)~(C)에 들어갈 말로 알맞은 것을 고르시오.

➡ (A) _____ (B) _____ (C) _____

10 위 대화의 내용과 일치하는 것은?

① Dad liked his tomato soup so much.
② The tomato came from Italy in Europe.
③ Sujin learns social studies from Ms. Song.
④ Ms. Song has been to South America.
⑤ Sujin knows when the tomato came from South America.

11 다음 우리말을 주어진 단어를 이용하여 영작하시오.

(1) 그 산맥은 많은 독특한 식물과 동물의 서식지이다. (range, unique, home)

➡ _____
_____

(2) 나는 처음에는 그를 전혀 이해할 수 없었다. (at, couldn't, all)

➡ _____

(3) 솔직히 말하면, 나는 집에 머물며 TV를 보고 싶어. (honest)

➡ _____
_____

12 우리말과 일치하도록 빈칸을 채우시오.

(1) 고래는 바다에서 가장 큰 동물들이다.

➡ _____ are the largest animals in the ocean.

(2) 이 천연 돌다리는 이 마을의 상징이다.

➡ This _____ stone bridge is the symbol of this town.

(3) 이 음료에는 어떤 알코올도 포함되어 있지 않다.

➡ This drink does not _____ any alcohol.

13 다음 중 밑줄 친 부분의 쓰임이 나머지와 다른 하나는?

① Can you tell me if she will come?
② I wonder if he wants to see me.
③ I'm not sure if the news is true.
④ I will go if they invite me.
⑤ I don't know if she locked the door.

14 다음 중 빈칸에 들어갈 말로 적절한 것을 모두 고르시오.

> No other waterfall in the world is as wide as Iguazu Falls.
> = Iguazu Falls is _____ in the world.

① as wide as all the other waterfalls
② more wider than any other waterfall
③ the widest waterfall
④ wider than all the other waterfalls
⑤ the most widest waterfall

15 다음 중 어법상 바르지 않은 것은?

① That was the most wonderful trip.
② Can you tell me why you didn't help her?
③ Bob thinks he is the most handsome student in his school.
④ I need to know when they booked the restaurant.
⑤ Tell me who your book found.

16 주어진 단어를 활용하여 다음 우리말을 영어로 옮기시오. 필요하다면 어형을 바꿀 것.

> 싱가포르는 내가 방문해 본 도시 중 가장 흥미로운 곳 중 하나야. (Singapore / interesting / place / ever / visit)

➡ _____

_____

17 다음 두 문장을 하나의 문장으로 쓰시오.

(1) Do you know? Why is she upset?

➡ _____

(2) I wonder. Does he sing well?

➡ _____

[18~19] 다음 글을 읽고 물음에 답하시오.

> Atacama Desert
> ⓐThe Atacama is the driest desert on Earth.
>
> [A] The ground in some areas is so dry that no plants can grow. Do you know what scientists do in such a dry place?
> [B] In some parts, it gets almost no rain at all — only 1–3 millimeters per year!
> [C] The soil in this desert is very similar to the soil on Mars, so they prepare for trips to outer space.
>
> The Atacama is also one of the best places on Earth to watch stars.

18 다음 중 밑줄 친 ⓐ를 대신하여 쓸 수 있는 문장은?

① The Atacama is not drier than all the other deserts on Earth.
② The Atacama is not as dry as all the other deserts on Earth.
③ No other desert on Earth is drier than the Atacama.
④ No deserts on Earth are not as dry as the Atacama.
⑤ The Atacama is as dry as all the other deserts on Earth.

19 자연스러운 내용이 되도록 [A]~[C]를 바르게 나열하시오.

➡ _____

[20~22] 다음 글을 읽고 물음에 답하시오.

Angel Falls

If you go to Venezuela, you can see the world's highest waterfall. It is 979 meters high. Clouds often cover the top, so you need patience and a little luck to get a good view. Actually, the waterfall is named after Jimmie Angel, a pilot from the United States who first flew over the waterfall in 1933. You can still get to the top of the beautiful waterfall only by plane.

20 다음 중 Angel Falls에 관하여 언급된 것을 <u>모두</u> 고르시오.

① its height
② its width
③ the number of visitors
④ the origin of its name
⑤ its depth

21 How can you get to the top of Angel Falls? Answer in English with a full sentence. Use the word 'there.'

➡ _____

22 다음 중 위 글을 읽고 답할 수 <u>없는</u> 것은?

① Where is Angel Falls?
② What is the highest waterfall in the world?
③ Who first flew over the waterfall?
④ When did Jimmie Angel first fly over Angel Falls?
⑤ How old was Jimmie Angel when he first flew over the waterfall?

23 ①~⑤ 중 주어진 문장이 들어가기에 가장 적합한 곳은?

In fact, the salt flat makes any tourist a great photographer.

Salar de Uyuni in Bolivia is the world's largest salt flat. ① Thousands of years ago, there was water, but it all dried up. ② Now, a large salt desert is left about 3,656 meters above sea level. ③ Salar de Uyuni is one of the most visited natural wonders of South America, too. ④ All year round a lot of people visit this place to take pictures of its unique natural beauty. ⑤ Every picture you take in Salar de Uyuni will be a beautiful work of art!

①   ②   ③   ④   ⑤

[24~25] 다음 글을 읽고 물음에 답하시오.

The Amazon runs across the continent through seven countries. It travels from Peru in the west and flows into the Atlantic Ocean. The Amazon River is interesting in many ways. For the most part, it has no bridges. That is because it usually runs through rainforests and wet areas, not cities or towns. Also, in many places the river is very wide, so you cannot see the other side! You probably do not want to swim in this river. It is home to some very big snakes and fish that eat meat.

24 Write the reason why for the most part, the Amazon doesn't have bridges. Answer in English starting with 'Because'.

➡ _____

_____

25 위 글의 내용에 맞게 빈칸에 알맞은 말을 쓰시오.

The Amazon runs across _____ _____ in South America. For the most part, there are no _____ over the river. Some very big _____ and meat-eating _____ live in the river.

Reading for Fun 4

Play

The Two Stones

Words & Expressions

Key Words

□ **allow** [əláu] 통 허락하다, 허가하다

□ **anymore** [ènimɔ́ːr] 부 (부정문 · 의문문에서) 지금은, 이제는 (더 이상) (= **any longer**)

□ **borrow** [bárou] 통 빌리다

□ **carefully** [kέərfəli] 부 주의 깊게

□ **celebrate** [séləbrèit] 통 축하하다

□ **character** [kǽriktər] 명 등장인물

□ **drop** [drɑp] 통 떨어뜨리다

□ **either** [íːðər] 부 (부정문에서) 역시, 또한

□ **happen** [hǽpən] 통 일어나다, 생기다, 발생하다

□ **instead** [instéd] 부 대신에

□ **loudly** [láudli] 부 큰소리로

□ **mean** [miːn] 형 비열한, 못된

□ **million** [míljən] 명 백만

□ **narrator** [nǽreitər] 명 (연극 · 영화 · TV 등의) 해설자, 내레이터

□ **peso** [péisou] 명 페소《필리핀 · 멕시코 및 중남미 여러 나라의 화폐 단위》

□ **pick** [pik] 통 고르다

□ **poor** [puər] 형 가난한

□ **prison** [prízn] 명 감옥

□ **save** [seiv] 통 (목숨을) 구하다

□ **servant** [sə́ːrvənt] 명 하인

□ **terrible** [térəbl] 형 끔찍한

□ **trick** [trik] 명 속임수

Key Expressions

□ **don't[doesn't] have to** ~할 필요가 없다

□ **money lender** 대부업자

□ **pay back** (돈을) 갚다

□ **right away** 즉시, 바로

□ **say to oneself** 중얼거리다

□ **to oneself** 혼자

Word Power

※ 희곡 용어

☐ **해설 (narration)**: 희곡의 첫머리에 등장하여 인물, 배경 등을 설명하고, 관객에게 이야기의 내용을 설명하는 말로 해설자(**narrator**)가 직접 관객에게 말을 함

☐ **대화 (dialog)**: 등장인물끼리 주고받는 말

☐ **독백 (monolog)**: 등장인물이 상대역 없이 혼자 하는 말

☐ **방백 (aside)**: 관객에게는 들리나 상대역에게는 들리지 않는 것으로 약속하고 하는 말

☐ **지시문 (direction)**: 등장인물들의 대사와 대사 사이에서 무대 장치, 분위기, 등장인물의 행동, 표정, 퇴장 시기, 말투 등을 지시하는 말

※ 연극의 배역과 관련된 표현 (Roles for Actors)

☐ **lead role** 주연

☐ **supporting role** 조연

☐ **bit part** 단역

☐ **extra** 엑스트라

☐ **cameo** 카메오, 유명인이 잠시 출연하는 역할

☐ **villain** 악역

English Dictionary

☐ **borrow** 빌리다
→ to take something and promise to return it
어떤 것을 가져가고 그것을 돌려주기로 약속하다

☐ **celebrate**: 축하하다
→ to do something enjoyable because of a special occasion or to mark someone's success
특별한 행사나 누군가의 성공을 기념하기 위해 즐거운 것을 하다

☐ **character**: 등장인물
→ a person who appears in a story, book, play, movie, or television show
이야기, 책, 연극, 영화, 텔레비전 프로에 나오는 인물

☐ **happen**: 발생하다, 일어나다
→ to take place, especially without being planned
특히 계획 없이 일어나다

☐ **instead** 대신에
→ in place of
~을 대신해서, ~ 대신에

☐ **mean** 비열한, 못된
→ not kind to people
사람들에게 친절하지 않은

☐ **narrator**: 해설자, 내레이터
→ a person who tells a story, especially in a book, play, or movie
특히 책이나 연극이나 영화에서 이야기를 하는 사람

☐ **pick** 고르다
→ to choose from a group
한 무리로부터 선택하다

☐ **prison**: 감옥
→ a building where people are kept as a punishment for a crime they have committed
사람들이 저지른 범죄에 대한 처벌로 갇혀 있는 건물

☐ **save** (목숨을) 구하다
→ to help someone get away from danger or harm
누군가를 위험이나 해로부터 빠져나가도록 돕다

☐ **servant** 하인
→ a person whose job is to do another person's housework, often living in the home
직업이 다른 사람의 집안일을 하는 것이고, 종종 그 집에서 사는 사람

☐ **trick** 속임수
→ a plan to deceive someone
누군가를 속이려는 계획

The Two Stones

Characters: Father, Daughter, <u>Money Lender</u>, Friends, Narrator
등장인물   대부업자

Narrator: <u>A long time ago</u>, <u>in a small village</u> <u>in South America</u>, there
오래 전에   부사구   형용사구
<u>lived a farmer and his daughter</u>. The farmer was poor, and <u>had to</u>
'~가 살았다'. there는 부사로 의미가 없다.   must(= have to)의 과거형 '~해야 했다'
borrow three <u>million</u> pesos from a money lender. But the money
millions(×)
lender was not kind, and <u>when</u> the farmer <u>asked for</u> one month
부사절 접속사 '~할 때'   ~을 요구했다
<u>to pay back</u> the money, she didn't <u>allow him anymore time.</u>
부사적 용법(목적) '~하기 위해'   allow+간접목적어+직접목적어

Money Lender: <u>You have no money?</u> That's okay. Your daughter will
Do you have no money?에서 Do가 생략된 형태
become my servant instead.

Father and Daughter: Oh, no!

Daughter: I <u>don't want to be</u> your servant.
want는 to부정사를 목적어로 취하는 동사다
Father: I don't want that, <u>either</u>! *(to Money Lender)* No, thank you.
부정문에서 '또한'
Money Lender: Do you want to go to prison? Then, <u>let's play</u> a game. I
let's+동사원형: ~하자
will put two stones in a bag. <u>One</u> is white, and <u>the other</u> is black.
가리키는 대상이 두 개일 때, 하나는 one, 다른 하나는 the other로 지칭한다.
Your daughter will pick <u>one</u>.
= a stone
Daughter: What happens <u>if</u> I pick the white <u>one</u>?
조건 부사절로 '~한다면'   = stone을 가리키는 부정대명사
Money Lender: Then you will be my servant.

Friends: Oh, no! She's mean. <u>How terrible!</u>
'How+형용사+주어+동사' 어순의 감탄문으로 뒤에 'it is'가 생략되어 있다.
Daughter: What happens if I pick the black one?

Glossary
character 등장인물
money lender 대부업자
narrator 해설자
borrow 빌리다
million 백만
pay back (돈을) 갚다
allow 허락하다
servant 하인
instead 대신에
pick 고르다
mean 야비한, 못된
terrible 끔찍한

📎 **확인문제**

● 다음 문장이 본문의 내용과 일치하면 T, 일치하지 <u>않으면</u> F를 쓰시오.

1 The farmer and his daughter had to borrow money. ☐

2 The money lender was mean. ☐

3 The money lender suggested playing a game with the farmer. ☐

4 If the daughter picks the white stone, she will be the money lender's servant. ☐

Money Lender: Then you will be free, and your father doesn't have to
_{~할 필요가 없다}

pay back my money.
_{갚다}

Father: What happens if she doesn't play this game with you?

Money Lender: *(loudly)* Then you will go to prison!

Father, Daughter, and Friends: Oh, no! Prison!

(Money Lender picks up two stones. Daughter looks carefully at her.)
_{동사 'look at'을 수식하는 부사가 와야 한다.}

Daughter: *(to herself)* Oh! She has picked up two white stones! She
_{혼잣말로}   _{현재완료}

will make me become her servant. What should I do?
_{사역동사+목적어+동사원형}

Narrator: Stop and think. What should she do? She cannot pick a

black one.
_{= stone}

(Daughter picks a stone from the bag. She drops it right away.)

Daughter: Oh, no! I'm sorry, I've dropped it. *(to Money Lender)* But
_{딸이 돌을 떨어뜨린 것}

it's okay. Show us the stone in the bag. Then we will know
       _{= Show the stone in the bag to us.}

which one I picked.
_{간접의문문으로 의문사(which one)+주어(I)+동사(picked)}

Money Lender: *(to herself)* I cannot tell them about my trick! Oh, no!

(Money Lender shows everyone the white stone. Friends and Father
       _{= Money Lender shows the white stone to everyone}

start celebrating.)
_{start+동명사/to부정사}

Friends: She picked the black one! They are free!

Narrator: Good thinking has saved Father and Daughter!

---

don't[doesn't] have to ~할 필요가
없다

loudly 큰소리로

prison 감옥

carefully 주의 깊게

to oneself 혼자서

drop 떨어뜨리다

right away 즉시, 바로

trick 속임수

save 구하다

📎 **확인문제**

- 다음 문장이 본문의 내용과 일치하면 T, 일치하지 <u>않으면</u> F를 쓰시오.

1   If the farmer's daughter doesn't play the game with the money lender, she will go to

prison. ☐

2   The daughter found out the money lender's trick. ☐

3   The daughter dropped the stone to win the game. ☐

4   The money lender told the farmer and his daughter about her trick. ☐

● 우리말을 참고하여 빈칸에 알맞은 말을 쓰시오.

1 The _____ _____

2 _____ : Father, Daughter, _____ _____, Friends, _____

3 Narrator: A long time _____, in a small _____ in South America, _____ _____ a farmer and his daughter.

4 The farmer was poor, and _____ _____ _____ three _____ pesos _____ a money lender.

5 But _____ _____ _____ was not kind, and when the farmer _____ _____ one month _____ _____ _____ the money, she didn't _____ him _____ time.

6 Money Lender: You have _____ money? That's okay.

7 Your daughter will become my _____ _____.

8 Father and Daughter: Oh, no!

9 Daughter: I don't want _____ _____ your _____.

10 Father: I don't want that, _____! *(to Money Lender)* No, _____ _____.

11 Money Lender: Do you want to go to _____?

12 Then, _____ _____ a game. I will _____ two stones in a bag.

13 _____ is white, and _____ _____ is black. Your daughter will _____ one.

14 Daughter: What _____ _____ I pick the white one?

15 Money Lender: _____ you will be my _____.

16 Friends: Oh, no! She's _____. _____!

17 Daughter: What happens _____ I _____ the black one?

1 두 개의 돌

2 등장인물: 아버지, 딸, 대부업자, 친구들, 해설자

3 해설자: 오래 전 남아메리카의 작은 마을에 농부와 그의 딸이 살았습니다.

4 농부는 가난했고, 대부업자로부터 3백만 페소를 빌려야 했습니다.

5 하지만 대부업자는 친절하지 않았고, 농부가 돈을 갚을 때까지 한 달을 기다려 달라고 하자, 더 이상의 시간을 허락해 주지 않았습니다.

6 대부업자: 돈이 없다는 거죠? 좋아요

7 대신 당신 딸이 내 하녀가 돼야겠네요.

8 아버지와 딸: 오, 안 돼!

9 딸: 저는 당신의 하녀가 되고 싶지 않아요.

10 아버지: 나도 그것을 원하지 않아! *(대부업자에게)* 사양하겠습니다.

11 대부업자: 감옥에 가고 싶은가요?

12 그렇다면, 게임을 하나 합시다. 내가 가방에 돌 두 개를 넣겠어요.

13 하나는 흰색이고, 다른 하나는 검은색이죠. 당신 딸이 하나를 집을 거예요.

14 딸: 제가 흰 돌을 집으면 어떻게 되죠?

15 대부업자: 그러면 넌 내 하녀가 될 거야.

16 친구들: 오, 안 돼! 그녀는 야비해. 정말 끔찍해!

17 딸: 제가 검은 돌을 집으면 어떻게 되죠?

18 Money Lender: Then you will be _____, and your father
_____ _____ _____ pay back my money.

19 Father: What happens if she _____ _____ this game
_____ you?

20 Money Lender: (_____) _____ you will go to _____!

21 Father, Daughter, and Friends: Oh, no! _____!

22 *(Money Lender _____ _____ two stones. Daughter _____*
_____ _____ her.)

23 Daughter: (_____ _____) Oh! She has _____
two white stones!

24 She will _____ me _____ her servant. What _____ I do?

25 Narrator: _____ _____ _____. What should she do?

26 She _____ _____ a black one.

27 *(Daughter picks a stone from the bag. She _____ it _____*
_____.)

28 Daughter Oh, no! I'm sorry, I've _____ it.

29 *(to Money Lender)* But it's _____.

30 _____ _____ _____ _____ in the bag.

31 Then we will know _____ _____ I picked.

32 Money Lender: (_____ _____) I _____ _____ them
about my _____! Oh, no!

33 *(Money Lender _____ _____ _____ _____ _____.*

34 *Friends and Father start _____.)*

35 Friends: She _____ the black one! They are _____!

36 Narrator: _____ _____ has _____ Father and Daughter!

18 대부업자: 그러면 넌 자유로워
질 것이고, 네 아버지는 내 돈을
갚을 필요가 없어.

19 아버지: 내 딸이 당신과 이 게임
을 하지 않으면 어떻게 되죠?

20 대부업자: *(큰소리로)* 그러면 당
신은 감옥에 가게 되겠죠!

21 아버지, 딸, 친구들: 오, 안 돼!
감옥이라니!

22 *(대부업자는 두 개의 돌을 집는
다. 딸은 주의 깊게 그녀를 본
다.)*

23 딸: *(혼잣말로)* 오! 그녀는 두 개
의 흰 돌을 집었어!

24 그녀는 나를 자신의 하녀로 만
들 거야. 어떻게 하면 좋지?

25 해설자: 가만히 생각해 보세요.
그녀는 어떻게 하면 좋을까요?

26 그녀는 검은 돌을 집을 수 없어
요.

27 *(딸은 가방에서 돌을 하나 집는
다. 그녀는 그것을 바로 떨어뜨
린다.)*

28 딸: 오, 안 돼! 미안해요, 제가
돌을 떨어뜨렸어요.

29 *(대부업자에게)* 하지만 괜찮아
요.

30 가방에 있는 돌을 우리에게 보
여주세요.

31 그러면 제가 무엇을 집었는지
우리가 알게 될 테니까요.

32 대부업자: *(혼잣말로)* 그들에게
내 속임수를 말할 수 없어! 오,
안 돼!

33 *(대부업자는 모두에게 흰 돌을
보여 준다.*

34 친구들과 아버지는 축하하기 시
작한다.)*

35 친구들: 그녀는 검은 돌을 집었
어! 그들은 자유야!

36 해설자: 현명한 생각이 아버지
와 딸을 구했습니다!

● 우리말을 참고하여 본문을 영작하시오.

1 두 개의 돌
➡ _____

2 등장인물: 아버지, 딸, 대부업자, 친구들, 해설자
➡ _____

3 해설자: 오래 전 남아메리카의 작은 마을에 농부와 그의 딸이 살았습니다.
➡ _____

4 농부는 가난했고, 대부업자로부터 3백만 페소를 빌려야 했습니다.
➡ _____

5 하지만 대부업자는 친절하지 않았고, 농부가 돈을 갚을 때까지 한 달을 기다려 달라고 하자,
더 이상의 시간을 허락해 주지 않았습니다.
➡ _____
_____

6 대부업자: 돈이 없다는 거죠? 좋아요
➡ _____

7 대신 당신 딸이 내 하녀가 돼야겠네요.
➡ _____

8 아버지와 딸: 오, 안 돼!
➡ _____

9 딸: 저는 당신의 하녀가 되고 싶지 않아요.
➡ _____

10 아버지: 나도 그것을 원하지 않아! *(대부업자에게)* 사양하겠습니다.
➡ _____

11 대부업자: 감옥에 가고 싶은가요?
➡ _____

12 그렇다면, 게임을 하나 합시다. 내가 가방에 돌 두 개를 넣겠어요.
➡ _____

13 하나는 흰색이고, 다른 하나는 검은색이죠. 당신 딸이 하나를 집을 거예요.
➡ _____

14 딸: 제가 흰 돌을 집으면 어떻게 되죠?
➡ _____

15 대부업자: 그러면 넌 내 하녀가 될 거야.
➡ _____

16 친구들: 오, 안 돼! 그녀는 야비해. 정말 끔찍해!
➡ _____

17 딸: 제가 검은 돌을 집으면 어떻게 되죠?
➡ _____

18 대부업자: 그러면 넌 자유로워질 것이고, 네 아버지는 내 돈을 갚을 필요가 없어.
➡ _____

19 아버지: 내 딸이 당신과 이 게임을 하지 않으면 어떻게 되죠?
➡ _____

20 대부업자: *(큰소리로)* 그러면 당신은 감옥에 가게 되겠죠!
➡ _____

21 아버지, 딸, 친구들: 오, 안 돼! 감옥이라니!
➡ _____

22 *(대부업자는 두 개의 돌을 집는다. 딸은 주의 깊게 그녀를 본다.)*
➡ _____

23 딸: *(혼잣말로)* 오! 그녀는 두 개의 흰 돌을 집었어!
➡ _____

24 그녀는 나를 자신의 하녀로 만들 거야. 어떻게 하면 좋지?
➡ _____

25 해설자: 가만히 생각해 보세요. 그녀는 어떻게 하면 좋을까요?
➡ _____

26 그녀는 검은 돌을 집을 수 없어요.
➡ _____

27 *(딸은 가방에서 돌을 하나 집는다. 그녀는 그것을 바로 떨어뜨린다.)*
➡ _____

28 딸: 오, 안 돼! 미안해요, 제가 돌을 떨어뜨렸어요. *(대부업자에게)* 하지만 괜찮아요.
➡ _____

29 가방에 있는 돌을 우리에게 보여주세요.
➡ _____

30 그러면 제가 무엇을 집었는지 우리가 알게 될 테니까요.
➡ _____

31 대부업자: *(혼잣말로)* 그들에게 내 속임수를 말할 수 없어! 오, 안 돼!
➡ _____

32 *(대부업자는 모두에게 흰 돌을 보여 준다. 친구들과 아버지는 축하하기 시작한다.)*
➡ _____

33 친구들: 그녀는 검은 돌을 집었어! 그들은 자유야!
➡ _____

34 해설자: 현명한 생각이 아버지와 딸을 구했습니다!
➡ _____

01 다음 빈칸에 알맞은 말을 〈보기〉에서 골라 쓰시오.

---- 보기 ----
instead, borrow, right away, mean, servant, pick, pay back

(1) The old man had _____ to do all the cleaning and cooking for him.

(2) I'll _____ the money with interest.

(3) She has to _____ the right answer.

(4) Would you be able to start working _____?

(5) I don't care for the mountains, so let's go to the beach _____.

(6) May I _____ your camera for a few days?

(7) It was _____ of you not to invite him to the party.

02 다음 영영풀이에 해당하는 단어를 〈보기〉에서 찾아 쓰시오.

---- 보기 ----
save, borrow, mean, trick

(1) a plan to deceive someone

➡ _____

(2) not kind to people

➡ _____

(3) to help someone get away from danger or harm

➡ _____

(4) to take something and promise to return it

➡ _____

03 주어진 우리말에 맞게 빈칸에 알맞은 말을 쓰시오.

(1) 하나는 고속도로이고 다른 하나는 샛길입니다.
• _____ is the expressway and _____ _____ is a side road.

(2) 제가 흰 것을 집으면 어떻게 되죠?
• What happens if I pick the white _____?

(3) 당신이 할 수 없는 일을 나한테 시키지 마세요!
• Don't make _____ _____ what you can't do!

(4) 어느 것을 갖고 싶은지 말해 줘.
• Tell me _____ _____ you want to have.

(5) 지금까지 그녀는 200마리의 길 잃은 개들을 구했다.
• So far, she _____ _____ 200 lost dogs.

04 다음 문장을 어법에 맞게 고쳐 쓰시오.

(1) He has served this school since twenty years.

➡ _____

(2) He has two balls. One is white and another is red.

➡ _____

05 다음 두 문장을 한 문장으로 바꿔 쓰시오.

(1) I don't know. What did Sarah want me to do?

➡ _____
_____

(2) Will you tell me? Do you want to go shopping with me?

　➡ _____

　　_____

(3) Do you think? What does he want?

　➡ _____

　　_____

(4) Let me know. Will you go there?

　➡ _____

　　_____

[06~08] 다음 글을 읽고 물음에 답하시오.

> **Characters:** Father, Daughter, Money Lender, Friends, Narrator
>
> **Narrator:** A long time ago, in a small village in South America, (A)농부와 그의 딸이 살았습니다. The farmer was poor, and had to borrow three million pesos from a money lender. But the money lender was not kind, and when the farmer asked for one month to pay back the money, she didn't allow him anymore time.
>
> **Money Lender:** You have no money? That's okay. Your daughter will become my servant instead.
>
> **Father and Daughter:** Oh, no!
>
> **Daughter:** I don't want to be your servant.
>
> **Father:** I don't want that, either!
>
> *(to Money Lender)* No, thank you.

06 위 글의 밑줄 친 (A)의 우리말에 맞게 주어진 단어를 이용하여 영어로 쓰시오.

> there

➡ _____

07 위 글에서 다음 영영풀이에 해당하는 단어를 찾아 쓰시오.

> a person whose job is to do another person's housework, often living in the home

➡ _____

08 Where is the setting of the story?

➡ It _____ .

[09~12] 다음 글을 읽고 물음에 답하시오.

> **Money Lender:** You have no money? That's okay. Your daughter will become my servant instead.
>
> **Father and Daughter:** Oh, no!
>
> **Daughter:** I don't want to be your servant.
>
> **Father:** (A)I don't want that, either!
>
> *(to Money Lender)* No, thank you.
>
> **Money Lender:** Do you want to go to prison? Then, let's play a game. I will put two stones in a bag. (B)One is white, and another is black. Your daughter will pick one.
>
> **Daughter:** What happens if I pick the white one?
>
> **Money Lender:** Then you will be my servant.
>
> **Friends:** Oh, no! She's mean. (C)정말 끔찍해!
>
> **Daughter:** What happens if I pick the black one?
>
> **Money Lender:** Then you will be free, and (D)네 아버지는 내 돈을 갚을 필요가 없어.

09 위 글의 밑줄 친 (A)와 같은 의미의 문장으로 바꾸어 쓸 때 빈칸에 알맞은 말을 쓰시오.

➡ I don't _____ my daughter _____

　_____ _____ _____, either!

★ 중요

10 위 글의 밑줄 친 (B)에서 어법상 어색한 것을 찾아 바르게 고쳐 문장을 쓰시오.

➡ _____

11 위 글의 밑줄 친 (C)의 우리말에 맞게 주어진 단어를 사용하여 '주어+동사'가 있는 완전한 문장으로 감탄문을 완성하시오.

terrible

➡ _____

12 위 글의 밑줄 친 (D)의 우리말에 맞게 주어진 단어를 활용하여 영어로 쓰시오.

have to / pay back

➡ _____

[13~15] 다음 글을 읽고 물음에 답하시오.

> **Father:** What happens if she doesn't play this game with you?
> **Money Lender:** *(loudly)* Then you will go to prison!
> **Father, Daughter, and Friends:** Oh, no! Prison!
> *(Money Lender picks up two stones. Daughter looks carefully at her.)*
> **Daughter:** *(to herself)* Oh! She has picked up two white stones! (A)그녀는 나를 자신의 하녀로 만들 거야. What should I do?
> **Narrator:** Stop and think. What should she do? She cannot pick a black one.
> *(Daughter picks a stone from the bag. She drops it right away.)*
> **Daughter:** Oh, no! I'm sorry, I've dropped it. *(to Money Lender)* But it's okay. (B)Show us the stone in the bag. Then we will know which one I picked.

> **Money Lender:** *(to herself)* I cannot tell them about my trick! Oh, no!
> *(Money Lender shows everyone the white stone. Friends and Father start celebrating.)*
> **Friends:** She picked the black one! They are free!
> **Narrator:** Good thinking has saved Father and Daughter!

★ 중요

13 위 글의 밑줄 친 (A)의 우리말에 맞게 주어진 단어를 이용하여 영작하시오. (7 words)

make / become

➡ _____

14 위 글의 밑줄 친 (B)를 같은 의미의 문장으로 바꾸어 쓰시오.

➡ _____

15 위 글을 읽고, 글의 내용과 일치하지 <u>않는</u> 문장을 찾아 바르게 고쳐 쓰시오.

① If the farmer doesn't play the game with money lender, his daughter will go to prison.
② Money lender picked up two white stones.
③ The farmer's daughter picked a stone and dropped it right away.
④ Actually the farmer's daughter picked a black stone.

➡ 틀린 문장 번호: _____

➡ 바르게 고친 문장:

(1) _____

_____

(2) _____

_____

01 출제율 95%

다음 단어들 중 성격이 다른 하나를 고르시오.

① lead role ② villain
③ cameo ④ character
⑤ bit part

02 출제율 95%

다음 영영풀이의 빈칸에 해당하는 단어로 알맞은 것은?

> If someone is _____ed to do something, it is all right for them to do it and they will not get into trouble

① borrow ② celebrate ③ drop
④ mean ⑤ allow

03 출제율 90%

다음 빈칸에 알맞은 말을 고르시오.

> • I did not need the brush _____, so I threw it out.

① also ② anymore
③ too ④ away
⑤ either

04 출제율 90%

다음 우리말에 맞게 빈칸에 알맞은 말을 쓰시오.

(1) 길을 건너기 전에 양쪽을 주의 깊게 살펴라.
  • Look both ways _____ before crossing the street.
(2) 내가 네 책을 빌려도 될까?
  • Can I _____ your book?

05 출제율 90%

다음 영영풀이에 해당하는 단어를 주어진 철자로 시작하여 쓰시오.

> to do something enjoyable because of a special occasion or to mark someone's success

➡ c_____

06 출제율 90%

다음 중 밑줄 친 부분의 뜻풀이가 바르지 않은 것은?

① I don't like Jack, either. (역시)
② I can't hear you if you don't speak loudly. (큰소리로)
③ It's just a trick of hers. (재능)
④ The police sent him to prison. (감옥)
⑤ The man is mean and careless, and stupid. (사악한, 못된)

07 출제율 95%

다음 중 어법상 어색한 것은?

① I don't like to say things twice, too.
② Do you know who she is?
③ I need a pen. Can you lend me one?
④ How happy she was!
⑤ We will know which one she liked.

08 출제율 100%

다음 중 어법상 적절한 것은?

① She picked black one.
② Do you think why she left the party so early?
③ Friends and Father start to celebrate.
④ I have two sisters. One is older than me and another is younger than me.
⑤ What nice the old lady is!

09 다음 문장을 어법에 맞게 고쳐 쓰시오.

(1) You can choose one or another of the two rooms.

➡ _____

(2) I'm not sure that he will come or not.

➡ _____

[10~12] 다음 희곡을 읽고 물음에 답하시오.

_____(A)_____ : Father, Daughter, Money Lender, Friends, Narrator

Narrator: A long time ago, in a small village in South America, there ⓐlived a farmer and his daughter. The farmer was poor, and ⓑhad to borrowing three million pesos from a money lender. But the money lender was not kind, and ⓒwhen the farmer asked for one month to pay back the money, she didn't allow him ⓓanymore time.

Money Lender: You have no money? That's okay. Your daughter will become my servant instead.

Father and Daughter: Oh, no!

Daughter: I don't want to be your servant.

Father: I don't want that, ⓔeither!

(to Money Lender) No, thank you.

10 아래의 영영풀이를 보고, 빈칸 (A)에 들어갈 말을 쓰시오. (복수형으로 쓸 것)

<영영풀이> a person represented in a film, play, or story

➡ _____

11 위 글의 밑줄 친 ⓐ~ⓔ 중 어법상 어색한 것은?

① ⓐ ② ⓑ ③ ⓒ ④ ⓓ ⑤ ⓔ

12 위 글의 내용과 일치하지 않는 것은?

① A farmer and his daughter lived in a small village in South America.

② The farmer had to lend three million pesos to a money lender.

③ The money lender was mean.

④ The farmer asked for one month to pay back the money.

⑤ Unless the farmer pays back the money, his daughter will be the money lender's servant.

[13~16] 다음 글을 읽고 물음에 답하시오.

Money Lender: You have no money? That's okay. (①) Your daughter will become my servant instead.

Father and Daughter: Oh, no! (②)

Daughter: I don't want to be your servant.

Father: I don't want that, either!

(to Money Lender) No, thank you.

Money Lender: (③) Do you want to go to prison? Then, let's play a game. (④) One is white, and the other is black. Your daughter will pick one. (⑤)

Daughter: What happens if I pick the white one?

Money Lender: Then you will be my servant.

Friends: Oh, no! She's _____ⓐ_____. How terrible!

Daughter: What happens if I pick the black one?

Money Lender: Then you will be free, and your father doesn't have to pay back my money.

13 위 글의 빈칸 ⓐ에 들어갈 'the money lender'의 성격으로 알맞은 것은?

① kind ② smart

③ stupid ④ thoughtful

⑤ mean

14 위 글에서 주어진 문장이 들어갈 위치로 알맞은 것은?

> I will put two stones in a bag.

① ② ③ ④ ⑤

15 위 글은 희곡의 일부분이다. 이야기의 전개 구조상 해당되는 부분은?

① Setting ② Characters

③ Conflict ④ Climax

⑤ Solution

16 위 글을 읽고 다음 물음에 영어로 답하시오. (should를 사용할 것)

Q: Which color stone should the daughter pick if she doesn't want to be the money lender's servant?

➡ _____

[17~21] 다음 글을 읽고 물음에 답하시오.

Father: What happens if she doesn't play this game with you?

Money Lender: (ⓐ) Then you will go to prison! (①)

Father, Daughter, and Friends: Oh, no! Prison! (②)

Daughter: (ⓑ) Oh! She has picked up two white stones! (③) She will make me become her servant. What should I do? (④)

Narrator: Stop and think. What should she do? She cannot pick a black one.

(*Daughter picks a stone from the bag. She ___ⓒ___.*)

Daughter: Oh, no! I'm sorry, I've dropped it. (ⓓ) But it's okay. Show us the stone in the bag. Then we will know which one I picked. (⑤)

Money Lender: (ⓔ) I cannot tell them about my trick! Oh, no!

(*Money Lender shows everyone the white stone. Friends and Father start celebrating.*)

Friends: She picked the ___ⓕ___ one! They are free!

Narrator: Good thinking has saved Father and Daughter!

17 주어진 문장은 희곡의 '지시문'에 해당한다. (①)~(⑤) 중 들어갈 위치로 알맞은 것은?

> (*Money Lender picks up two stones. Daughter looks carefully at her.*)

① ② ③ ④ ⑤

18 위 글의 빈칸 ⓐ~ⓔ에 들어갈 말로 어색한 것은?

① loudly

② to herself

③ drops it right away

④ to her father

⑤ to herself

19 위 글의 흐름상 빈칸 ⓕ에 들어갈 단어를 본문에서 찾아 쓰시오.

➡ _____

단원별 예상문제 **123**

✎ 출제율 90%

20 위 글을 읽고 다음 질문에 대한 답의 빈칸을 채우시오.

Q: What did the daughter do when she knew the two stones in the money lender's bag were both white?

➡ She _____ the stone that she _____ from the bag _____.

✎ 출제율 95%

21 위 글은 희곡의 전개 방식에서 어디에 해당되는 부분인가?

① Conflict → Climax

② Development → Conflict

③ Conflict → Development

④ Development → Climax

⑤ Climax → Solution

[22~24] 다음 글을 읽고 물음에 답하시오.

Characters: Father, Daughter, Money Lender, Friends, Narrator

Narrator: A long time ago, in a small village in South America, there lived a farmer and his daughter. The farmer was poor, and had to borrow three million pesos from a money lender. But the money lender was not kind, and when the farmer asked for one month to pay back the money, she didn't allow him anymore time.

_____ⓐ_____ : You have no money? That's okay. Your daughter will become my servant __(A)__.

Father and Daughter: Oh, no!

Daughter: I don't want to be your servant.

_____ⓑ_____ : I don't want that, either! *(to Money Lender)* No, thank you.

Money Lender: Do you want to go to prison? Then, let's play a game. I will put two stones in a bag. One is white, and the other is black. Your daughter will pick one.

_____ⓒ_____ : What happens if I pick the white one?

Money Lender: Then you will be my servant.

_____ⓓ_____ : Oh, no! (B)She's mean. How terrible!

Daughter: What happens if I pick the black one?

Money Lender: Then you will be free, and your father doesn't have to pay back my money.

✎ 출제율 90%

22 위 글의 등장인물을 참고하여, 빈칸 ⓐ~ⓓ는 각각 누구의 대사인지 쓰시오.

➡ ⓐ _____ ⓑ _____

ⓒ _____ ⓓ _____

✎ 출제율 95%

23 위 글의 빈칸 (A)에 들어갈 말로 알맞은 것은?

① however ② though

③ instead ④ unless

⑤ otherwise

✎ 출제율 100%

24 위 글의 밑줄 친 (B)의 정보를 바탕으로 'the money lender'가 다음에 취하는 행동으로 알맞은 것은?

① The money lender praises the farmer's daughter.

② The money lender puts one black stone and one white stone in a bag.

③ The money lender puts two black stones in a bag.

④ The money lender puts two white stones in a bag.

⑤ The money lender frees the farmer from his debt.

INSIGHT
on the textbook

교과서 파헤치기

Lesson **7** **A Life Full of Fun**

Lesson **8** **Viva, South America!**

Lesson **S** **The Two Stones**

※ 다음 영어를 우리말로 쓰시오.

01 chef _____

02 pollute _____

03 boil _____

04 showtime _____

05 probably _____

06 fascinating _____

07 appear _____

08 machine _____

09 education _____

10 pour _____

11 select _____

12 lastly _____

13 creative _____

14 movement _____

15 common _____

16 alive _____

17 amusing _____

18 plate _____

19 taste _____

20 develop _____

21 simple _____

22 publish _____

23 usual _____

24 recipe _____

25 among _____

26 remain _____

27 silly _____

28 well-known _____

29 sunscreen _____

30 translate _____

31 choose _____

32 caricature _____

33 animated movie _____

34 cartoonist _____

35 pay for _____

36 jump out at _____

37 make fun of _____

38 can't wait to _____

39 ups and downs _____

40 watch out _____

41 cut A into pieces _____

42 play a role _____

43 come together _____

※ 다음 우리말을 영어로 쓰시오.

01	나타나다, 등장하다	_____
02	요리사	_____
03	오염시키다	_____
04	번역하다	_____
05	창의적인, 독창적인	_____
06	개발하다, 만들다	_____
07	만화가	_____
08	더러운	_____
09	살아 있는	_____
10	교육	_____
11	출판하다	_____
12	볶다, 튀기다	_____
13	마지막으로	_____
14	평소의, 보통의	_____
15	붓다	_____
16	~ 중에	_____
17	자외선 차단제	_____
18	기계	_____
19	상영 시간	_____
20	어리석은	_____
21	끓이다	_____

22	간단한, 단순한	_____
23	극장 매표소	_____
24	공통의	_____
25	만화영화	_____
26	선택하다	_____
27	조리법, 비법	_____
28	고추	_____
29	접시	_____
30	맛보다, 먹다	_____
31	유명한, 잘 알려진	_____
32	아마도	_____
33	매력적인	_____
34	움직임	_____
35	조심하다	_____
36	역할을 하다	_____
37	~로 만들어지다	_____
38	살펴보다	_____
39	~가 기대되다	_____
40	기복	_____
41	~을 놀리다	_____
42	~에 대한 돈을 내다	_____
43	모든 연령의	_____

※ 다음 영영풀이에 알맞은 단어를 <보기>에서 골라 쓴 후, 우리말 뜻을 쓰시오.

1　_____ : the act of moving: _____

2　_____ : normal, happening most often: _____

3　_____ : the time when a play, movie, etc., begins: _____

4　_____ : causing laughter: _____

5　_____ : a process of teaching and learning: _____

6　_____ : to start to be seen: _____

7　_____ : showing little thought; foolish: _____

8　_____ : to invent something new: _____

9　_____ : extremely interesting: _____

10　_____ : to be changed from one language to another: _____

11　_____ : to cook something in hot fat or oil: _____

12　_____ : to stay in the same place or in the same condition: _____

13　_____ : a funny drawing of somebody that exaggerates some of their features:

_____

14　_____ : to make information available to people in a book, magazine, or newspaper:

_____

15　_____ : a type of lotion that you put on your skin to protect it from being damaged

by the sun: _____

16　_____ : a professional cook who usually is in charge of a kitchen in a restaurant:

_____

※ 다음 우리말과 일치하도록 빈칸에 알맞은 말을 쓰시오.

Communication: Listen – Dialog 1

Jane: Kevin, you _____ _____.

Kevin: Nothing _____. _____ my feelings change _____ _____.

Jane: I understand. Many _____ have _____ _____ in their feelings.

Kevin: Oh, _____?

Jane: _____ _____ _____ the _____ _____ "Shining Days"?

Kevin: No, _____ _____. _____ do you _____?

Jane: It is about a _____ _____. It _____ _____ you _____ your feelings _____.

Kevin: That _____ good! I'll _____ it.

Communication: Listen – Dialog 2

Emily: Oh, _____ _____ the long _____ at the box office.

Tony: Yeah, there's a _____ _____ over there. _____ _____ the tickets _____ the _____.

Emily: All right. Do you know _____ _____ _____ _____ _____?

Tony: Sure. It's easy. First, _____ a movie and a _____.

Emily: Okay. We can _____ the seven o'clock show. Then _____?

Tony: Well, _____ the number of tickets and _____ our _____.

Emily: Okay. Two tickets, and I want to _____ _____ _____.

Tony: No _____. _____, _____ _____ the tickets.

Emily: It's very _____.

Communication: Listen More

Suji: Good morning, Chef Garcia!

Garcia: Hello, Suji. _____ _____ _____ _____ nacho pizza?

Suji: Nacho pizza? _____, _____ _____.

Garcia: Kids will love it, and I'll tell you _____ _____ _____ it.

Suji: _____ good!

Garcia: It's easy to make. _____, _____ nacho chips _____ a _____ and _____ pizza sauce on them.

Suji: Okay. Let me _____ you _____ the pizza sauce.

Garcia: Thanks. _____, put some ham, onions, and _____ on top.

Suji: Okay. Then?

Garcia: _____ cheese and _____ _____ _____ 12 minutes in the _____.

Suji: I _____ _____ _____ _____ it!

Communicate: Speak

Anna: Do you know _____ _____ make _____ _____?

Jinsu: Sure. It's easy. First, _____ the vegetables _____ small pieces.

Anna: Okay. What do you do _____?

Jinsu: _____ some oil in the pan. Then, _____ the vegetables _____ _____.

Anna: Wow, it's really _____.

Wrap Up – Listening ❺

Judy: _____ you ever _____ _____ Sokcho?

Minsu: Yes, I _____. _____ my uncle lives there, so I visit him _____ _____.

Judy: Really? Then, _____ _____ Mt. Seorak, _____ _____?

Minsu: Yes, I've climbed to the top of the mountain _____.

Wrap Up – Listening ❻

Mike: Today, I'll tell you _____ _____ _____ a bear's face. _____, draw a big _____ for the face. _____, make two circles on top of the face. After that, _____ two circles for its eyes and _____ them black. Then, _____ a small _____ for the nose. _____, _____ a mouth.

Suji: 안녕하세요, Garcia 셰프님!

Garcia: 안녕하세요, 수지 씨. 나초 피자를 만들어 본 적 있나요?

Suji: 나초 피자요? 아뇨, 만들어 본 적 없어요.

Garcia: 아이들이 그걸 매우 좋아할 거예요. 그럼 제가 어떻게 만드는지 알려 드리죠.

Suji: 좋아요!

Garcia: 만들기 쉬워요. 첫째로 접시 위에 나초 칩을 올려놓고 그것들 위에 피자 소스를 바르세요.

Suji: 네, 피자 소스를 제가 도와드릴게요.

Garcia: 고맙습니다. 다음으로 햄, 양파, 피망을 위에 올리세요.

Suji: 네. 그다음에는요?

Garcia: 치즈를 올리고 오븐에서 약 12분 동안 구우세요.

Suji: 빨리 맛보고 싶군요!

Anna: 너는 볶음밥을 만드는 법을 아니?

Jinsu: 물론이야. 그건 쉬워. 먼저 채소를 작은 조각으로 잘라.

Anna: 알았어. 다음엔 뭘 하니?

Jinsu: 팬에 기름을 둘러. 그러고는 채소를 밥과 함께 볶아.

Anna: 와, 정말 간단하구나.

Judy: 너는 속초에 가 본 적이 있니?

Minsu: 응, 가 본 적이 있어. 사실은 내 삼촌이 거기 살아서, 나는 매년 그를 방문해.

Judy: 정말? 그러면, 너는 설악산을 올라 본 적이 있지, 그렇지 않니?

Judy: 응, 그 산의 정상에 올라간 적이 두 번 있어.

Mike: 오늘 나는 곰의 얼굴을 그리는 방법을 네게 말해 줄게. 첫 번째로, 얼굴에 해당하는 큰 원을 그려. 다음에, 얼굴 위에 두 개의 원을 그려. 그 후에 눈에 해당하는 두 개의 원을 그리고 그것들을 검게 색칠해. 그리고 코에 해당하는 작은 원을 그려. 마지막으로 입을 만들어.

※ 다음 우리말에 맞도록 대화를 영어로 쓰시오.

Communication: Listen – Dialog 1

Jane: _____

Kevin: _____

Jane: _____

Kevin: _____

Jane: _____

Kevin: _____

Jane: _____

_____

Kevin: _____

Jane: Kevin, 너 기분이 안 좋아 보이는구나.
Kevin: 별거 아니에요. 때때로 제 감정이 많이 바뀌어요.
Jane: 이해한단다. 많은 십 대가 감정의 기복이 있지.
Kevin: 아, 정말요?
Jane: 'Shining Days'라는 만화영화를 본 적이 있니?
Kevin: 아니요, 본 적이 없어요. 왜 물으세요?
Jane: 그건 십 대의 감정에 관한 거야. 그건 네가 네 감정을 더 잘 이해하도록 도와줄 거야.
Kevin: 괜찮은 거 같네요! 그걸 볼게요.

Communication: Listen – Dialog 2

Emily: _____

Tony: _____

_____

Emily: _____

Tony: _____

Emily: _____

Tony: _____

Emily: _____

Tony: _____

Emily: _____

Emily: 아, 극장 매표소에 길게 늘어선 줄을 좀 봐.
Tony: 네, 저쪽에 발매기가 하나 있어요. 저 기계에서 표를 사요.
Emily: 좋아. 그 기계를 어떻게 쓰는지 아니?
Tony: 그럼요. 쉬워요. 먼저, 영화와 상영 시간을 골라요.
Emily: 알았어. 우리는 7시 영화를 볼 수 있겠네. 그리고 뭘 하니?
Tony: 음, 표 매수를 선택하고 우리의 좌석을 골라요.
Emily: 좋아. 표 두 장, 그리고 나는 뒤에 앉고 싶어.
Tony: 좋아요. 마지막으로 표 값을 내요.
Emily: 정말 간단하구나.

Communication: Listen More

Suji: _____

Garcia: _____

Suji: _____

Garcia: _____

Suji: _____

Garcia: _____

_____

Suji: _____

Garcia: _____

Suji: _____

Garcia: _____

Suji: _____

Communicate: Speak

Anna: _____

Jinsu: _____

Anna: _____

Jinsu: _____

Anna: _____

Wrap Up – Listening ❺

Judy: _____

Minsu: _____

Judy: _____

Minsu: _____

Wrap Up – Listening ❻

Mike: _____

_____

_____

_____

Suji: 안녕하세요, Garcia 셰프님!

Garcia: 안녕하세요, 수지 씨. 나초 피자를 만들어 본 적 있나요?

Suji: 나초 피자요? 아뇨, 만들어 본 적 없어요.

Garcia: 아이들이 그걸 매우 좋아할 거예요, 그럼 제가 어떻게 만드는지 알려 드리죠.

Suji: 좋아요!

Garcia: 만들기 쉬워요. 첫째로 접시 위에 나초 칩을 올려놓고 그것들 위에 피자 소스를 바르세요.

Suji: 네, 피자 소스를 제가 도와드릴게요.

Garcia: 고맙습니다. 다음으로 햄, 양파, 피망을 위에 올리세요.

Suji: 네. 그다음에는요?

Garcia: 치즈를 올리고 오븐에서 약 12분 동안 구우세요.

Suji: 빨리 맛보고 싶군요!

Anna: 너는 볶음밥을 만드는 법을 아니?

Jinsu: 물론이야. 그건 쉬워. 먼저 채소를 작은 조각으로 잘라.

Anna: 알았어. 다음엔 뭘 하니?

Jinsu: 팬에 기름을 둘러. 그러고는 채소를 밥과 함께 볶아.

Anna: 와, 정말 간단하구나.

Judy: 너는 속초에 가 본 적이 있니?

Minsu: 응, 가 본 적이 있어. 사실은 내 삼촌이 거기 살아서, 나는 매년 그를 방문해.

Judy: 정말? 그러면, 너는 설악산을 올라 본 적이 있지, 그렇지 않니?

Judy: 응, 그 산의 정상에 올라간 적이 두 번 있어.

Mike: 오늘 나는 곰의 얼굴을 그리는 방법을 네게 말해 줄게. 첫 번째로, 얼굴에 해당하는 큰 원을 그려. 다음에, 얼굴 위에 두 개의 원을 그려. 그 후에 눈에 해당하는 두 개의 원을 그리고 그것들을 검게 색칠해. 그리고 코에 해당하는 작은 원을 그려. 마지막으로 입을 만들어.

※ 다음 우리말과 일치하도록 빈칸에 알맞은 것을 골라 쓰시오.

1 _____! _____!
    A. Land   B. Boat

2 Did you _____ when you _____ the cartoon _____?
    A. above   B. saw   C. laugh

3 If _____, the cartoonist was _____.
    A. successful   B. so

4 Cartoonists are the people _____ _____ _____.
    A. cartoons   B. make   C. who

5 They want to _____ your interest, and usually, _____ you _____ with simple language and _____ drawings.
    A. catch   B. laugh   C. creative   D. make

6 People _____ _____ cartoons _____ _____ of years.
    A. hundreds   B. made   C. have   D. for

7 There are many _____ of _____, and they play _____ _____.
    A. roles   B. types   C. different   D. cartoons

8 _____ form of cartoon _____ a picture with _____ _____ words.
    A. few   B. one   C. is   D. a

9 It _____ sometimes _____ a "gag cartoon."
    A. called   B. is

10 The cartoonist _____ a funny _____, and the character makes you _____ by doing or _____ silly things.
    A. laugh   B. saying   C. character   D. makes

11 _____ type of cartoon _____ _____ a caricature.
    A. is   B. another   C. called

12 In a caricature, some _____ of a character are _____ or _____ than _____.
    A. bigger   B. parts   C. different   D. usual

13 Look _____ the picture _____ the _____.
    A. on   B. at   C. right

14 _____ _____ of the man's face _____ _____ at you?
    A. out   B. parts   C. which   D. jump

15 Artists _____ _____ this type of cartoon to _____ _____ of well-known people.
    A. used   B. fun   C. have   D. make

16 When _____ cartoon pictures _____ _____ and tell a story, we have a comic _____.
    A. together   B. come   C. strip   D. several

1 배다! 육지다!

2 위의 만화를 보고 웃었는가?

3 그랬다면 그 만화가는 성공했다.

4 만화가들은 만화를 만드는 사람들이다.

5 그들은 여러분의 관심을 끌고, 대개는 간단한 말과 독창적인 그림으로 여러분을 웃게 하고 싶어 한다.

6 사람들은 수백 년 동안 만화를 만들어 왔다.

7 만화에는 많은 종류가 있으며, 그것들은 다양한 역할을 한다.

8 만화의 한 형태로 몇 마디 말을 쓴 그림이 있다.

9 간혹 그것은 '개그 만화'라고 불린다.

10 만화가는 웃긴 캐릭터를 만들고, 그 캐릭터는 우스꽝스러운 행동이나 말을 함으로써 여러분을 웃게 만든다.

11 다른 종류의 만화는 캐리커처라고 불린다.

12 캐리커처에서 캐릭터의 어떤 부분은 평소와 다르거나 더 크다.

13 오른쪽의 그림을 보아라.

14 남자 얼굴의 어떤 부분이 여러분에게 분명히 보이는가?

15 미술가들은 유명한 사람들을 풍자하기 위해 이런 종류의 만화를 그려 왔다.

16 몇 가지 만화 그림이 모여서 이야기를 들려주게 되면, 그것이 연재만화가 된다.

17 Comic strips _____ _____ in newspapers _____ many _____.

    A. for   B. been   C. years   D. have

18 They are often _____ _____ _____.

    A. just   B. stories   C. amusing

19 People _____ _____ _____ comic strips for _____.

    A. education   B. have   C. used   D. also

20 Comics can _____ information _____ and _____ to _____.

    A. learn   B. easier   C. make   D. clearer

21 You _____ _____ _____ comic history or science books.

    A. seen   B. probably   C. have

22 You _____ _____ _____ many cartoon movies, or _____ movies, too.

    A. animated   B. surely   C. seen   D. have

23 These are very _____ _____ people of _____ _____.

    A. among   B. ages   C. popular   D. all

24 Movement and sounds are _____ _____ pictures, so they _____ _____.

    A. come   B. added   C. to   D. alive

25 Artists and writers can _____ _____ characters and tell _____ stories _____ animation.

    A. interesting   B. develop   C. through   D. fascinating

26 In the 1990s, a new _____ of cartoon _____ _____.

    A. was   B. type   C. developed

27 It _____ _____ a webtoon.

    A. called   B. is

28 Webtoons _____ _____ online, so you can _____ them anytime, anywhere _____ your phone or computer.

    A. read   B. on   C. published   D. are

29 They are very _____, and some of _____ are _____ made _____ TV dramas or movies.

    A. them   B. into   C. popular   D. even

30 New _____ of cartoons _____ _____ in the future.

    A. appear   B. forms   C. may

31 They could be _____ and even more _____ than now, but one thing will _____ the same: they will help us laugh, _____, and learn.

    A. relax   B. different   C. remain   D. exciting

---

17 연재만화는 여러 해 동안 신문에 실려 왔다.

18 그것들은 종종 그저 재미있는 이야기이다.

19 사람들은 연재만화를 교육용으로 사용해 오기도 했다.

20 만화는 정보를 더 명료하고 더 배우기 쉽게 만들 수 있다.

21 여러분은 아마 만화 역사책이나 과학책을 본 적이 있을 것이다.

22 여러분은 많은 만화영화도 당연히 봤을 것이다.

23 이것들은 모든 연령대의 사람들에게 매우 인기가 많다.

24 동작이나 소리가 그림에 더해져서 그림들이 생생하게 살아난다.

25 미술가들과 작가들은 매력적인 캐릭터를 개발하고 만화영화 제작을 통해 재미있는 이야기를 들려준다.

26 1990년대에 새로운 형식의 만화가 개발되었다.

27 그건 웹툰이라고 불린다.

28 웹툰은 온라인으로 출판되기 때문에 여러분이 휴대 전화나 컴퓨터로 언제 어디서나 볼 수 있다.

29 그것은 매우 인기가 있고, 그들 가운데 일부는 심지어 텔레비전 드라마나 영화로 만들어지기도 한다.

30 미래에는 새로운 형태의 만화가 나타날지도 모른다.

31 그것은 지금과는 다르고 한층 더 재미있겠지만, 한 가지는 같을 것이다. 그것은 우리가 웃고, 쉬고, 배우도록 도와줄 것이다.

※ 다음 우리말과 일치하도록 빈칸에 알맞은 말을 쓰시오.

1 Boat! _____!

2 Did you _____ _____ you _____ the cartoon _____?

3 If _____, the _____ was _____.

4 Cartoonists are the people _____ _____ _____.

5 They want _____ _____ your interest, and usually, _____ _____ _____ with simple language and _____ _____.

6 People _____ _____ cartoons _____ _____ _____ _____.

7 There are _____ _____ _____ _____, and they play _____ _____.

8 _____ _____ of cartoon _____ a picture with _____ _____ _____.

9 It _____ _____ _____ a "gag cartoon."

10 The cartoonist _____ _____ _____ _____, and the character _____ you _____ by _____ or _____ silly things.

11 _____ type of cartoon _____ _____ a caricature.

12 In a caricature, _____ _____ of a character _____ or _____ _____ _____.

13 _____ _____ the picture _____ the right.

14 _____ _____ of the man's face _____ _____ at you?

15 Artists _____ _____ this type of cartoon _____ _____ _____ _____ _____.

16 When _____ cartoon pictures _____ _____ and tell a story, we have _____ _____ _____.

1 배다! 육지다!

2 위의 만화를 보고 웃었는가?

3 그랬다면 그 만화가는 성공했다.

4 만화가들은 만화를 만드는 사람들이다.

5 그들은 여러분의 관심을 끌고, 대개는 간단한 말과 독창적인 그림으로 여러분을 웃게 하고 싶어 한다.

6 사람들은 수백 년 동안 만화를 만들어 왔다.

7 만화에는 많은 종류가 있으며, 그것들은 다양한 역할을 한다.

8 만화의 한 형태로 몇 마디 말을 쓴 그림이 있다.

9 간혹 그것은 '개그 만화'라고 불린다.

10 만화가는 웃긴 캐릭터를 만들고, 그 캐릭터는 우스꽝스러운 행동이나 말을 함으로써 여러분을 웃게 만든다.

11 다른 종류의 만화는 캐리커처라고 불린다.

12 캐리커처에서 캐릭터의 어떤 부분은 평소와 다르거나 더 크다.

13 오른쪽의 그림을 보아라.

14 남자 얼굴의 어떤 부분이 여러분에게 분명히 보이는가?

15 미술가들은 유명한 사람들을 풍자하기 위해 이런 종류의 만화를 그려 왔다.

16 몇 가지 만화 그림이 모여서 이야기를 들려주게 되면, 그것이 연재만화가 된다.

17 Comic strips _____ _____ in newspapers _____ _____ _____.

18 They are often _____ _____ _____.

19 People _____ _____ _____ comic strips _____ _____.

20 Comics can _____ information _____ and _____ _____.

21 You _____ _____ _____ comic history or science books.

22 You _____ _____ _____ many cartoon movies, or _____ _____, _____.

23 These are very _____ _____ _____ _____ _____ _____.

24 _____ and sounds _____ _____ _____ pictures, so they _____ _____.

25 Artists and writers can _____ _____ and tell _____ stories _____ animation.

26 In the 1990s, a new _____ _____ cartoon _____.

27 It _____ _____ a webtoon.

28 Webtoons _____ _____ online, so you can _____ _____ anytime, anywhere _____ your phone or computer.

29 They are very _____, and some of _____ _____ even _____ _____ TV dramas or movies.

30 New _____ of cartoons _____ _____ in the future.

31 They could be _____ and even more _____ _____ now, but one thing will _____ the same: they will help us _____, _____, and _____.

17 연재만화는 여러 해 동안 신문에 실려 왔다.

18 그것들은 종종 그저 재미있는 이야기이다.

19 사람들은 연재만화를 교육용으로 사용해 오기도 했다.

20 만화는 정보를 더 명료하고 더 배우기 쉽게 만들 수 있다.

21 여러분은 아마 만화 역사책이나 과학책을 본 적이 있을 것이다.

22 여러분은 많은 만화영화도 당연히 봤을 것이다.

23 이것들은 모든 연령대의 사람들에게 매우 인기가 많다.

24 동작이나 소리가 그림에 더해져서 그림들이 생생하게 살아난다.

25 미술가들과 작가들은 매력적인 캐릭터를 개발하고 만화영화 제작을 통해 재미있는 이야기를 들려준다.

26 1990년대에 새로운 형식의 만화가 개발되었다.

27 그건 웹툰이라고 불린다.

28 웹툰은 온라인으로 출판되기 때문에 여러분이 휴대 전화나 컴퓨터로 언제 어디서나 볼 수 있다.

29 그것은 매우 인기가 있고, 그들 가운데 일부는 심지어 텔레비전 드라마나 영화로 만들어지기도 한다.

30 미래에는 새로운 형태의 만화가 나타날지도 모른다.

31 그것은 지금과는 다르고 한층 더 재미있겠지만, 한 가지는 같을 것이다. 그것은 우리가 웃고, 쉬고, 배우도록 도와줄 것이다.

※ 다음 문장을 우리말로 쓰시오.

1 Boat! Land!

➡ _____

2 Did you laugh when you saw the cartoon above?

➡ _____

3 If so, the cartoonist was successful.

➡ _____

4 Cartoonists are the people who make cartoons.

➡ _____

5 They want to catch your interest, and usually, make you laugh with simple language and creative drawings.

➡ _____

6 People have made cartoons for hundreds of years.

➡ _____

7 There are many types of cartoons, and they play different roles.

➡ _____

8 One form of cartoon is a picture with a few words.

➡ _____

9 It is sometimes called a "gag cartoon."

➡ _____

10 The cartoonist makes a funny character, and the character makes you laugh by doing or saying silly things.

➡ _____

11 Another type of cartoon is called a caricature.

➡ _____

12 In a caricature, some parts of a character are different or bigger than usual.

➡ _____

13 Look at the picture on the right.

➡ _____

14 Which parts of the man's face jump out at you?

➡ _____

15 Artists have used this type of cartoon to make fun of well-known people.

➡ _____

16 When several cartoon pictures come together and tell a story, we have a comic strip.
➡ _____

17 Comic strips have been in newspapers for many years.
➡ _____

18 They are often just amusing stories.
➡ _____

19 People have also used comic strips for education.
➡ _____

20 Comics can make information clearer and easier to learn.
➡ _____

21 You have probably seen comic history or science books.
➡ _____

22 You have surely seen many cartoon movies, or animated movies, too.
➡ _____

23 These are very popular among people of all ages.
➡ _____

24 Movement and sounds are added to pictures, so they come alive.
➡ _____

25 Artists and writers can develop fascinating characters and tell interesting stories through animation.
➡ _____

26 In the 1990s, a new type of cartoon was developed.
➡ _____

27 It is called a webtoon.
➡ _____

28 Webtoons are published online, so you can read them anytime, anywhere on your phone or computer.
➡ _____

29 They are very popular, and some of them are even made into TV dramas or movies.
➡ _____

30 New forms of cartoons may appear in the future.
➡ _____

31 They could be different and even more exciting than now, but one thing will remain the same: they will help us laugh, relax, and learn.
➡ _____
_____

※ 다음 괄호 안의 단어들을 우리말에 맞도록 바르게 배열하시오.

1 (land! / boat!)
➡ _____

2 (you / did / when / laugh / saw / you / cartoon / above? / the)
➡ _____

3 (so, / if / cartoonist / the / successful. / was)
➡ _____

4 (are / cartoonists / people / the / make / who / cartoons.)
➡ _____

5 (want / they / catch / to / interest, / your / usually, / and / you / make / laugh / simple / with / language and / and / drawings. / creative)
➡ _____

6 (have / people / cartoons / made / hundreds / for / years. / of)
➡ _____

7 (are / there / many / of / types / cartoons, / and / play / they / roles. / different)
➡ _____

8 (form / one / cartoon / of / is / picture / a / with / words. / few / a)
➡ _____

9 (is / it / sometimes / a / called / cartoon." / "gag)
➡ _____

10 (cartoonist / the / a / makes / character, / funny / and / character / the / you / makes / laugh / doing / by / or / silly / things. / saying)
➡ _____

11 (type / another / cartoon / of / called / is / caricature. / a)
➡ _____

12 (a / in / caricature, / parts / some / a / of / character / different / are / than / or / bigger / usual.)
➡ _____

13 (at / look / picture / the / the / right. / on)
➡ _____

14 (parts / which / the / of / face / man's / out / jump / you? / at)
➡ _____

15 (have / artists / used / type / this / of / cartoon / make / to / fun / make / of / people. / well-known)
➡ _____

16 (several / when / pictures / cartoon / together / come / and / a / tell / story, / have / we / comic / a / strip.)
➡ _____

1 배다! 육지다!

2 위의 만화를 보고 웃었는가?

3 그랬다면 그 만화는 성공했다.

4 만화가들은 만화를 만드는 사람들이다.

5 그들은 여러분의 관심을 끌고, 대개는 간단한 말과 독창적인 그림으로 여러분을 웃게 하고 싶어 한다.

6 사람들은 수백 년 동안 만화를 만들어 왔다.

7 만화에는 많은 종류가 있으며, 그것들은 다양한 역할을 한다.

8 만화의 한 형태로 몇 마디 말을 쓴 그림이 있다.

9 간혹 그것은 '개그 만화'라고 불린다.

10 만화가는 웃긴 캐릭터를 만들고, 그 캐릭터는 우스꽝스러운 행동이나 말을 함으로써 여러분을 웃게 만든다.

11 다른 종류의 만화는 캐리커처라고 불린다.

12 캐리커처에서 캐릭터의 어떤 부분은 평소와 다르거나 더 크다.

13 오른쪽의 그림을 보아라.

14 남자 얼굴의 어떤 부분이 여러분에게 분명히 보이는가?

15 미술가들은 유명한 사람들을 풍자하기 위해 이런 종류의 만화를 그려 왔다.

16 몇 가지 만화 그림이 모여서 이야기를 들려주게 되면, 그것이 연재만화가 된다.

17 (strips / comic / been / have / newspapers / in / for / years. / many)
➡ _____

18 (are / they / just / often / stories. / amusing)
➡ _____

19 (have / people / also / comic / used / for / strips / education.)
➡ _____

20 (can / comics / make / clearer / information / and / to / learn. / easier)
➡ _____

21 (have / you / seen / probably / history / comic / or / books. / science)
➡ _____

22 (have / you / seen / surely / cartoon / many / movies, / or / movies, / too. / animated)
➡ _____

23 (are / these / popular / very / people / among / all / of / ages.)
➡ _____

24 (sounds / and / movement / added / are / pictures, / to / they / so / alive. / come)
➡ _____

25 (writers / and / artists / develop / can / characters / fascinating / and / interesting / tell / stories / animation. / through)
➡ _____

26 (the / in /. 1990s, / new / a / of / type / was / cartoon / developed.)
➡ _____

27 (is / it / called / webtoon. / a)
➡ _____

28 (are / webtoons / published / online, / you / so / read / can / anytime. / them / anywhere / your / on / computer. / or / phone)
➡ _____

29 (are / they / popular, / very / some / and / them / of / even / are / into / made / dramas / TV / movies. / or)
➡ _____

30 (forms / new / cartoons / of / appear / may / future. / the / in)
➡ _____

31 (could / they / different / be / even / and / exciting / more / now, / than / one / but / will / thing / remain / same: / the / will / they / us / help / laugh, / and / relax, / learn.)
➡ _____
_____

17 연재만화는 여러 해 동안 신문에 실려 왔다.

18 그것들은 종종 그저 재미있는 이야기이다.

19 사람들은 연재만화를 교육용으로 사용해 오기도 했다.

20 만화는 정보를 더 명료하고 더 배우기 쉽게 만들 수 있다.

21 여러분은 아마 만화 역사책이나 과학책을 본 적이 있을 것이다.

22 여러분은 많은 만화영화도 당연히 봤을 것이다.

23 이것들은 모든 연령대의 사람들에게 매우 인기가 많다.

24 동작이나 소리가 그림에 더해져서 그림들이 생생하게 살아난다.

25 미술가들과 작가들은 매력적인 캐릭터를 개발하고 만화영화 제작을 통해 재미있는 이야기를 들려준다.

26 1990년대에 새로운 형식의 만화가 개발되었다.

27 그건 웹툰이라고 불린다.

28 웹툰은 온라인으로 출판되기 때문에 여러분이 휴대 전화나 컴퓨터로 언제 어디서나 볼 수 있다.

29 그것은 매우 인기가 있고, 그들 가운데 일부는 심지어 텔레비전 드라마나 영화로 만들어지기도 한다.

30 미래에는 새로운 형태의 만화가 나타날지도 모른다.

31 그것은 지금과는 다르고 한층 더 재미있겠지만, 한 가지는 같을 것이다. 그것은 우리가 웃고, 쉬고, 배우도록 도와줄 것이다.

※ **다음 우리말을 영어로 쓰시오.**

1 배다! 육지다!

➡ _____

2 위의 만화를 보고 웃었는가?

➡ _____

3 그랬다면 그 만화가는 성공했다.

➡ _____

4 만화가들은 만화를 만드는 사람들이다.

➡ _____

5 그들은 여러분의 관심을 끌고, 대개는 간단한 말과 독창적인 그림으로 여러분을 웃게 하고 싶어 한다.

➡ _____

6 사람들은 수백 년 동안 만화를 만들어 왔다.

➡ _____

7 만화에는 많은 종류가 있으며, 그것들은 다양한 역할을 한다.

➡ _____

8 만화의 한 형태로 몇 마디 말을 쓴 그림이 있다.

➡ _____

9 간혹 그것은 '개그 만화'라고 불린다.

➡ _____

10 만화가는 웃긴 캐릭터를 만들고, 그 캐릭터는 우스꽝스러운 행동이나 말을 함으로써 여러분을 웃게 만든다.

➡ _____

11 다른 종류의 만화는 캐리커처라고 불린다.

➡ _____

12 캐리커처에서 캐릭터의 어떤 부분은 평소와 다르거나 더 크다.

➡ _____

13 오른쪽의 그림을 보아라.

➡ _____

14 남자 얼굴의 어떤 부분이 여러분에게 분명히 보이는가?

➡ _____

15 미술가들은 유명한 사람들을 풍자하기 위해 이런 종류의 만화를 그려 왔다.

➡ _____

16 몇 가지 만화 그림이 모여서 이야기를 들려주게 되면, 그것이 연재만화가 된다.

➡ _____

17 연재만화는 여러 해 동안 신문에 실려 왔다.

➡ _____

18 그것들은 종종 그저 재미있는 이야기이다.

➡ _____

19 사람들은 연재만화를 교육용으로 사용해 오기도 했다.

➡ _____

20 만화는 정보를 더 명료하고 더 배우기 쉽게 만들 수 있다.

➡ _____

21 여러분은 아마 만화 역사책이나 과학책을 본 적이 있을 것이다.

➡ _____

22 여러분은 많은 만화영화도 당연히 봤을 것이다.

➡ _____

23 이것들은 모든 연령대의 사람들에게 매우 인기가 많다.

➡ _____

24 동작이나 소리가 그림에 더해져서 그림들이 생생하게 살아난다.

➡ _____

25 미술가들과 작가들은 매력적인 캐릭터를 개발하고 만화영화 제작을 통해 재미있는 이야기를 들려준다.

➡ _____

26 1990년대에 새로운 형식의 만화가 개발되었다.

➡ _____

27 그건 웹툰이라고 불린다.

➡ _____

28 웹툰은 온라인으로 출판되기 때문에 여러분이 휴대 전화나 컴퓨터로 언제 어디서나 볼 수 있다.

➡ _____

29 그것은 매우 인기가 있고, 그들 가운데 일부는 심지어 텔레비전 드라마나 영화로 만들어지기도 한다.

➡ _____

30 미래에는 새로운 형태의 만화가 나타날지도 모른다.

➡ _____

31 그것은 지금과는 다르고 한층 더 재미있겠지만, 한 가지는 같을 것이다. 그것은 우리가 웃고, 쉬고, 배우도록 도와줄 것이다.

➡ _____

_____

※ 다음 우리말과 일치하도록 빈칸에 알맞은 말을 쓰시오.

My Speaking Portfolio – Step 3

1. _____ is a _____ _____ for you.

2. I've _____ my sneakers this way _____ _____.

3. First, put the sneakers, _____ water, and _____ _____ in a plastic bag.

4. _____ close the bag and _____ it _____ _____ _____.

5. _____, take the sneakers _____ _____ the bag and wash _____.

6. They'll _____ _____ new sneakers.

1. 여기 당신을 위한 유용한 조언이 있어요.
2. 나는 내 운동화를 여러 번 이런 방식으로 세탁했어요.
3. 첫째, 운동화, 온수, 그리고 세제를 비닐봉지에 넣으세요.
4. 그리고 비닐봉지를 묶어 7분 동안 두세요.
5. 마지막으로 운동화를 비닐봉지에서 꺼내 씻으세요.
6. 그들은 새 운동화처럼 보일 거예요.

My Writing Portfolio

1. Giyeong, My Favorite _____ _____

2. My _____ _____ _____ is Giyeong of *Black Rubber Shoes*.

3. He is an _____ _____ student. He is _____ and _____.

4. _____, he is not very smart and sometimes _____ _____.

5. I like him _____ he looks on the _____ _____ of everything and always _____ _____ help _____.

1. 기영, 내가 가장 좋아하는 만화 캐릭터
2. 내가 가장 좋아하는 만화 캐릭터는 〈검정 고무신〉의 기영이다.
3. 그는 초등학교 학생이다. 그는 재미있고 친절하다.
4. 하지만, 그는 그렇게 똑똑진 않고, 때때로 말썽을 피운다.
5. 그는 모든 것의 긍정적인 면을 보고 항상 다른 이들을 도우려 하기 때문에 나는 그를 좋아한다.

Words in Action B

1. The Best _____ _____ for Children's Education

2. Animals welcome the city's plan _____ _____ an amusement park _____ _____ _____.

3. However, they _____ _____ _____ serious _____.

4. An old elephant _____ _____ _____.

5. The animals and the city _____ _____ _____ _____ _____ a better world for everyone.

1. 아이들의 교육을 위한 최고의 만화영화
2. 동물들은 숲속에 놀이공원을 지으려는 도시의 계획을 환영한다.
3. 하지만, 그들은 곧 심각한 오염에 시달린다.
4. 나이 든 코끼리가 한 가지 제안을 한다.
5. 동물들과 도시는 모든 이들을 위한 더 좋은 세상을 만들기 위한 합의에 이른다.

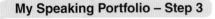

※ 다음 우리말을 영어로 쓰시오.

My Speaking Portfolio – Step 3

1. 여기 당신을 위한 유용한 조언이 있어요.
   ➡ _____

2. 나는 내 운동화를 여러 번 이런 방식으로 세탁했어요.
   ➡ _____

3. 첫째, 운동화, 온수, 그리고 세제를 비닐봉지에 넣으세요.
   ➡ _____

4. 그리고 비닐봉지를 묶어 7분 동안 두세요.
   ➡ _____

5. 마지막으로 운동화를 비닐봉지에서 꺼내 씻으세요.
   ➡ _____

6. 그들은 새 운동화처럼 보일 거예요.
   ➡ _____

My Writing Portfolio

1. 기영, 내가 가장 좋아하는 만화 캐릭터
   ➡ _____

2. 내가 가장 좋아하는 만화 캐릭터는 〈검정 고무신〉의 기영이다.
   ➡ _____

3. 그는 초등학교 학생이다. 그는 재미있고 친절하다.
   ➡ _____

4. 하지만, 그는 그렇게 똑똑하진 않고, 때때로 말썽을 피운다.
   ➡ _____

5. 그는 모든 것의 긍정적인 면을 보고 항상 다른 이들을 도우려 하기 때문에 나는 그를 좋아한다.
   ➡ _____

Words in Action B

1. 아이들의 교육을 위한 최고의 만화영화
   ➡ _____

2. 동물들은 숲속에 놀이공원을 지으려는 도시의 계획을 환영한다.
   ➡ _____

3. 하지만, 그들은 곧 심각한 오염에 시달린다.
   ➡ _____

4. 나이 든 코끼리가 한 가지 제안을 한다.
   ➡ _____

5. 동물들과 도시는 모든 이들을 위한 더 좋은 세상을 만들기 위한 합의에 이른다.
   ➡ _____

※ 다음 영어를 우리말로 쓰시오.

01	pilot	
02	sunrise	
03	benefit	
04	prepare	
05	bridge	
06	area	
07	per	
08	natural	
09	probably	
10	capital	
11	view	
12	continent	
13	scared	
14	similar	
15	fantastic	
16	flow	
17	shy	
18	sunscreen	
19	mountain range	
20	unique	
21	waterfall	

22	soil	
23	ocean	
24	wonder	
25	patience	
26	work of art	
27	outer space	
28	especially	
29	origin	
30	rainforest	
31	contain	
32	sea level	
33	through	
34	wide	
35	go away	
36	be similar to	
37	to be honest	
38	all year round	
39	be full of	
40	name after	
41	by oneself	
42	throw a party	
43	by the way	

※ 다음 우리말을 영어로 쓰시오.

01	준비하다	
02	이익, 혜택	
03	전망	
04	넓은	
05	수도	
06	경이, 놀라움	
07	다리	
08	기원, 원산	
09	인내심	
10	폭포	
11	특히	
12	해돋이, 일출	
13	관광객	
14	자외선 차단제	
15	환상적인, 엄청난	
16	독특한	
17	흐르다	
18	화성	
19	수줍은, 부끄럼 타는	
20	산맥	
21	비슷한, 유사한	

22	~을 통하여	
23	흙, 토양	
24	대륙	
25	~당, ~마다	
26	지역	
27	해수면	
28	겁먹은, 무서워하는	
29	자연의, 천연의	
30	포함하다	
31	아마도	
32	열대 우림	
33	대양	
34	건너서, 가로질러	
35	~을 따라 이름 짓다	
36	그건 그렇고	
37	없어지다	
38	일 년 내내, 연중	
39	~으로 가득하다	
40	~와 비슷하다	
41	솔직히 말하면	
42	파티를 열다	
43	혼자서, 홀로	

※ 다음 영영풀이에 알맞은 단어를 <보기>에서 골라 쓴 후, 우리말 뜻을 쓰시오.

1 _____ : to make a plan for something that will happen: _____

2 _____ : an advantage that something gives you: _____

3 _____ : a part of country, town: _____

4 _____ : a forest in a tropical area that receives a lot of rain: _____

5 _____ : a large mass of land surrounded by sea: _____

6 _____ : from one side of something to the other: _____

7 _____ : a thing that causes a feeling of great surprise or admiration: _____

8 _____ : the ability to stay calm without becoming angry: _____

9 _____ : the top layer of the earth in which plants and trees grow: _____

10 _____ : existing in nature; not made or caused by humans: _____

11 _____ : a large area of land that has very little water and very few plants growing on it: _____

12 _____ : measuring a large distance from one side to the other: _____

13 _____ : the point from which something starts; the cause of something:

_____

14 _____ : a person who operates the controls of an aircraft, especially as a job:

_____

15 _____ : a place where a stream or river falls from a high place, for example over a cliff or rock: _____

16 _____ : a structure built over something such as a river so that people or vehicles can get across: _____

pilot	wonder	bridge	soil
across	area	wide	benefit
waterfall	origin	continent	desert
prepare	rainforest	natural	patience

※ 다음 우리말과 일치하도록 빈칸에 알맞은 말을 쓰시오.

Communication: Listen – Dialog 1

Sujin: Dad, I like this _____ _____.

Dad: I'm _____ you _____ it.

Sujin: _____ _____ _____, do you know _____ the tomato _____ _____ _____?

Dad: Italy or _____ _____ _____?

Sujin: No, the tomato _____ _____ _____ _____.

Dad: Really? _____ did you know that?

Sujin: I learned it from Ms. Song, my _____ _____ teacher.

Dad: That's good.

Communication: Listen – Dialog 2

Jenny: _____ you _____ the pictures Ms. Song _____?

Brian: _____ pictures?

Jenny: She _____ _____ South America _____ _____ last summer.

Brian: Really? What a _____!

Jenny: She _____ _____ _____ _____ of beautiful places. I _____ liked the pictures of _____.

Brian: _____ _____ pyramids in _____ _____?

Jenny: Yes. She said some pyramids are _____ 3,800 meters _____ _____ _____.

Brian: I _____ _____ _____.

Sujin: 아빠, 저는 이 토마토 수프가 마음에 들어요.
Dad: 네가 좋아하니 기쁘구나.
Sujin: 그런데 아빠는 토마토가 처음에 어디에서 재배되었는지 아세요?
Dad: 이탈리아나 유럽 어딘가가 아닐까?
Sujin: 아니에요, 토마토는 남아메리카에서 왔어요.
Dad: 정말? 너는 그걸 어떻게 알았니?
Sujin: 저는 그걸 사회 선생님이신 송 선생님께 배웠어요.
Dad: 훌륭하구나.

Jenny: 너 송 선생님께서 찍은 사진들을 봤니?
Brian: 무슨 사진?
Jenny: 선생님께서는 지난여름에 혼자 남아메리카로 여행을 다녀오셨대.
Brian: 정말? 그것 참 놀랍다!
Jenny: 선생님께서 우리들에게 아름다운 장소들의 사진을 보여 주셨어. 나는 특히 피라미드 사진이 마음에 들더라.
Brian: 남아메리카에 피라미드가 있어?
Jenny: 응. 선생님께서 몇몇 피라미드는 해발 3,800미터 정도에 위치하고 있다고 하셨어.
Brian: 정말 놀랍다.

Communication: Listen More

Hana: _____ _____ the roller coaster ride, Jongha?

Jongha: It was _____ . I _____ _____ it.

Hana: Ha ha. You _____ your eyes _____ _____ .

Jongha: Did you see? _____ _____ _____ , I was really _____

_____ _____ .

Hana: Do you know _____ _____ this roller coaster _____ ?

Jongha: I have _____ _____ .

Hana: It goes _____ _____ _____ 140 km per hour.

Jongha: Wow! That's _____ !

Hana: _____ _____ it one more time!

Jongha: Look at the _____ . We can't ride it _____ 8 p.m.

Hana: Oh, _____ _____ _____ .

Communicate: Speak

Amy: Do you know _____ _____ _____ _____

_____ ?

Jinsu: I have _____ _____ . What is it?

Amy: It's Lima.

Jinsu: I _____ _____ that.

Wrap Up – Listening ❺

Jack: Do you know Junha _____ _____ _____ ?

Minji: No. _____ did he get it? From a _____ _____ ?

Jack: No. I _____ he got the puppy from his _____ .

Minji: I _____ one, _____ .

Wrap Up – Listening ❻

Mike: Do you know Sumin _____ _____ _____ at the speech

contest?

Sue: I can't believe it. She was very _____ and _____ last year.

Mike: Yeah. She _____ the drama club this year, and she _____

_____ _____ _____ .

Sue: I see. I _____ _____ _____ the club, _____ .

Hana: 롤러코스터 어땠어, 종하야?
Jongha: 신나더라. 난 정말 재미있었어.
Hana: 하하. 너는 타는 동안에 눈을 감고 있던걸.
Jongha: 봤어? 솔직히 말하면 처음에는 정말 무서웠어.
Hana: 너 이 롤러코스터가 얼마나 빠른지 알고 있니?
Jongha: 모르겠어.
Hana: 이건 시속 140km로 달린대.
Jongha: 와! 정말 놀랍다!
Hana: 우리 한 번 더 타자!
Jongha: 표지판을 봐. 저녁 8시 이후에는 그것을 탈 수 없어.
Hana: 아, 다음에 타지 뭐.

Amy: 너는 페루의 수도가 어디인지 알고 있니?
Jinsu: 아니 모르겠어. 어디야?
Amy: 리마야.
Jinsu: 그건 몰랐네.

Jack: 너는 준하에게 강아지가 생긴 걸 알고 있니?
Minji: 아니. 어디에서 났대? 애완동물 가게에서?
Jack: 아니. 나는 그가 강아지를 삼촌 댁에서 얻었다고 들었어.
Minji: 나도 강아지를 키우고 싶다.

Mike: 너는 수민이가 말하기 대회에서 우승한 걸 알고 있니?
Sue: 그것 참 놀랍다. 작년에 그 애는 정말 조용하고 수줍음이 많았는데.
Mike: 맞아. 그 애가 올해 연극 동아리에 가입했는데, 많이 바뀌었대.
Sue: 그렇구나. 나도 그 동아리에 가입하고 싶다.

※ 다음 우리말에 맞도록 대화를 영어로 쓰시오.

Communication: Listen – Dialog 1

Sujin: _____

Dad: _____

Sujin: _____

Dad: _____

Sujin: _____

Dad: _____

Sujin: _____

Dad: _____

 해석

Sujin: 아빠, 저는 이 토마토 수프가 마음에 들어요.
Dad: 네가 좋아하니 기쁘구나.
Sujin: 그런데 아빠는 토마토가 처음에 어디에서 재배되었는지 아세요?
Dad: 이탈리아나 유럽 어딘가가 아닐까?
Sujin: 아니에요, 토마토는 남아메리카에서 왔어요.
Dad: 정말? 너는 그걸 어떻게 알았니?
Sujin: 저는 그걸 사회 선생님이신 송 선생님께 배웠어요.
Dad: 훌륭하구나.

Communication: Listen – Dialog 2

Jenny: _____

Brian: _____

Jenny: _____

Brian: _____

Jenny: _____

_____

Brian: _____

Jenny: _____

Brian: _____

Jenny: 너 송 선생님께서 찍은 사진들을 봤니?
Brian: 무슨 사진?
Jenny: 선생님께서는 지난여름에 혼자 남아메리카로 여행을 다녀오셨대.
Brian: 정말? 그것 참 놀랍다!
Jenny: 선생님께서 우리들에게 아름다운 장소들의 사진을 보여 주셨어. 나는 특히 피라미드 사진이 마음에 들더라.
Brian: 남아메리카에 피라미드가 있어?
Jenny: 응. 선생님께서 몇몇 피라미드는 해발 3,800미터 정도에 위치하고 있다고 하셨어.
Brian: 정말 놀랍다.

Communication: Listen More

Hana: _____

Jongha: _____

Hana: _____

Jongha: _____

Hana: _____

Jongha: _____

Hana: _____

Jongha: _____

Hana: _____

Jongha: _____

Hana: _____

Hana: 롤러코스터 어땠어, 종하야?

Jongha: 신나더라. 난 정말 재미있었어.

Hana: 하하. 너는 타는 동안에 눈을 감고 있던걸.

Jongha: 봤어? 솔직히 말하면 처음에는 정말 무서웠어.

Hana: 너 이 롤러코스터가 얼마나 빠른지 알고 있니?

Jongha: 모르겠어.

Hana: 이건 시속 140km로 달린대.

Jongha: 와! 정말 놀랍다!

Hana: 우리 한 번 더 타자!

Jongha: 표지판을 봐. 저녁 8시 이후에는 그것을 탈 수 없어.

Hana: 아, 다음에 타지 뭐.

Communicate: Speak

Amy: _____

Jinsu: _____

Amy: _____

Jinsu: _____

Amy: 너는 페루의 수도가 어디인지 알고 있니?

Jinsu: 아니 모르겠어. 어디야?

Amy: 리마야.

Jinsu: 그건 몰랐네.

Wrap Up – Listening ❺

Jack: _____

Minji: _____

Jack: _____

Minji: _____

Jack: 너는 준하에게 강아지가 생긴 걸 알고 있니?

Minji: 아니. 어디에서 났대? 애완동물 가게에서?

Jack: 아니. 나는 그가 강아지를 삼촌 댁에서 얻었다고 들었어.

Minji: 나도 강아지를 키우고 싶다.

Wrap Up – Listening ❻

Mike: _____

Sue: _____

Mike: _____

Sue: _____

Mike: 너는 수민이가 말하기 대회에서 우승한 걸 알고 있니?

Sue: 그것 참 놀랍다. 작년에 그 애는 정말 조용하고 수줍음이 많았는데.

Mike: 맞아. 그 애가 올해 연극 동아리에 가입했는데, 많이 바뀌었대.

Sue: 그렇구나. 나도 그 동아리에 가입하고 싶다.

※ 다음 우리말과 일치하도록 빈칸에 알맞은 것을 골라 쓰시오.

1 Do you know _____ the _____ _____ on Earth is?
  A. driest   B. where   C. desert

2 How _____ _____ _____ waterfall?
  A. highest   B. about   C. the

3 Yes, _____ are _____ in _____ America.
  A. both   B. they   C. South

4 This continent is _____ of natural _____ _____ will _____ you.
  A. wonders   B. full   C. surprise   D. that

5 The Atacama is _____ _____ _____ on Earth.
  A. desert   B. driest   C. the

6 In some _____, it _____ almost no rain at _____ — only 1–3 millimeters _____ year!
  A. all   B. per   C. gets   D. parts

7 The ground in some _____ is _____ dry _____ no plants can _____.
  A. that   B. so   C. grow   D. areas

8 Do you know _____ _____ do in _____ a _____ place?
  A. dry   B. such   C. what   D. scientists

9 The soil in this desert is very _____ to the soil on Mars, _____ they _____ for tips to _____ space.
  A. prepare   B. similar   C. outer   D. so

10 The Atacama is also _____ of the _____ _____ on Earth to _____ stars.
  A. places   B. one   C. best   D. watch

11 _____ you go _____ Venezuela, you can see the _____ _____ waterfall.
  A. highest   B. world's   C. to   D. if

12 It is 979 _____ _____.
  A. high   B. meters

13 Clouds often _____ the top, so you need _____ and a little _____ to get a good _____.
  A. view   B. patience   C. luck   D. cover

14 Actually, the waterfall is _____ _____ Jimmie Angel, a pilot from the United States who first _____ _____ the waterfall in 1933.
  A. after   B. flew   C. named   D. over

1 여러분은 지구에서 가장 건조한 사막이 어디인지 알고 있나요?

2 가장 높은 폭포는 어떠한가요?

3 그렇습니다. 그것들은 둘 다 남아메리카에 있습니다.

4 이 대륙은 여러분을 놀라게 할 자연 경관으로 가득하답니다.

5 아타카마 사막은 지구에서 가장 건조한 사막입니다.

6 몇몇 지역은 비가 전혀 오지 않아서, 연간 강수량이 1~3mm에 그칩니다!

7 어떤 지역의 토양은 너무 건조해서 어떤 식물도 자랄 수가 없습니다.

8 이처럼 건조한 곳에서 과학자들이 무슨 일을 하는지 알고 있나요?

9 이 사막의 토양은 화성의 토양과 아주 비슷해서, 그들은 우주로의 여행을 준비합니다.

10 또한 아타카마 사막은 지구에서 별을 관측하기에 가장 좋은 장소 가운데 하나이기도 합니다.

11 여러분이 베네수엘라에 간다면, 세계에서 가장 높은 폭포를 볼 수 있을 것입니다.

12 그것은 높이가 979m입니다.

13 구름이 꼭대기 부분을 자주 에워싸기 때문에, 멋진 경치를 보려면 인내심과 약간의 운이 필요합니다.

14 사실 그 폭포는 1933년에 처음으로 폭포 너머 비행을 한 미국의 비행사 Jimmie Angel에게서 이름을 따왔습니다.

15 You can still _____ _____ the _____ of the beautiful waterfall only _____ plane.

A. by   B. get   C. top   D. to

16 The Amazon _____ _____ the continent _____ seven countries.

A. across   B. through   C. runs

17 It _____ _____ Peru in the west and _____ _____ the Atlantic Ocean.

A. flows   B. travels   C. into   D. from

18 The Amazon River is _____ _____ many _____.

A. ways   B. interesting   C. in

19 For the _____ part, it has _____ _____.

A. no   B. most   C. bridges

20 That is _____ it usually _____ _____ rainforests and _____ areas, not cities or towns.

A. through   B. because   C. runs   D. wet

21 Also, in many _____ the river is very _____, so you cannot see the _____ _____!

A. wide   B. other   C. places   D. side

22 You _____ do not want to _____ _____ this river.

A. swim   B. probably   C. in

23 It is _____ to some very big snakes and fish _____ eat _____.

A. that   B. home   C. meat

24 The Andes are _____ _____ _____ mountain _____.

A. longest   B. range   C. world's   D. the

25 Do you know _____ _____ the _____ _____ is?

A. range   B. long   C. how   D. mountain

26 It is _____ 7,000 kilometers _____!

A. long   B. about

27 It also _____ the highest _____ _____ of Asia.

A. mountains   B. contains   C. outside

28 _____ a _____ of the _____ in South America live in the Andes.

A. third   B. about   C. people

29 Many _____ animals _____ _____ there.

A. live   B. unique   C. also

15 여전히 비행기로만 그 아름다운 폭포의 꼭대기에 갈 수 있습니다.

16 아마존강은 일곱 개의 나라를 거쳐 대륙을 가로질러 흐릅니다.

17 그것은 서쪽의 페루에서 시작하여 대서양으로 흘러갑니다.

18 아마존강은 많은 점에서 흥미롭습니다.

19 강의 대부분에는 다리가 없습니다.

20 그것은 강이 대개 도시나 마을이 아닌, 열대 우림과 습지를 지나 흐르기 때문입니다.

21 또한 많은 곳에서 강이 너무 넓어서 그 건너편을 볼 수조차 없습니다!

22 여러분은 아마도 이 강에서 헤엄치고 싶지 않을 것입니다.

23 이곳은 몇몇 아주 큰 뱀과 고기를 먹는 물고기들의 서식지입니다.

24 안데스 산맥은 세계에서 가장 긴 산맥입니다.

25 여러분은 그 산맥의 길이가 얼마인지 아시나요?

26 그것은 약 7,000km입니다.

27 또한 그곳에는 아시아 외의 지역에서 가장 높은 산이 있습니다.

28 남아메리카 인구의 3분의 1 정도가 안데스 산맥에 살고 있습니다.

29 그리고 독특한 동물들이 많이 서식하고 있기도 합니다.

※ 다음 우리말과 일치하도록 빈칸에 알맞은 말을 쓰시오.

1 Do you know _____ _____ _____ _____ on Earth is?

2 How _____ _____ _____ _____?

3 Yes, _____ _____ _____ in South America.

4 This continent _____ _____ _____ natural wonders _____ _____ _____ you.

5 The Atacama is _____ _____ _____ on Earth.

6 In some parts, _____ _____ almost no rain _____ _____ — only 1–3 millimeters _____ _____!

7 The ground in some areas _____ _____ _____ _____ _____ no plants _____ _____.

8 Do you know _____ _____ _____ in _____ _____ _____ _____?

9 The soil in this desert is very _____ _____ the soil on Mars, so _____ _____ _____ _____ _____ to _____ _____.

10 The Atacama is also _____ _____ _____ _____ on Earth _____ _____ _____.

11 If you go to Venezuela, you can _____ _____ _____ _____.

12 _____ is 979 _____ _____.

13 Clouds often _____ the top, so you need _____ and a little _____ to get a _____ _____.

14 Actually, the waterfall is _____ _____ Jimmie Angel, a pilot from the United States _____ first _____ over the waterfall in 1933.

1 여러분은 지구에서 가장 건조한 사막이 어디인지 알고 있나요?

2 가장 높은 폭포는 어떠한가요?

3 그렇습니다, 그것들은 둘 다 남아메리카에 있습니다.

4 이 대륙은 여러분을 놀라게 할 자연 경관으로 가득하답니다.

5 아타카마 사막은 지구에서 가장 건조한 사막입니다.

6 몇몇 지역은 비가 전혀 오지 않아서, 연간 강수량이 1~3mm에 그칩니다!

7 어떤 지역의 토양은 너무 건조해서 어떤 식물도 자랄 수가 없습니다.

8 이처럼 건조한 곳에서 과학자들이 무슨 일을 하는지 알고 있나요?

9 이 사막의 토양은 화성의 토양과 아주 비슷해서, 그들은 우주로의 여행을 준비합니다.

10 또한 아타카마 사막은 지구에서 별을 관측하기에 가장 좋은 장소 가운데 하나이기도 합니다.

11 여러분이 베네수엘라에 간다면, 세계에서 가장 높은 폭포를 볼 수 있을 것입니다.

12 그것은 높이가 979m입니다.

13 구름이 꼭대기 부분을 자주 에워싸기 때문에, 멋진 경치를 보려면 인내심과 약간의 운이 필요합니다.

14 사실 그 폭포는 1933년에 처음으로 폭포 너머 비행을 한 미국의 비행사 Jimmie Angel에게서 이름을 따왔습니다.

15 You can _____ _____ _____ the top of the beautiful waterfall _____ _____ _____.

16 The Amazon _____ _____ the continent _____ seven countries.

17 It _____ _____ Peru in the west and _____ _____ the _____ _____.

18 The Amazon River _____ _____ in _____ _____.

19 For the most part, it has _____ _____.

20 That is _____ _____ _____ _____ _____ rainforests and _____ _____, not cities or towns.

21 Also, in many places the river is very wide, so you cannot _____ _____ _____ _____!

22 You _____ do not want to _____ _____ this river.

23 It is _____ to some very big snakes and fish _____ eat meat.

24 The Andes are _____ _____ _____ _____ _____.

25 Do you know _____ _____ _____ _____ _____ is?

26 It is _____ 7,000 kilometers _____!

27 It also _____ the highest _____ _____ of Asia.

28 About _____ _____ _____ _____ _____ in South America _____ _____ the Andes.

29 Many _____ _____ also _____ _____.

15 여전히 비행기로만 그 아름다운 폭포의 꼭대기에 갈 수 있습니다.

16 아마존강은 일곱 개의 나라를 거쳐 대륙을 가로질러 흐릅니다.

17 그것은 서쪽의 페루에서 시작하여 대서양으로 흘러갑니다.

18 아마존강은 많은 점에서 흥미롭습니다.

19 강의 대부분에는 다리가 없습니다.

20 그것은 강이 대개 도시나 마을이 아닌, 열대 우림과 습지를 지나 흐르기 때문입니다.

21 또한 많은 곳에서 강이 너무 넓어서 그 건너편을 볼 수조차 없습니다!

22 여러분은 아마도 이 강에서 헤엄치고 싶지 않을 것입니다.

23 이곳은 몇몇 아주 큰 뱀과 고기를 먹는 물고기들의 서식지입니다.

24 안데스 산맥은 세계에서 가장 긴 산맥입니다.

25 여러분은 그 산맥의 길이가 얼마인지 아시나요?

26 그것은 약 7,000km입니다.

27 또한 그곳에는 아시아 외의 지역에서 가장 높은 산이 있습니다.

28 남아메리카 인구의 3분의 1 정도가 안데스 산맥에 살고 있습니다.

29 그리고 독특한 동물들이 많이 서식하고 있기도 합니다.

※ 다음 문장을 우리말로 쓰시오.

1 Do you know where the driest desert on Earth is?

➡ _____

2 How about the highest waterfall?

➡ _____

3 Yes, they are both in South America.

➡ _____

4 This continent is full of natural wonders that will surprise you.

➡ _____

5 The Atacama is the driest desert on Earth.

➡ _____

6 In some parts, it gets almost no rain at all — only 1–3 millimeters per year!

➡ _____

7 The ground in some areas is so dry that no plants can grow.

➡ _____

8 Do you know what scientists do in such a dry place?

➡ _____

9 The soil in this desert is very similar to the soil on Mars, so they prepare for trips to outer space.

➡ _____

10 The Atacama is also one of the best places on Earth to watch stars.

➡ _____

11 If you go to Venezuela, you can see the world's highest waterfall.

➡ _____

12 It is 979 meters high.

➡ _____

13 Clouds often cover the top, so you need patience and a little luck to get a good view.

➡ _____

14 Actually, the waterfall is named after Jimmie Angel, a pilot from the United States who first flew over the waterfall in 1933.

➡ _____

15 You can still get to the top of the beautiful waterfall only by plane.

➡ _____

16 The Amazon runs across the continent through seven countries.

➡ _____

17 It travels from Peru in the west and flows into the Atlantic Ocean.

➡ _____

18 The Amazon River is interesting in many ways.

➡ _____

19 For the most part, it has no bridges.

➡ _____

20 That is because it usually runs through rainforests and wet areas, not cities or towns.

➡ _____

21 Also, in many places the river is very wide, so you cannot see the other side!

➡ _____

22 You probably do not want to swim in this river.

➡ _____

23 It is home to some very big snakes and fish that eat meat.

➡ _____

24 The Andes are the world's longest mountain range.

➡ _____

25 Do you know how long the mountain range is?

➡ _____

26 It is about 7,000 kilometers long!

➡ _____

27 It also contains the highest mountains outside of Asia.

➡ _____

28 About a third of the people in South America live in the Andes.

➡ _____

29 Many unique animals also live there.

➡ _____

※ 다음 괄호 안의 단어들을 우리말에 맞도록 바르게 배열하시오.

1 (you / do / know / where / the / desert / driest / on / is? / Earth)
➡ _____

2 (about / how / the / waterfall? / highest)
➡ _____

3 (yes, / are / they / borth / South / in / America.)
➡ _____

4 (continent / this / is / of / full / wonders / natural / will / that / you. / surpeise)
➡ _____

5 (Atacama / the / is / the / desert / driest / Earth. / on)
➡ _____

6 (some / in / parts, / gets / it / no / almost / rain / all / at / — / 1-3 / only / per / millimeters / year!)
➡ _____

7 (ground / the / some / in / areas / is / dry / so / no / that / plants / grow. / can)
➡ _____

8 (you / do / what / know / do / scientists / in / do / such / place? / dry / a)
➡ _____

9 (soil / the / this / in / desert / very / is / to / similar / soil / the / Mars, / on / so / prepare / they / trips / for / outer / to / space.)
➡ _____

10 (Atacama / the / also / is / of / one / best / the / places / Earth / on / stars. / watch / to)
➡ _____

11 (you / if / to / go / Venezuela, / you / see / can / world's / the / waterfall. / highest)
➡ _____

12 (is / it / meters / 979 / high.)
➡ _____

13 (often / clouds / the / cover / top, / you / so / patience / need / and / little / a / to / luck / get / view. / good / a)
➡ _____

14 (actually, / waterfall / the / named / is / after / Angel, / Jimmie / pilot / a / from / United / the / States / first / who / over / flew / waterfall / the / 1933. / in)
➡ _____
_____

1 여러분은 지구에서 가장 건조한 사막이 어디인지 알고 있나요?

2 가장 높은 폭포는 어떠한가요?

3 그렇습니다. 그것들은 둘 다 남아메리카에 있습니다.

4 이 대륙은 여러분을 놀라게 할 자연 경관으로 가득하답니다.

5 아타카마 사막은 지구에서 가장 건조한 사막입니다.

6 몇몇 지역은 비가 전혀 오지 않아서, 연간 강수량이 1~3mm에 그칩니다!

7 어떤 지역의 토양은 너무 건조해서 어떤 식물도 자랄 수가 없습니다.

8 이처럼 건조한 곳에서 과학자들이 무슨 일을 하는지 알고 있나요?

9 이 사막의 토양은 화성의 토양과 아주 비슷해서, 그들은 우주로의 여행을 준비합니다.

10 또한 아타카마 사막은 지구에서 별을 관측하기에 가장 좋은 장소 가운데 하나이기도 합니다.

11 여러분이 베네수엘라에 간다면, 세계에서 가장 높은 폭포를 볼 수 있을 것입니다.

12 그것은 높이가 979m입니다.

13 구름이 꼭대기 부분을 자주 에워싸기 때문에, 멋진 경치를 보려면 인내심과 약간의 운이 필요합니다.

14 사실 그 폭포는 1933년에 처음으로 폭포 너머 비행을 한 미국의 비행사 Jimmie Angel에게서 이름을 따왔습니다.

15 (can / you / get / still / to / top / the / of / beautiful / the / waterfall / by / plane. / only)

➡ _____

16 (Amazon / the / across / runs / the / through / continent / countries. / seven)

➡ _____

17 (travels / it / Peru / from / the / in / west / and / into / flows / Atlantic / the / Ocean.)

➡ _____

18 (Amazon / the / River / is / interesting / many / ways. / in)

➡ _____

19 (the / for / part, / most / has / it / bridges. / no)

➡ _____

20 (is / that / because / usually / it / through / runs / rainforests / wet / and / areas, / cities / not / towns. / or)

➡ _____

➡ _____

21 (also, / many / in / places / river / the / is / wide, / very / you / so / see / cannot / the / side! / other)

➡ _____

➡ _____

22 (probably / you / not / do / want / swim / to / in / river. / this)

➡ _____

23 (is / it / to / home / some / big / very / snakes / and / that / fish / meat. / eat)

➡ _____

24 (Andes / the / are / world's / the / mountain / longest / range.)

➡ _____

25 (you / do / how / know / the / long / range / mountain / is?)

➡ _____

26 (is / it / about / kilometers / 7,000 / long!)

➡ _____

27 (also / it / contains / highest / the / mountains / of / Asia. / outside)

➡ _____

28 (a / about / third / of / people / the / South / in / live / America / the / in / Andes.)

➡ _____

29 (unique / many / also / animals / there. / live)

➡ _____

15 여전히 비행기로만 그 아름다운 폭포의 꼭대기에 갈 수 있습니다.

16 아마존강은 일곱 개의 나라를 거쳐 대륙을 가로질러 흐릅니다.

17 그것은 서쪽의 페루에서 시작하여 대서양으로 흘러갑니다.

18 아마존강은 많은 점에서 흥미롭습니다.

19 강의 대부분에는 다리가 없습니다.

20 그것은 강이 대개 도시나 마을이 아닌, 열대 우림과 습지를 지나 흐르기 때문입니다.

21 또한 많은 곳에서 강이 너무 넓어서 그 건너편을 볼 수조차 없습니다!

22 여러분은 아마도 이 강에서 헤엄치고 싶지 않을 것입니다.

23 이곳은 몇몇 아주 큰 뱀과 고기를 먹는 물고기들의 서식지입니다.

24 안데스 산맥은 세계에서 가장 긴 산맥입니다.

25 여러분은 그 산맥의 길이가 얼마인지 아시나요?

26 그것은 약 7,000km입니다.

27 또한 그곳에는 아시아 외의 지역에서 가장 높은 산이 있습니다.

28 남아메리카 인구의 3분의 1 정도가 안데스 산맥에 살고 있습니다.

29 그리고 독특한 동물들이 많이 서식하고 있기도 합니다.

※ 다음 우리말을 영어로 쓰시오.

1 여러분은 지구에서 가장 건조한 사막이 어디인지 알고 있나요?

➡ _____

2 가장 높은 폭포는 어떠한가요?

➡ _____

3 그렇습니다, 그것들은 둘 다 남아메리카에 있습니다.

➡ _____

4 이 대륙은 여러분을 놀라게 할 자연 경관으로 가득하답니다.

➡ _____

5 아타카마 사막은 지구에서 가장 건조한 사막입니다.

➡ _____

6 몇몇 지역은 비가 전혀 오지 않아서, 연간 강수량이 1~3mm에 그칩니다!

➡ _____

7 어떤 지역의 토양은 너무 건조해서 어떤 식물도 자랄 수가 없습니다.

➡ _____

8 이처럼 건조한 곳에서 과학자들이 무슨 일을 하는지 알고 있나요?

➡ _____

9 이 사막의 토양은 화성의 토양과 아주 비슷해서, 그들은 우주로의 여행을 준비합니다.

➡ _____

10 또한 아타카마 사막은 지구에서 별을 관측하기에 가장 좋은 장소 가운데 하나이기도 합니다.

➡ _____

11 여러분이 베네수엘라에 간다면, 세계에서 가장 높은 폭포를 볼 수 있을 것입니다.

➡ _____

12 그것은 높이가 979m입니다.

➡ _____

13 구름이 꼭대기 부분을 자주 에워싸기 때문에, 멋진 경치를 보려면 인내심과 약간의 운이 필요합니다.

➡ _____

14 사실 그 폭포는 1933년에 처음으로 폭포 너머 비행을 한 미국의 비행사 Jimmie Angel에게서 이름을 따왔습니다.

➡ _____

_____

15 여전히 비행기로만 그 아름다운 폭포의 꼭대기에 갈 수 있습니다.

➡ _____

16 아마존강은 일곱 개의 나라를 거쳐 대륙을 가로질러 흐릅니다.

➡ _____

17 그것은 서쪽의 페루에서 시작하여 대서양으로 흘러갑니다.

➡ _____

18 아마존강은 많은 점에서 흥미롭습니다.

➡ _____

19 강의 대부분에는 다리가 없습니다.

➡ _____

20 그것은 강이 대개 도시나 마을이 아닌, 열대 우림과 습지를 지나 흐르기 때문입니다.

➡ _____

21 또한 많은 곳에서 강이 너무 넓어서 그 건너편을 볼 수조차 없습니다!

➡ _____

22 여러분은 아마도 이 강에서 헤엄치고 싶지 않을 것입니다.

➡ _____

23 이곳은 몇몇 아주 큰 뱀과 고기를 먹는 물고기들의 서식지입니다.

➡ _____

24 안데스 산맥은 세계에서 가장 긴 산맥입니다.

➡ _____

25 여러분은 그 산맥의 길이가 얼마인지 아시나요?

➡ _____

26 그것은 약 7,000km입니다.

➡ _____

27 또한 그곳에는 아시아 외의 지역에서 가장 높은 산이 있습니다.

➡ _____

28 남아메리카 인구의 3분의 1 정도가 안데스 산맥에 살고 있습니다.

➡ _____

29 그리고 독특한 동물들이 많이 서식하고 있기도 합니다.

➡ _____

※ 다음 우리말과 일치하도록 빈칸에 알맞은 말을 쓰시오.

My Speaking Portfolio

1. A: _____ _____ do you want _____ _____?

2. B: Brazil. Do you know _____ _____ _____?

3. A: Yes, I do. It's _____ _____ _____. Do you know that Brazil is _____ _____ _____ in South America?

4. B: _____ _____ _____! I didn't know that. So, what's _____ _____ _____ you want to see in Brazil?

5. A: I want _____ _____ Iguazu Falls _____ the sky.

My Writing Portfolio

1. A _____ in _____

2. I _____ _____ Kaieteur Falls _____ my family.

3. The waterfall _____ _____ the Amazon Rainforest in Guyana, and it is 226 _____ _____.

4. I _____ _____ _____ the size of the waterfall.

5. I could see the _____ _____ and _____ _____ there.

6. _____ _____ _____ Kaieteur Falls _____ _____ _____ good.

7. I _____ _____ all my stress _____ _____.

Wrap Up - Reading

1. Salar de Uyuni in Bolivia is _____ _____ _____ salt flat.

2. _____ _____ _____ ago, there was water, but it _____ _____ _____ _____.

3. Now, a large salt desert _____ _____ _____ 3,656 meters _____ _____ _____.

4. Salar de Uyuni is _____ _____ _____ _____ of South America, too.

5. _____ _____ _____ a lot of people visit this place to take pictures of its _____ _____ _____.

6. _____ _____, the salt flat _____ any _____ a great photographer.

7. _____ _____ you _____ in Salar de Uyuni will be a _____ _____ _____ _____!

---

1. A: 너는 어느 나라를 가 보고 싶니?
2. B: 브라질. 너는 브라질이 어디에 있는지 알고 있니?
3. A: 응, 알아. 그건 남아메리카에 있어. 너는 남아메리카에서 브라질이 가장 큰 나라라는 거 알고 있니?
4. B: 정말 놀랍다! 그건 몰랐네. 그러면 너는 브라질에서 가장 처음으로 보고 싶은 게 뭐야?
5. A: 나는 하늘에서 이구아수폭포를 보고 싶어.

1. 자연에서의 하루
2. 나는 가족과 함께 카이에투 폭포에 갔다.
3. 그 폭포는 가이아나에 있는 아마존 열대우림에 위치하고 있고, 높이는 226m이다.
4. 나는 폭포의 크기에 놀랐다.
5. 나는 그곳에서 갈색 바위와 초록색 나무를 볼 수 있었다.
6. 카이에투 폭포로의 여행은 나를 기분 좋게 만들어 주었다.
7. 내 모든 스트레스가 사라진 것 같았다.

1. 볼리비아에 있는 살라르 데 우유니는 세계에서 가장 큰 솔트 플랫(소금 평원)이다.
2. 수천 년 전에는 그곳에 물이 있었지만, 모두 말라버렸다.
3. 지금은 해발 약 3,656미터에 큰 소금 사막이 남겨져 있다.
4. 살라르 데 우유니는 또한 방문객이 가장 많은 남아메리카의 자연 경관 중의 하나이다.
5. 일 년 내내 많은 사람들이 독특한 자연의 아름다움을 사진으로 찍기 위해 이 장소를 방문한다.
6. 사실, 그 솔트 플랫은 어떤 방문객도 훌륭한 사진작가로 만든다.
7. 살라르 데 우유니에서 당신이 찍은 모든 사진은 아름다운 예술 작품이 될 것이다!

※ 다음 우리말을 영어로 쓰시오.

My Speaking Portfolio

1. A: 너는 어느 나라를 가 보고 싶니?
➡ _____

2. B: 브라질. 너는 브라질이 어디에 있는지 알고 있니?
➡ _____

3. A: 응, 알아. 그건 남아메리카에 있어. 너는 남아메리카에서 브라질이 가장 큰 나라라는 거 알고 있니?
➡ _____

4. B: 정말 놀랍다! 그건 몰랐네. 그러면 너는 브라질에서 가장 처음으로 보고 싶은 게 뭐야?
➡ _____

5. A: 나는 하늘에서 이구아수폭포를 보고 싶어.
➡ _____

My Writing Portfolio

1. 자연에서의 하루
➡ _____

2. 나는 가족과 함께 카이에투 폭포에 갔다.
➡ _____

3. 그 폭포는 가이아나에 있는 아마존 열대우림에 위치하고 있고, 높이는 226m이다.
➡ _____

4. 나는 폭포의 크기에 놀랐다.
➡ _____

5. 나는 그곳에서 갈색 바위와 초록색 나무를 볼 수 있었다.
➡ _____

6. 카이에투 폭포로의 여행은 나를 기분 좋게 만들어 주었다.
➡ _____

7. 내 모든 스트레스가 사라진 것 같았다.
➡ _____

Wrap Up - Reading

1. 볼리비아에 있는 살라르 데 우유니는 세계에서 가장 큰 솔트 플랫(소금 평원)이다.
➡ _____

2. 수천 년 전에는 그곳에 물이 있었지만, 모두 말라버렸다.
➡ _____

3. 지금은 해발 약 3,656미터에 큰 소금 사막이 남겨져 있다.
➡ _____

4. 살라르 데 우유니는 또한 방문객이 가장 많은 남아메리카의 자연 경관 중의 하나이다.
➡ _____

5. 일 년 내내 많은 사람들이 독특한 자연의 아름다움을 사진으로 찍기 위해 이 장소를 방문한다.
➡ _____

6. 사실, 그 솔트 플랫은 어떤 방문객도 훌륭한 사진작가로 만든다.
➡ _____

7. 살라르 데 우유니에서 당신이 찍은 모든 사진은 아름다운 예술 작품이 될 것이다!
➡ _____

※ 다음 영어를 우리말로 쓰시오.

01 pick _____

02 celebrate _____

03 either _____

04 happen _____

05 trick _____

06 mean _____

07 borrow _____

08 carefully _____

09 million _____

10 anymore _____

11 servant _____

12 narrator _____

13 poor _____

14 instead _____

15 loudly _____

16 prison _____

17 save _____

18 allow _____

19 terrible _____

20 character _____

21 drop _____

22 don't[doesn't] have to _____

23 money lender _____

24 pay back _____

25 right away _____

26 say to oneself _____

27 to oneself _____

※ 다음 우리말을 영어로 쓰시오.

01 가난한 _____

02 빌리다 _____

03 떨어뜨리다 _____

04 백만 _____

05 주의 깊게 _____

06 (목숨을) 구하다 _____

07 속임수 _____

08 해설자, 내레이터 _____

09 끔찍한 _____

10 일어나다, 생기다 _____

11 허락하다, 허가하다 _____

12 대신에 _____

13 고르다 _____

14 큰소리로 _____

15 등장인물 _____

16 비열한, 못된 _____

17 지금은, 이제는 (더 이상) _____

18 감옥 _____

19 하인 _____

20 (부정문에서) 역시, 또한 _____

21 축하하다 _____

22 즉시, 바로 _____

23 중얼거리다 _____

24 대부업자 _____

25 (돈을) 갚다 _____

26 혼잣말로 _____

27 ~할 필요가 없다 _____

※ 다음 영영풀이에 알맞은 단어를 <보기>에서 골라 쓴 후, 우리말 뜻을 쓰시오.

1 _____ : in place of: _____

2 _____ : a plan to deceive someone: _____

3 _____ : to choose from a group: _____

4 _____ : not kind to people: _____

5 _____ : to take something and promise to return it: _____

6 _____ : a person who appears in a story, book, play, movie, or television show:

     _____

7 _____ : to take place, especially without being planned: _____

8 _____ : a person who tells a story, especially in a book, play, or movie:

     _____

9 _____ : a building where people are kept as a punishment for a crime they have

     committed: _____

10 _____ : to help someone get away from danger or harm: _____

11 _____ : to do something enjoyable because of a special occasion or to mark

     someone's success: _____

12 _____ : a person whose job is to do another person's housework, often living in

     the home: _____

보기			
save	celebrate	pick	mean
instead	servant	character	borrow
prison	trick	happen	narrator

※ 다음 우리말과 일치하도록 빈칸에 알맞은 것을 골라 쓰시오.

1 The _____ _____
    A. Stones   B. Two

2 _____ : Father, Daughter, _____ _____, Friends, _____
    A. Lender   B. Characters   C. Narrator   D. Money

3 Narrator: A long time _____, in a small _____ in South America, _____ _____ a farmer and his daughter.
    A. there   B. ago   C. lived   D. village

4 The farmer was poor, and _____ to _____ three _____ pesos _____ a money lender.
    A. borrow   B. from   C. million   D. had

5 But the money lender was not kind, and when the farmer asked _____ one month to _____ back the money, she didn't _____ him _____ time.
    A. allow   B. for   C. anymore   D. pay

6 Money Lender: You _____ _____ money? That's okay.
    A. no   B. have

7 Your daughter will _____ my _____ _____.
    A. servant   B. become   C. instead

8 Father and _____ : Oh, _____ !
    A. no   B. Daughter

9 Daughter: I don't want _____ _____ your _____.
    A. be   B. servant   C. to

10 Father: I don't _____ that, _____ ! *(to Money Lender)* No, _____ you.
    A. either   B. thank   C. want

11 Money Lender: Do you want _____ _____ to _____ ?
    A. to   B. go   C. prison

12 Then, _____ _____ a game. I will _____ two stones in a bag.
    A. play   B. put   C. let's

13 _____ is white, and _____ _____ is black. Your daughter will _____ one.
    A. the   B. pick   C. one   D. other

14 Daughter: What _____ _____ I pick the white _____ ?
    A. one   B. if   C. happens

15 Money Lender: _____ you will _____ my _____.
    A. be   B. then   C. servant

16 Friends: Oh, no! She's _____. _____ _____ !
    A. how   B. mean   C. terrible

17 Daughter: _____ happens _____ I _____ the black one?
    A. if   B. pick   C. what

1 두 개의 돌

2 등장인물: 아버지, 딸, 대부업자, 친구들, 해설자

3 해설자: 오래 전 남아메리카의 작은 마을에 농부와 그의 딸이 살았습니다.

4 농부는 가난했고, 대부업자로부터 3백만 페소를 빌려야 했습니다.

5 하지만 대부업자는 친절하지 않았고, 농부가 돈을 갚을 때까지 한 달을 기다려 달라고 하자, 더 이상의 시간을 허락해 주지 않았습니다.

6 대부업자: 돈이 없다는 거죠? 좋아요

7 대신 당신 딸이 내 하녀가 돼야겠네요.

8 아버지와 딸: 오, 안 돼!

9 딸: 저는 당신의 하녀가 되고 싶지 않아요.

10 아버지: 나도 그것을 원하지 않아! *(대부업자에게)* 사양하겠습니다.

11 대부업자: 감옥에 가고 싶은가요?

12 그렇다면, 게임을 하나 합시다. 내가 가방에 돌 두 개를 넣겠어요.

13 하나는 흰색이고, 다른 하나는 검은색이죠. 당신 딸이 하나를 집을 거예요.

14 딸: 제가 흰 돌을 집으면 어떻게 되죠?

15 대부업자: 그러면 넌 내 하녀가 될 거야.

16 친구들: 오, 안 돼! 그녀는 야비해. 정말 끔찍해!

17 딸: 제가 검은 돌을 집으면 어떻게 되죠?

18 Money Lender: Then you will be _____, and your father doesn't _____ to _____ _____ my money.

A. have   B. back   C. free   D. pay

19 Father: What _____ if she _____ play this game _____ you?

A. with   B. doesn't   C. happens

20 Money Lender: (_____) _____ you will go to _____!

A. then   B. loudly   C. prison

21 Father, _____, and _____ : Oh, no! _____!

A. Prison   B. Friends   C. Daughter

22 (Money Lender _____ _____ two stones. Daughter looks _____ _____ her.)

A. carefully   B. picks   C. at   D. up

23 Daughter: (_____ _____) Oh! She has _____ _____ two white stones!

A. picked   B. herself   C. up   D. to

24 She will _____ me _____ her servant. What _____ I do?

A. should   B. become   C. make

25 Narrator: _____ and _____ . What _____ she do?

A. should   B. think   C. stop

26 She _____ _____ a black _____ .

A. pick   B. one   C. cannot

27 (Daughter picks a stone _____ the bag. She _____ it _____ .)

A. drops   B. away   C. right   D. from

28 Daughter Oh, no! I'm _____, I've _____ it.

A. dropped   B. sorry

29 (to Money Lender) _____ it's _____ .

A. okay   B. but

30 _____ _____ the _____ in the bag.

A. us   B. show   C. stone

31 Then we will know _____ _____ I _____ .

A. one   B. which   C. picked

32 Money Lender: (_____ _____) I _____ tell them about my _____! Oh, no!

A. herself   B. trick   C. to   D. cannot

33 (Money Lender _____ _____ the white _____ .

A. everyone   B. shows   C. stone

34 Friends and Father _____ _____ .)

A. celebrating   B. start

35 Friends: She _____ the black _____ ! They are _____ !

A. free   B. picked   C. one

36 Narrator: _____ has _____ Father and Daughter!

A. thinking   B. saved   C. good

18 대부업자: 그러면 넌 자유로워 질 것이고, 네 아버지는 내 돈을 갚을 필요가 없어.

19 아버지: 내 딸이 당신과 이 게임을 하지 않으면 어떻게 되죠?

20 대부업자: (큰소리로) 그러면 당신은 감옥에 가게 되겠죠!

21 아버지, 딸, 친구들: 오, 안 돼! 감옥이라니!

22 (대부업자는 두 개의 돌을 집는다. 딸은 주의 깊게 그녀를 본다.)

23 딸: (혼잣말로) 오! 그녀는 두 개의 흰 돌을 집었어!

24 그녀는 나를 자신의 하녀로 만들 거야. 어떻게 하면 좋지?

25 해설자: 가만히 생각해 보세요. 그녀는 어떻게 하면 좋을까요?

26 그녀는 검은 돌을 집을 수 없어요.

27 (딸은 가방에서 돌을 하나 집는다. 그녀는 그것을 바로 떨어뜨린다.)

28 딸: 오, 안 돼! 미안해요. 제가 돌을 떨어뜨렸어요.

29 (대부업자에게) 하지만 괜찮아요.

30 가방에 있는 돌을 우리에게 보여주세요.

31 그러면 제가 무엇을 집었는지 우리가 알게 될 테니까요.

32 대부업자: (혼잣말로) 그들에게 내 속임수를 말할 수 없어! 오, 안 돼!

33 (대부업자는 모두에게 흰 돌을 보여 준다.

34 친구들과 아버지는 축하하기 시작한다.)

35 친구들: 그녀는 검은 돌을 집었어! 그들은 자유야!

36 해설자: 현명한 생각이 아버지와 딸을 구했습니다!

※ 다음 우리말과 일치하도록 빈칸에 알맞은 말을 쓰시오.

1 The _____ _____

2 _____ : Father, Daughter, _____ _____ , Friends, _____

3 Narrator: A _____ _____ _____ , in a small _____ in South America, _____ _____ a farmer and his daughter.

4 The farmer was poor, and _____ _____ _____ three _____ pesos _____ a _____ _____ .

5 But _____ _____ _____ was not kind, and when the farmer _____ _____ one month _____ _____ _____ the money, she didn't _____ him _____ time.

6 Money Lender: You _____ _____ money? That's okay.

7 Your daughter _____ _____ my _____ _____ .

8 Father and Daughter: Oh, _____ !

9 Daughter: I don't want _____ _____ your _____ .

10 Father: I don't want that, _____ ! *(to Money Lender)* No, _____ _____ .

11 Money Lender: Do you want to _____ _____ _____ ?

12 Then, _____ _____ a game. I will _____ two stones in a bag.

13 _____ is white, and _____ _____ is black. Your daughter will _____ _____ .

14 Daughter: What _____ _____ I _____ the white one?

15 Money Lender: _____ you _____ _____ my _____ .

16 Friends: Oh, no! She's _____ . _____ _____ !

17 Daughter: What happens _____ I _____ the black one?

---

1 두 개의 돌

2 등장인물: 아버지, 딸, 대부업자, 친구들, 해설자

3 해설자: 오래 전 남아메리카의 작은 마을에 농부와 그의 딸이 살았습니다.

4 농부는 가난했고, 대부업자로부터 3백만 페소를 빌려야 했습니다.

5 하지만 대부업자는 친절하지 않았고, 농부가 돈을 갚을 때까지 한 달을 기다려 달라고 하자, 더 이상의 시간을 허락해 주지 않았습니다.

6 대부업자: 돈이 없다는 거죠? 좋아요

7 대신 당신 딸이 내 하녀가 돼야겠네요.

8 아버지와 딸: 오, 안 돼!

9 딸: 저는 당신의 하녀가 되고 싶지 않아요.

10 아버지: 나도 그것을 원하지 않아! *(대부업자에게)* 사양하겠습니다.

11 대부업자: 감옥에 가고 싶은가요?

12 그렇다면, 게임을 하나 합시다. 내가 가방에 돌 두 개를 넣겠어요.

13 하나는 흰색이고, 다른 하나는 검은색이죠. 당신 딸이 하나를 집을 거예요.

14 딸: 제가 흰 돌을 집으면 어떻게 되죠?

15 대부업자: 그러면 넌 내 하녀가 될 거야.

16 친구들: 오, 안 돼! 그녀는 야비해. 정말 끔찍해!

17 딸: 제가 검은 돌을 집으면 어떻게 되죠?

18 Money Lender: Then you will be _____, and your father _____ _____ _____ _____ _____ my money.

19 Father: What _____ if she _____ _____ this game _____ you?

20 Money Lender: (_____) _____ you will go to _____!

21 Father, Daughter, and Friends: Oh, no! _____!

22 (Money Lender _____ _____ two stones. Daughter _____ _____ _____ her.)

23 Daughter: (_____ _____) Oh! She has _____ _____ two _____ _____!

24 She will _____ me _____ her servant. _____ _____ I do?

25 Narrator: _____ _____ _____. What should she do?

26 She _____ _____ a black one.

27 (Daughter picks a stone from the bag. She _____ it _____ _____.)

28 Daughter Oh, no! I'm sorry, I've _____ it.

29 (to Money Lender) But it's _____.

30 _____ _____ _____ _____ _____ in the bag.

31 Then we will know _____ _____ _____ _____.

32 Money Lender: (_____ _____) I _____ _____ them about my _____! Oh, no!

33 (Money Lender _____ _____ _____ _____ _____.

34 Friends and Father _____ _____.)

35 Friends: She _____ the black one! They are _____!

36 Narrator: _____ _____ has _____ Father and Daughter!

18 대부업자: 그러면 넌 자유로워 질 것이고, 네 아버지는 내 돈을 갚을 필요가 없어.

19 아버지: 내 딸이 당신과 이 게임 을 하지 않으면 어떻게 되죠?

20 대부업자: (큰소리로) 그러면 당 신은 감옥에 가게 되겠죠!

21 아버지, 딸, 친구들: 오, 안 돼! 감옥이라니!

22 (대부업자는 두 개의 돌을 집는 다. 딸은 주의 깊게 그녀를 본다.)

23 딸: (혼잣말로) 오! 그녀는 두 개 의 흰 돌을 집었어!

24 그녀는 나를 자신의 하녀로 만 들 거야. 어떻게 하면 좋지?

25 해설자: 가만히 생각해 보세요. 그녀는 어떻게 하면 좋을까요?

26 그녀는 검은 돌을 집을 수 없어요.

27 (딸은 가방에서 돌을 하나 집는 다. 그녀는 그것을 바로 떨어뜨 린다.)

28 딸: 오, 안 돼! 미안해요, 제가 돌을 떨어뜨렸어요.

29 (대부업자에게) 하지만 괜찮아요.

30 가방에 있는 돌을 우리에게 보 여주세요.

31 그러면 제가 무엇을 집었는지 우리가 알게 될 테니까요.

32 대부업자: (혼잣말로) 그들에게 내 속임수를 말할 수 없어! 오, 안 돼!

33 (대부업자는 모두에게 흰 돌을 보여 준다.

34 친구들과 아버지는 축하하기 시 작한다.)

35 친구들: 그녀는 검은 돌을 집었 어! 그들은 자유야!

36 해설자: 현명한 생각이 아버지 와 딸을 구했습니다!

※ 다음 문장을 우리말로 쓰시오.

1 The Two Stones
➡ _____

2 Characters: Father, Daughter, Money Lender, Friends, Narrator
➡ _____

3 Narrator: A long time ago, in a small village in South America, there lived a farmer and his daughter.
➡ _____

4 The farmer was poor, and had to borrow three million pesos from a money lender.
➡ _____

5 But the money lender was not kind, and when the farmer asked for one month to pay back the money, she didn't allow him anymore time.
➡ _____
_____

6 Money Lender: You have no money? That's okay.
➡ _____

7 Your daughter will become my servant instead.
➡ _____

8 Father and Daughter: Oh, no!
➡ _____

9 Daughter: I don't want to be your servant.
➡ _____

10 Father: I don't want that, either! (to Money Lender) No, thank you.
➡ _____

11 Money Lender: Do you want to go to prison?
➡ _____

12 Then, let's play a game. I will put two stones in a bag.
➡ _____

13 One is white, and the other is black. Your daughter will pick one.
➡ _____

14 Daughter: What happens if I pick the white one?
➡ _____

15 Money Lender: Then you will be my servant.
➡ _____

16 Friends: Oh, no! She's mean. How terrible!
➡ _____

17 Daughter: What happens if I pick the black one?

➡ _____

18 Money Lender: Then you will be free, and your father doesn't have to pay back my money.

➡ _____

19 Father: What happens if she doesn't play this game with you?

➡ _____

20 *Money Lender: (loudly) Then you will go to prison!*

➡ _____

21 Father, Daughter, and Friends: Oh, no! Prison!

➡ _____

22 *(Money Lender picks up two stones. Daughter looks carefully at her.)*

➡ _____

23 Daughter: (*to herself*) Oh! She has picked up two white stones!

➡ _____

24 She will make me become her servant. What should I do?

➡ _____

25 Narrator: Stop and think. What should she do?

➡ _____

26 She cannot pick a black one.

➡ _____

27 *(Daughter picks a stone from the bag. She drops it right away.)*

➡ _____

28 Daughter: Oh, no! I'm sorry, I've dropped it. (*to Money Lender*) But it's okay.

➡ _____

29 Show us the stone in the bag.

➡ _____

30 Then we will know which one I picked.

➡ _____

31 Money Lender: (*to herself*) I cannot tell them about my trick! Oh, no!

➡ _____

32 *(Money Lender shows everyone the white stone. Friends and Father start celebrating.)*

➡ _____

33 Friends: She picked the black one! They are free!

➡ _____

34 Narrator: Good thinking has saved Father and Daughter!

➡ _____

※ 다음 괄호 안의 단어들을 우리말에 맞도록 바르게 배열하시오.

1 (Two / Stones / The)
➡ _____

2 (Characters: / Daughter, / Father, / Lender, / Money / Narrator / Friends,)
➡ _____

3 (Narrator: / long / a / ago, / time / a / in / village / small / South / in / America, / there / a / lived / farmer / his / and / daughter.)
➡ _____

4 (farmer / the / poor, / was / and / to / had / borrow / million / three / pesos / a / from / lender. / money)
➡ _____

5 (the / but / lender / money / was / kind, / not / and / the / when / farmer / for / asked / one / to / month / back / pay / money, / the / she / allow / didn't / anymore / time. / him)
➡ _____

6 (Lender: / Money / have / you / money? / no // okay. / that's)
➡ _____

7 (daughter / your / become / will / servant / instead. / my)
➡ _____

8 (Daughter: / and / Father / no! / oh,)
➡ _____

9 (Daughter: / I / want / don't / be / to / servant. / your)
➡ _____

10 (Father: / I / want / don't / either! / that, // Money / (to / Lender) // thank / no, / you.)
➡ _____

11 (Lender: / Money / you / do / want / go / to / prison? / to)
➡ _____

12 (then, / play / a / let's / game. // will / I / two / put / in / stones / bag. / a)
➡ _____

13 (white, / is / one / and / other / the / black. / is // daughter / your / will / one. / pick)
➡ _____

14 (Daughter: / happens / what / I / if / the / pick / one? / white)
➡ _____

15 (Lender: / Money / you / then / be / will / servant. / my)
➡ _____

16 (Friends: / no! / oh, // mean. / she's // terrible! / how)
➡ _____

17 (Daughter: / happens / what / I / if / pick / one? / black / the)
➡ _____

1 두 개의 돌

2 등장인물: 아버지, 딸, 대부업자, 친구들, 해설자

3 해설자: 오래 전 남아메리카의 작은 마을에 농부와 그의 딸이 살았습니다.

4 농부는 가난했고, 대부업자로부터 3백만 페소를 빌려야 했습니다.

5 하지만 대부업자는 친절하지 않았고, 농부가 돈을 갚을 때까지 한 달을 기다려 달라고 하자, 더 이상의 시간을 허락해 주지 않았습니다.

6 대부업자: 돈이 없다는 거죠? 좋아요

7 대신 당신 딸이 내 하녀가 돼야 겠네요.

8 아버지와 딸: 오, 안 돼!

9 딸: 저는 당신의 하녀가 되고 싶지 않아요.

10 아버지: 나도 그것을 원하지 않아! *(대부업자에게)* 사양하겠습니다.

11 대부업자: 감옥에 가고 싶은가요?

12 그렇다면, 게임을 하나 합시다. 내가 가방에 돌 두 개를 넣겠어요.

13 하나는 흰색이고, 다른 하나는 검은색이죠. 당신 딸이 하나를 집을 거예요.

14 딸: 제가 흰 돌을 집으면 어떻게 되죠?

15 대부업자: 그러면 넌 내 하녀가 될 거야.

16 친구들: 오, 안 돼! 그녀는 야비해. 정말 끔찍해!

17 딸: 제가 검은 돌을 집으면 어떻게 되죠?

18 (Lender: / Money / then / will / you / free, / be / and / father / your / doesn't / to / have / back / pay / money. / my)

➡ _____

_____

19 (Father: / happens / what / she / if / doesn't / this / play / with / you? / game)

➡ _____

20 (Lender: / Money / (*loudly*) / you / then / go / will / prison! / to)

➡ _____

21 (Daughter, / Father, / Friends: / and / no! / oh, / prison!)

➡ _____

22 ((Lender / Money / up / picks / stones. / two // looks / daughter / at / carefully / her.))

➡ _____

23 (Daughter: / *herself*) / (to / oh! // has / she / up / picked / white / stones! / two)

➡ _____

24 (will / she / me / make / become / servant. / her // should / what / do? / I)

➡ _____

25 (Narrator: / think. / and / stop // she / what / do? / should)

➡ _____

26 (cannot / she / a / pick / one. / black)

➡ _____

27 ((picks / daughter / stone / a / from / bag. / the // drops / she / right / it / away.))

➡ _____

28 (Daughter: / no! / oh, // sorry, / I'm / dropped / I've / it. // *Lender*) / *Money* / (to) // it's / but / okay.)

➡ _____

29 (us / show / stone / the / in / bag. / the)

➡ _____

30 (we / then / know / will / one / which / picked. / I)

➡ _____

31 (Lender: / Money / *herself*) / (to / cannot / I / them / tell / my / about / trick! // no! / oh,)

➡ _____

32 ((Lender / Money / everyone / shows / the / stone. / white // Father / and / Friends / celebrating. / start))

➡ _____

_____

33 (Friends: / picked / she / black / the / one! / are / free! / they)

➡ _____

34 (Narrator: / thinking / good / saved / has / Daughter! / and / Father)

➡ _____

18 대부업자: 그러면 넌 자유로워 질 것이고, 네 아버지는 내 돈을 갚을 필요가 없어.

19 아버지: 내 딸이 당신과 이 게임 을 하지 않으면 어떻게 되죠?

20 대부업자: (큰소리로) 그러면 당 신은 감옥에 가게 되겠죠!

21 아버지, 딸, 친구들: 오, 안 돼! 감옥이라니!

22 (대부업자는 두 개의 돌을 집는 다. 딸은 주의 깊게 그녀를 본다.)

23 딸: (혼잣말로) 오! 그녀는 두 개 의 흰 돌을 집었어!

24 그녀는 나를 자신의 하녀로 만 들 거야. 어떻게 하면 좋지?

25 해설자: 가만히 생각해 보세요. 그녀는 어떻게 하면 좋을까요?

26 그녀는 검은 돌을 집을 수 없어요.

27 (딸은 가방에서 돌을 하나 집는 다. 그녀는 그것을 바로 떨어뜨 린다.)

28 딸: 오, 안 돼! 미안해요, 제가 돌을 떨어뜨렸어요. (대부업자에 게) 하지만 괜찮아요.

29 가방에 있는 돌을 우리에게 보 여주세요.

30 그러면 제가 무엇을 집었는지 우리가 알게 될 테니까요.

31 대부업자: (혼잣말로) 그들에게 내 속임수를 말할 수 없어! 오, 안 돼!

32 (대부업자는 모두에게 흰 돌을 보여 준다. 친구들과 아버지는 축하하기 시작한다.)

33 친구들: 그녀는 검은 돌을 집었 어! 그들은 자유야!

34 해설자: 현명한 생각이 아버지 와 딸을 구했습니다!

※ 다음 우리말을 영어로 쓰시오.

1 두 개의 돌

➡ _____

2 등장인물: 아버지, 딸, 대부업자, 친구들, 해설자

➡ _____

3 해설자: 오래 전 남아메리카의 작은 마을에 농부와 그의 딸이 살았습니다.

➡ _____

4 농부는 가난했고, 대부업자로부터 3백만 페소를 빌려야 했습니다.

➡ _____

5 하지만 대부업자는 친절하지 않았고, 농부가 돈을 갚을 때까지 한 달을 기다려 달라고 하자, 더 이상의 시간을 허락해 주지 않았습니다.

➡ _____

  _____

6 대부업자: 돈이 없다는 거죠? 좋아요

➡ _____

7 대신 당신 딸이 내 하녀가 돼야겠네요.

➡ _____

8 아버지와 딸: 오, 안 돼!

➡ _____

9 딸: 저는 당신의 하녀가 되고 싶지 않아요.

➡ _____

10 아버지: 나도 그것을 원하지 않아! *(대부업자에게)* 사양하겠습니다.

➡ _____

11 대부업자: 감옥에 가고 싶은가요?

➡ _____

12 그렇다면, 게임을 하나 합시다. 내가 가방에 돌 두 개를 넣겠어요.

➡ _____

13 하나는 흰색이고, 다른 하나는 검은색이죠. 당신 딸이 하나를 집을 거예요.

➡ _____

14 딸: 제가 흰 돌을 집으면 어떻게 되죠?

➡ _____

15 대부업자: 그러면 넌 내 하녀가 될 거야.

➡ _____

16 친구들: 오, 안 돼! 그녀는 야비해. 정말 끔찍해!

➡ _____

17 딸: 제가 검은 돌을 집으면 어떻게 되죠?

  ➡ _____

18 대부업자: 그러면 넌 자유로워질 것이고, 네 아버지는 내 돈을 갚을 필요가 없어.

  ➡ _____

19 아버지: 내 딸이 당신과 이 게임을 하지 않으면 어떻게 되죠?

  ➡ _____

20 대부업자: *(큰소리로)* 그러면 당신은 감옥에 가게 되겠죠!

  ➡ _____

21 아버지, 딸, 친구들: 오, 안 돼! 감옥이라니!

  ➡ _____

22 *(대부업자는 두 개의 돌을 집는다. 딸은 주의 깊게 그녀를 본다.)*

  ➡ _____

23 딸: *(혼잣말로)* 오! 그녀는 두 개의 흰 돌을 집었어!

  ➡ _____

24 그녀는 나를 자신의 하녀로 만들 거야. 어떻게 하면 좋지?

  ➡ _____

25 해설자: 가만히 생각해 보세요. 그녀는 어떻게 하면 좋을까요?

  ➡ _____

26 그녀는 검은 돌을 집을 수 없어요.

  ➡ _____

27 *(딸은 가방에서 돌을 하나 집는다. 그녀는 그것을 바로 떨어뜨린다.)*

  ➡ _____

28 딸: 오, 안 돼! 미안해요, 제가 돌을 떨어뜨렸어요. *(대부업자에게)* 하지만 괜찮아요.

  ➡ _____

29 가방에 있는 돌을 우리에게 보여주세요.

  ➡ _____

30 그러면 제가 무엇을 집었는지 우리가 알게 될 테니까요.

  ➡ _____

31 대부업자: *(혼잣말로)* 그들에게 내 속임수를 말할 수 없어! 오, 안 돼!

  ➡ _____

32 *(대부업자는 모두에게 흰 돌을 보여 준다. 친구들과 아버지는 축하하기 시작한다.)*

  ➡ _____

33 친구들: 그녀는 검은 돌을 집었어! 그들은 자유야!

  ➡ _____

34 해설자: 현명한 생각이 아버지와 딸을 구했습니다!

  ➡ _____

영어 기출 문제집

적중100

2학기

정답 및 해설

천재 | 이재영

중 2

영어 기출 문제집

2학기

정답 및 해설

천재 | 이재영

중 2

A Life Full of Fun

하지만, 그들은 곧 심각한 오염에 시달린다. 나이 든 코끼리가 한 가지 제안을 한다. 동물들과 도시는 모든 이들을 위한 더 좋은 세상을 만들기 위해 합의에 이른다.

시험대비 실력평가 p.08

01 ⑤　　02 ⑤　　03 ①　　04 ④
05 (1) Lastly　(2) spread　(3) plate　(4) is made into
　　(5) caught my interest　(6) take a look
06 ①

01 pour: 붓다, bake: 굽다, fry: 볶다, cook: 요리하다, publish: 출판하다

02 agree의 명사형은 agreement이다.

03 하나의 언어에서 다른 언어로 바뀌는 것을 가리키는 말은 translate(번역하다)이다.

04 fascinating: 매력적인

05 lastly: 마지막으로, spread: 바르다. plate: 접시 be made into ~로 만들어지다, catch one's interest ~의 관심을 끌다, take a look 살펴보다

06 주어진 문장에서 spread는 '바르다'는 뜻으로 쓰였으며 이와 같은 의미로 쓰인 것은 ①번이다. ②, ③번은 '펼치다', ④, ⑤번은 '번지다, 확산시키다'는 뜻으로 쓰였다.

서술형 시험대비 p.09

01 dead　　02 (1) creative　(2) cartoonist
　　(3) silly　(4) usual　(5) well-known
03 (1) box office　(2) showtime　(3) pay for
04 (1) You should not make fun of your friends.
　　(2) Lucy is always calm through life's ups and downs.
　　(3) I take a look at the webtoons of the day.
05 Education, amusement, pollution, suggestion, agreement

01 주어진 문장은 반의어 관계를 나타낸다. dead: 죽은, alive: 살아 있는

02 creative: 창의적인, cartoonist: 만화가, silly: 어리석은, usual: 보통의, well-known: 유명한, 잘 알려진

03 box office: 매표소, showtime: 상영 시간, pay for: ~에 대한 돈을 내다

04 make fun of: ~을 놀리다, ups and downs: 기복, take a look: 살펴보다

05 동물들은 숲속에 놀이공원을 지으려는 도시의 계획을 환영한다.

교과서 Conversation

핵심 Check p.10~11

1 (1) met / haven't, Have / have
　(2) Have you ever been / have been / did
2 (1) how to / First, Second / next / Boil
　(2) fall asleep easily / First of all, Next, Lastly

교과서 대화문 익히기

Check(√) True or False p.12

1 F　2 T　3 T　4 F

교과서 확인학습 p.14~15

Communication: Listen – Dialog 1

down / serious, a lot / ups and downs / Have you watched / I haven't . Why / feelings, understand, better / sounds, watch

Communication: Listen – Dialog 2

line / ticket machine, from, machine / how to use the machine / select / watch, what / select, seats / back / Lastly , pay for / simple

Communication: Listen More

Have you ever made / No, I haven't / how to make / First, put, on, spread / help, with / Next, peppers / Add, bake, oven / wait, taste

Communicate: Speak

fried rice / cut, into / next / Put, fry / simple

Wrap Up – Listening ❺

Have, been / have. Actually / you've climbed, haven't you / twice

Wrap Up – Listening ❻

how to draw / First, circle, Next / draw, color, circle, Lastly

01 He needs six circles.   02 ⑤

03 Do you know how to make fried rice?

04 채소를 작은 조각으로 자르고 팬에 기름을 두른 후 채소를 밥과 함께 볶는다.

05 (1) I've never been to Baltimore before.

    (2) Have you ever been to China?

01 Mike는 곰의 얼굴을 그리기 위해 6개의 원이 필요하다.

02 마지막에 입을 만들어야 한다.

05 Have you ever p.p: ~해 본 적이 있니?

---

01 ②   02 ①

03 Have you watched the animated movie "Shining Days"?   04 ③   05 ④

06 ⓐ put   ⓑ help   ⓒ bake   ⓓ wait

07 ⑤   08 (E) → (C) → (A) → (D) → (B)

09 haven't you?

10 Have you ever been to Sokcho?

11 (1) Have you ever been to Dokdo?

    (2) I have read the Harry Potter series.

01 'Have you ever ~?'의 경험을 묻는 질문에 'Yes, I have.' 또는 'No, I haven't.'로 대답한다.

02 (A)의 'down'은 '우울한'을 의미한다.

04 (A) 기계를 사용하는 방법을 묻고 있으므로 how, (B) select와 병렬 구조로 동사 choose, (C) Lately: 최근에, Lastly: 마지막으로

05 표 매수와 좌석을 고른 후 표 값을 지불한다.

06 bake: 굽다

07 Garcia와 Suji가 피자 소스를 만들기 위해 무슨 재료를 준비해야 하는지 알 수 없다.

08 (E) 볶음밥 만드는 법 질문 → (C) 대답 및 첫 번째 단계 설명 → (A) 두 번째 단계 질문 → (D) 두 번째 단계 및 세 번째 단계 설명 → (B) 반응

09 선행하는 문장의 시제가 현재완료이므로 'haven't you?'가 적절하다

11 Have you ever been to ~?: ~에 가 본 적이 있니?

---

01 (3) → (4) → (2)

02 He will make nacho pizza.

03 He put nacho chips on a plate.

04 He put pizza sauce, ham, onions. peppers, and cheese.

05 (D) → (E) → (C) → (A) → (B)

06 Yes, he has.

07 Because his uncle lives there.

01 나초 칩을 접시 위에 올려놓고 피자 소스를 바른 후 햄, 양파, 피망을 위에 올린다. 그리고 피자를 올린다.

02 요리사는 나초 피자를 만들 것이다.다.

03 요리사는 첫 번째로 나초 칩을 접시 위에 올려놓았다.

04 나초 칩 위에 피자 소스, 햄, 양파, 피망 그리고 치즈를 올려놓았다.

05 (D) 기계를 사용하는 방법으로 첫 번째 단계 설명 → (E) 상영 시간 선택 → (C) 두 번째 단계 설명→ (A) 앉고 싶은 자리 설명 → (B) 마지막 단계 설명

06 민수는 설악산에 올라가 본 적이 있다.

07 민수는 그의 삼촌이 속초에 살고 계시기 때문에 매년 속초를 방문한다.

교과서

Grammar

1 (1) has been   (2) has, left   (3) have called

2 (1) typing   (2) boring   (3) sung

01 (1) hasn't gone → hasn't been

    (2) saw → have seen   (3) did → have done

    (4) have work → have worked

02 (1) living   (2) crying   (3) written   (4) made

    (5) barking

03 (1) I have read 500 books since I was six.

    (2) The boy has already drunk the milk.

    (3) Is this a baked potato?

    (4) Did you find your sleeping bag?

01 (1) 'have gone to ~'는 '~에 가고 없다'는 의미로 결과를 나타내는 현재완료이다. '~에 가 본 적이 없다'는 것은 'have[has] not been to ~'로 표현한다. (2) 지금까지 프로그램을 몇 번 보았다는 의미이므로 현재완료 시제로 표현하는 것이 적절하다. (3) 어제 이래로 아무것도 하지 않았다는 것이므로 과거의 일이 현재까지 이어지는 것이라 볼 수 있다. 따라서 현재완료 시제가 적절하다. (4) 현재완료의 형태는 'have+p.p.'이다.

02 (1) '그 마을에서 살고 있는'이라는 의미이므로 현재분사로 people을 수식한다. (2) 아기가 울고 있는 것이므로 현재분사로 baby를 수식하는 것이 적절하다. (3) 책이 유명한 작가에 의해 '쓰여진' 것이므로 과거분사를 쓴다. (4) '금으로 만들어진 수저'라는 의미이므로 과거분사로 spoon을 수식한다. (5) '짖는 개'라는 의미이므로 현재분사를 쓰는 것이 적절하다.

03 (1) 여섯 살 이후로 계속 책을 읽은 것이므로 현재완료 시제를 써서 나타낸다. (2) 벌써 우유를 마셨다는 완료를 나타내고 있으므로 현재완료 시제를 쓰는 것이 적절하다. (3) 감자는 구워지는 것이므로 과거분사로 potato를 수식한다. (4) 잠자는 용도로 쓰이는 자루를 말하는 것이므로 동명사 sleeping이 적절하다.

시험대비 실력평가   p.23~25

01 ④	02 ③	03 ③	04 ③
05 ⑤	06 ④	07 ④, ⑤	

08 Eunji has lived in Busan since she was five years old.

09 ⑤	10 ③	11 ④

12 I have just had a piece of frozen pizza.

13 ⑤	14 ③	15 ④

16 I bought a used car.   17 ③   18 ⑤

19 ④	20 ⑤

21 The surprising news is not true.   22 ⑤

23 Cold winds blew into the house through the broken window.

24 exciting / excited

01 현재완료 시제와 함께 쓰이면서 특정 시점을 이끌 수 있는 것은 since이다.

02 현재완료의 형태는 'have+p.p.'이다. 따라서 seen이 적절하다.

03 무언가가 '타고 있는' 것이므로 현재분사 burning으로 수식하고, 'Jessica라고 이름 지어진' 것이므로 과거분사로 a girl을 수식하는 것이 적절하다.

04 stop의 과거분사는 stopped이다.

05 주어진 문장은 경험을 나타내는 현재완료이다. 밑줄 친 현재완료의 용법은 각각 ① 결과 ②, ③ 완료 ④ 계속 ⑤ 경험을 나타내고 있다.

06 지금까지 3년 동안 그녀를 만나 왔다는 의미이므로 현재완료 시제를 사용하는 것이 적절하다.

07 목적격 보어로 과거분사를 취할 수 없는 동사는 help와 seem이다.

08 은지는 5살 때부터 부산에서 살기 시작하여 현재도 부산에서 살고 있다고 하였으므로 현재완료 시제를 활용하여 은지는 5살 이래로 부산에서 살고 있다는 문장으로 쓸 수 있다.

09 주어진 문장의 밑줄 친 부분은 현재분사로 쓰인 것이다. '손을 올리고 있는 소녀'라는 의미의 ⑤번이 현재분사로 쓰였으므로

⑤번이 답이다.

10 Has로 묻고 있으므로 has로 답하는 것이 적절하다.

11 ① that smiling girl ② the injured man ③ did you meet ⑤ for three years

12 '막 먹었다'는 완료의 의미는 현재완료 시제를 통하여 나타낼 수 있다.

13 (A) 흥분을 유발하는 게임이라는 의미이므로 현재분사로 game을 수식하는 것이 적절하다. (B) 5살 때부터 기타를 연주해 오고 있다는 의미이므로 현재완료 시제를 쓴다. (C) 과거를 나타내는 어구인 yesterday와 현재완료 시제는 함께 쓸 수 없다.

14 답변으로 미루어 보아 영화를 본 적이 있는지 경험을 묻는 말이 들어가는 것이 적절하다.

15 Paul이 10살 때부터 쭉 Tom이 가르치고 있다는 의미이므로 현재완료 시제가 적절하며, Tom이 Paul을 잘 안다는 것은 현재 상태를 나타내는 것이므로 현재시제를 쓴다.

16 중고차는 used car이다.

17 모두 특정 시점을 이끄는 since가 쓰이지만 ③번에는 기간을 이끄는 전치사 for가 쓰인다.

18 동생이 쇼핑몰에 가고서 현재 이곳에 없다는 의미이므로, 현재완료 시제를 사용하여 '동생은 쇼핑몰에 가고 없어.'라는 문장을 쓸 수 있다. 'have gone to'는 '~에 가고 없다'는 의미를 갖는다.

19 그는 오늘 아침 이래로 불타는 태양 아래에서 하루 종일 일해 왔다는 의미이다. 따라서 현재완료 시제를 쓰는 것이 적절하며, '불타는 태양'이므로 현재분사로 sun을 수식하는 것이 적절하다.

20 내가 즐거움을 느끼는 것이므로 과거분사 amused를 쓰는 것이 적절하다.

21 그 소식이 '놀라움을 주는'것이므로 현재분사로 news를 수식한다.

22 주어진 문장을 영어로 옮기면 I have fought with my brother before.이다.

23 blow의 과거형 blew를 쓰고, '부서진 창문'이라고 하였으므로 과거분사로 window를 수식하도록 문장을 쓰는 것이 적절하다.

24 콘서트는 흥분을 유발하는 것이므로 현재분사로. 팬들은 흥분을 느낀 것이므로 과거분사로 쓰는 것이 적절하다.

서술형 시험대비   p.26~27

01 (1) rising   (2) baked, sleeping   (3) dancing
   (4) cheering   (5) sliced

02 Jenny has been friends with Christina since 2010.

03 A: Have you ever cooked fried rice?
   B: Yes, I have cooked it many times.

04 Have you been to other countries before?

05 (1) drove　(2) has been　(3) has rained　(4) lost
　　(5) has read

06 Look at the boy wearing a red cap.

07 My brother has been sick since last night.

08 (1) 현재분사　이유: '수영하는 아기'라는 의미로 swimming이 baby를 수식하고 있다.
　　(2) 동명사　이유: 수영하는 용도로 쓰이는 풀'이라는 의미로 쓰이고 있다.

09 (1) I have been to Jejudo twice until now.
　　(2) I broke the window yesterday.
　　(3) We haven't seen the movie yet.

10 has lived, 2011, 2011, has learned, for

11 My grandmother has broken her right arm.

12 She made me bring a boiled egg and chopped carrot.

13 has worked

14 (1) boring → bored　(2) making → made
　　(3) excited → exciting　(4) barked → barking

01 분사의 수식을 받는 명사가 행위 주체인 경우에는 현재분사로, 그렇지 않은 경우에는 과거분사로 수식한다.

02 현재완료 시제를 이용하여 Jenny는 Christina와 2010년 이래로 쭉 친구라고 쓸 수 있다.

03 경험을 묻고 답하는 말이므로 현재완료 시제를 써서 나타낼 수 있다. '볶아진 밥'이라는 말로 '볶음밥'을 표현할 수 있음에 유의하자.

04 경험을 묻는 말이므로 현재완료 시제를 이용하여 문장을 만들 수 있다.

05 과거를 나타내는 어구와 현재완료는 함께 쓸 수 없다. 그러나 과거의 일이 현재까지 영향을 미치는 경우 현재완료 시제를 쓸 수 있다.

06 분사가 목적어나 부사구와 함께 쓰일 때는 명사를 뒤에서 수식한다.

07 어젯밤부터 아픈 것이 현재까지 이어지고 있으므로 현재완료시제를 활용하여 표현할 수 있다.

08 현재분사는 명사를 수식하고, 동명사는 '~한 용도로 쓰이는 명사'라고 해석된다.

09 (1) 지금까지의 경험을 나타내고 있으므로 현재완료 시제를 쓰는 것이 적절하다. (2) 어제 일어난 일을 말하고 있으므로 과거 시제를 쓴다. (3) 현재완료 시제의 용법 중 '완료'를 사용하여 나타낼 수 있다.

10 캐나다에서 태어난 Jason은 10살이던 2011년에 한국으로 이사를 오자마자 태권도를 배우기 시작했다. 그는 현재 18세이므로 8년간 태권도를 배워 왔다고 말할 수 있다.

11 지난달에 할머니의 오른팔이 부러졌고, 할머니는 여전히 오른팔을 쓰실 수 없으므로 현재완료 시제를 이용하여 오른팔이 부러진 상황이 지속됨을 말할 수 있다.

12 '삶은 달걀'은 삶아진 달걀을 뜻하므로 과거분사 boiled로 egg를 수식해야 하며, '다진 당근' 역시 다져진 당근을 뜻하므로 chopped carrot이라고 쓰는 것이 적절하다.

13 현재도 일을 하고 있고, 5년 동안 이 회사에서 일해 오고 있다는 의미이므로 현재완료 시제를 쓰는 것이 적절하다.

14 (1) 지루한 감정을 느낀 것이므로 과거분사 (2) 중국에서 만들어진 가방이므로 과거분사 (3) 흥분을 유발하는 모험영화이므로 현재분사를 쓰는 것이 적절하다. (4) 짖는 개라는 의미이므로 현재분사로 dog를 수식하는 것이 적절하다.

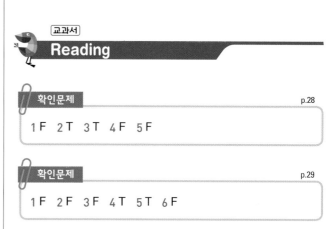

[교과서] **Reading**

확인문제　　　　　　　　　　p.28

1 F　2 T　3 T　4 F　5 F

확인문제　　　　　　　　　　p.29

1 F　2 F　3 F　4 T　5 T　6 F

교과서 확인학습 A　　　　　p.30~31

01 Land　　　　　02 laugh, saw, above

03 so, successful　　04 who make cartoons

05 to catch, make you laugh, creative drawings.

06 have made, for　　07 many types of cartoons

08 is, a few words　　09 is, called

10 makes a funny character, laugh, doing, saying

11 Another, is called

12 some parts, are different, bigger than usual

13 on　　　　　　14 Which parts, jump

15 have used, to make fun of

16 several, come together, a comic strip

17 have been, for　　18 just amusing stories

19 have also used, for education

20 make, clearer, easier to learn

21 have probabiy seen

22 have surely seen, animated movies

23 popular among people of all ages

24 are added to, come alive

25 develop fascinating, interesting, through

26 was developed　　27 is called

28 are published, read them, on

29 popular, them are, into　30 may appear

31 different, exciting than, remain, laugh, relax, learn

1 Boat! Land!

2 Did you laugh when you saw the cartoon above?

3 If so, the cartoonist was successful.

4 Cartoonists are the people who make cartoons.

5 They want to catch your interest, and usually, make you laugh with simple language and creative drawings.

6 People have made cartoons for hundreds of years.

7 There are many types of cartoons, and they play different roles.

8 One form of cartoon is a picture with a few words.

9 It is sometimes called a "gag cartoon."

10 The cartoonist makes a funny character, and the character makes you laugh by doing or saying silly things.

11 Another type of cartoon is called a caricature.

12 In a caricature, some parts of a character are different or bigger than usual.

13 Look at the picture on the right.

14 Which parts of the man's face jump out at you?

15 Artists have used this type of cartoon to make fun of well-known people.

16 When several cartoon pictures come together and tell a story, we have a comic strip.

17 Comic strips have been in newspapers for many years.

18 They are often just amusing stories.

19 People have also used comic strips for education.

20 Comics can make information clearer and easier to learn.

21 You have probably seen comic history or science books.

22 You have surely seen many cartoon movies, or animated movies, too.

23 These are very popular among people of all ages.

24 Movement and sounds are added to pictures, so they come alive.

25 Artists and writers can develop fascinating characters and tell interesting stories through animation.

26 In the 1990s, a new type of cartoon was developed.

27 It is called a webtoon.

28 Webtoons are published online, so you can read them anytime, anywhere on your phone or computer.

29 They are very popular, and some of them are even made into TV dramas or movies.

30 New forms of cartoons may appear in the future.

31 They could be different and even more exciting than now, but one thing will remain the same: they will help us laugh, relax, and learn.

01 ③   02 ⑤

03 It is called a caricature.

04 A cartoonist makes a funny character in a gag cartoon.

05 ②   06 ④   07 They make cartoons.

08 ③   09 ②   10 ③   11 ④

12 It's because they are published online. 13 ④

14 ②, ④   15 ③   16 successful

17 The characters in a gag cartoon make people laugh by doing or saying silly things.

18 ②   19 ④   20 We call it a gag cartoon.   21 ②   22 ③

23 A comic strip is made of several cartoon pictures and tells a story.

24 It's because comics can make information clearer and easier to learn.

25 ③   26 우리가 웃고, 쉬고, 배우도록 돕는 것

01 이어지는 글의 내용을 보면 다양한 종류의 만화는 서로 다른 역할을 한다. 따라서 different라고 쓰는 것이 적절하다.

02 빈칸 (A)에는 by+Ving로 '~함으로써'라는 의미를 완성하는 전치사 by가 들어간다. be interested in: ~에 흥미를 갖 다, give up: ~을 포기하다, turn off: ~을 끄다, be proud of: ~을 자랑스러워하다, one by one: 하나씩

03 두 번째 종류의 만화는 캐리커처라고 하였다.

04 만화가는 개그 만화에서 웃긴 캐릭터를 만든다고 하였다.

05 캐리커처는 유명한 사람들을 풍자하는 것이다.

06 글에는 두 가지 종류의 만화만 제시되어 있다.

07 만화가들은 만화를 만드는 사람들이다.

08 빈칸 (A)에는 기간을 이끄는 전치사 for가 쓰인다. ③번에는 특정 시점을 이끄는 since가 쓰인다.

09 연재만화는 여러 해 동안 신문에 실려 옴 - [B] 연재만화는 종종 단지 재미있는 이야기이고 교육용으로도 쓰임 - [A] 교육용 만화 역사책이나 과학책이 있음. 또한 만화영화도 있는데 - [C] 이는 모든 연령의 사람들에게 인기가 있고 동작이나 소리가 더해져서 그림들이 생생하게 살아남.

10 몇 가지 만화 그림을 모아 연재만화를 만든다고 하였다.

11 (A) 웹툰이라고 불리는 것이므로 수동태, (B) 지칭하는 것이 복수명사 webtoons이므로 복수 대명사, (C) appear는 자동사

이므로 수동태로 쓰일 수 없다.

12 우리가 휴대 전화나 컴퓨터로 언제 어디서나 웹툰을 읽을 수 있는 이유는 웹툰이 온라인으로 출판되기 때문이다.

13 웹툰을 주로 누가 보는지는 알 수 없다.

14 사람을 선행사로 받아주는 주격 관계대명사 who가 쓰이며, who를 대신하여 that을 쓸 수 있다.

15 다양한 종류의 만화가 있다고 하였으므로 만화의 종류가 이어지는 것이 가장 적절하다.

16 바라던 결과를 성취하는 것은 '성공적인(successful)'이다.

17 개그 만화에 등장하는 캐릭터는 우스꽝스러운 행동이나 말을 함으로써 사람들을 웃게 만든다고 하였다.

18 one과 another로 만화의 종류를 소개하고 있으므로 만화의 종류에는 두 가지 이상이 있음을 알 수 있다. another는 남아 있는 것 중 하나를 가리키는 대명사이다.

19 개그 만화에서는 우스꽝스러운 행동이나 말을 함으로써 독자를 웃게 만드는 캐릭터를 볼 수 있다고 하였다.

20 몇 마디 말을 쓴 그림은 '개그 만화'라고 부른다.

21 주어진 문장의 대명사 It은 a new type of cartoon을 지칭하는 것이다.

22 (A) 즐거움을 유발하는 이야기이므로 현재분사로 stories를 수식, (B) 긍정에 대한 동의이므로 too, (C) come alive: 생생하게 살아나다, 활기를 띠다, come live: 생방송하다

23 연재만화는 몇 가지 만화 그림으로 이루어져 있으며 이야기를 들려준다고 하였다.

24 만화는 정보를 더 명료하고 더 배우기 쉽게 만들 수 있기 때문에 사람들은 연재만화를 교육용으로 사용해 오기도 했다.

25 웹툰은 온라인으로 출판되기 때문에 여러분이 휴대 전화나 컴퓨터로 언제 어디서나 볼 수 있다고 하였다.

26 미래에 새로운 형태의 만화가 나타날지라도 우리가 웃고, 쉬고, 배우도록 돕는 것은 여전히 같을 것이라고 하였다.

🦉 서술형 시험대비 p.38~39

01 People have made cartoons for hundreds of years.

02 They use simple language and creative drawings.

03 If you laughed when you saw the cartoon above

04 many types of cartoons 05 It makes us laugh.

06 It is a gag cartoon.

07 many words → a few words wise → silly[foolish]

08 We can use comic strips.

09 movement and sounds are added to pictures

10 They can develop fascinating characters and tell interesting stories through animation.

11 Webtoons were developed in the 1990s.

12 a comic strip / amusing / education

13 will help us laugh, relax, and learn

01 사람들은 수 백 년 전에 만화를 만들었고 현재도 만들고 있다고 하였으므로, 현재완료 시제를 이용하여 '사람들은 수 백 년 동안 만화를 만들어 왔다'는 문장을 쓸 수 있다.

02 만화가들은 사람들을 웃게 하기 위해서 간단한 말과 독창적인 그림을 사용한다고 하였다.

03 If so는 '만약 그렇다면'이라는 뜻으로, '위 만화를 보고 웃었다면'이라는 의미로 쓰였다.

04 많은 종류의 만화를 가리키는 대명사이다.

05 개그 만화는 우리를 웃게 만든다.

06 간단한 말을 쓴 그림이므로 개그 만화이다.

07 만화의 한 형태로 몇 마디 말을 쓴 그림이 있고, 웃긴 캐릭터가 우스꽝스러운 행동을 한다고 하였다.

08 만화는 정보를 더 명료하고 더 배우기 쉽게 만들 수 있다고 하였다. 만약 정보를 좀 더 분명하게 전달하기를 원한다면 연재만화를 사용할 수 있다.

09 동작이나 소리가 그림에 더해져서 그림들이 생생하게 살아난다고 하였다.

10 미술가들과 작가들은 매력적인 캐릭터를 개발하고 만화영화 제작을 통해 재미있는 이야기를 들려준다고 하였다.

11 웹툰이 개발된 시기는 1990년대라고 하였다.

12 만화 그림이 모여 이야기를 들려주면 연재만화가 되고, 연재만화는 재미있는 이야기라고 하였다. 또한 연재만화는 교육용으로 사용된다.

13 해석: 비록 미래에 새로운 형태의 만화가 나타난다 할지라도, 그것은 지금처럼 우리가 웃고, 쉬고, 배우도록 도와줄 것이다.

🦉 영역별 핵심문제 p.41~45

01 ①   02 ③

03 (1) Emma poured orange juice into a glass and drank it.

   (2) We have lots of[a lot of] plates to wash.

   (3) I like to fry eggs and lots of vegetables.

04 (1) come together (2) comic strip (3) Watch out

   (4) of all ages (5) jumps out at me

05 ③   06 (B) → (D) → (C) → (A)   07 ⑤

08 (A) a movie (B) a showtime (C) choose seats

   (D) pay for the tickets

09 Have you ever made nacho pizza?

10 ⓐ nacho pizza ⓑ nacho chips

11 ④   12 ⑤

13 (A) down (B) serious (C) understand

14 ⑤   15 ⑤   16 ②

17 Do you know the boy jumping on the stage?

18 ④   19 ④   20 ②

21 I have had this problem since last year.

22 ⑤   23 ⑤   24 stolen, found
25 They have been in the library since noon.
26 ②   27 ③   28 ④   29 usual
30 ③

01 태양에 의해 손상되는 것으로부터 피부를 보호하기 위해 피부에 바르는 로션의 한 유형을 가리키는 말은 sunscreen(자외선 차단제)이다.

02 spread는 '바르다'는 의미로 쓰였다.

03 pour: 붓다, plate: 접시, fry: 볶다

04 of all ages: 모든 연령의, watch out for: ~을 조심하다, comic strip: 신문 연재만화 / jump out at: ~에게 금방 눈에 띄다, come together: 합쳐지다

05 주어진 문장에서 down은 '우울한'을 뜻하며 이와 같은 의미로 쓰인 것은 ③번이다. 나머지는 모두 '아래로, ~ 아래쪽으로'를 뜻한다.

06 (B) 속초 방문한 경험 질문 → (D) 대답 및 이유 설명 → (C) 설악산에 올라가 본 적이 있는지 확인 → (A) 대답 및 올라간 횟수 설명

07 빈칸 (A)에 들어갈 말로 나머지는 모두 제안을 나타내지만 ⑤번은 경험을 묻는 표현이다.

09 'Have you ever ~?' 표현을 사용하여 경험을 물어 볼 수 있다.

11 위 대화에서 피자 소스를 무엇으로 만드는지는 알 수 없다.

12 Anna가 Jinsu가 채소를 작게 자르는 것을 돕는지 대화를 통해 알 수 없다.

13 (A)에서 down은 '우울한'을 가리킨다. (B)에는 대명사를 수식하는 형용사 serious가 적절하다. (C)에는 help 뒤에 원형 부정사 understand가 적절하다.

14 drive의 과거분사형은 driven이다.

15 경험을 나타내는 문장은 현재완료로 표현할 수 있으며, '~에 가 본 적이 있다'는 'have been to'를 쓴다.

16 첫 번째 빈칸에는 경험을 나타내어 once, twice, before 등이 들어갈 수 있다. 특정 시점을 이끄는 것은 since, 기간을 이끄는 것은 for를 쓴다.

17 '무대 위에서 뛰고 있는'이 '소년'을 수식하는 구조이므로 the boy jumping on the stage라고 쓰는 것이 적절하다. 분사가 부사구와 함께 쓰이고 있으므로 명사를 뒤에서 수식하도록 문장을 만든다.

18 명백히 과거를 나타내는 어구인 when, ~ ago 등은 현재완료 시제와 함께 쓰일 수 없다. 현재완료의 과거형은 haven't p.p.이다.

19 주소를 잊고 여전히 기억할 수 없다고 하였으므로 현재완료 시제를 이용하여 주소를 잊은 상황을 말할 수 있다.

20 모두 baking이 들어가지만 ②번에는 baked가 들어간다. ⑤번에 쓰인 baking은 동명사로 '빵을 굽는 용도로 쓰이는 소다'라는 의미를 완성한다.

21 작년부터 지금까지 이 문제를 가지고 있었다고 하였으므로 현재완료 시제로 나타낼 수 있다.

22 주어진 문장의 밑줄 친 부분은 현재완료의 용법 중 '경험'을 나타낸다. 각각 ① 결과 ② 결과 ③ 계속 ④ 계속 ⑤ 경험 용법으로 쓰였다.

23 과거를 나타내는 어구인 the other day가 있으므로 과거시제를 쓰는 것이 적절하다. put은 과거와 과거완료의 형태가 모두 동일한 put–put–put이다.

24 '도난당한 차'이므로 과거분사 stolen으로 car를 수식하고, '발견되었다'고 하였으므로 수동태를 완성하는 과거분사 found를 쓴다.

25 정오에 도서관을 가서 여전히 도서관에 있다고 하였으므로, 현재완료 시제를 이용하여 그들이 정오 이래로 도서관에 계속 있다는 말을 쓸 수 있다.

26 ②번 문장의 주어인 They가 지칭하는 것은 주어진 문장의 Cartoonists이다. 따라서 ②번에 들어가는 것이 가장 적절하다.

27 밑줄 친 (A)는 현재완료의 '계속' 용법으로 쓰였다. ① 경험 ② 결과 ③ 계속 ④ 경험 ⑤ 결과

28 만화가들은 창의적인 그림으로 우리를 웃게 만든다고 하였다.

29 보통의; 아주 자주 발생하는 usual(평소의, 보통의)

30 글의 서두를 만화의 또 다른 종류(Another type of cartoon)라는 말로 이끌고 있으므로, 앞에서 다른 종류의 만화에 대해 언급했음을 알 수 있다.

단원별 예상문제   p.46~49

01 ⓒ → watched   02 ①

03 They want to buy them from the ticket machine.

04 They will watch it at seven o'clock.

05 She wants to sit in the back.

06 (C) → (A) → (E) → (D) → (B)   07 ③

08 They should fry the vegetables with rice.

09 They should prepare vegetables, oil, and rice.

10 ③   11 ④   12 ⑤   13 ⑤

14 ②   15 (1) named   (2) broken   (3) surprising

16 I will buy the recommended book.

17 Mr. Smith has taught me English since last year.

18 interesting   19 New forms of cartoons

20 ④   21 ④

22 Movement and sounds make the pictures come alive.

23 ④   24 ④   25 ②

26 Because he looks on the bright side of everything and always tries to help others.

01 경험을 묻는 현재완료 시제를 사용하여야 하므로 watched가 적절하다.

02 위 대화를 통해 Kevin이 어떻게 생겼는지는 알 수 없다.

03 Tony와 Emily는 발매기에서 표를 사고 싶어 한다.

04 Tony와 Emily는 영화를 7시에 볼 것이다.

05 Emily는 뒤에 앉고 싶어 한다.

06 (C) 첫 번째 단계 설명 → (A) 도움 제공 → (E) 두 번째 단계 설명 → (D) 다음 단계 질문 → (B) 마지막 단계 설명

07 (A) cut: 자르다, put: 놓다 (B) bake: 굽다, (C) fry: 볶다, spread: 바르다

08 그들은 팬에 기름을 두른 후 채소와 밥을 함께 볶아야 한다.

09 Anna와 Jinsu는 볶음밥을 만들기 위해 채소, 기름, 밥이 필요하다.

10 경험을 묻는 질문에 'Yes, I have.'라고 대답하는 것이 알맞다.

11 모두 '완료'를 나타내지만 ④번은 '계속'을 의미하는 현재완료이다.

12 ① made ② has practiced ③ frozen food ④ The boy walking with his friends가 적절하다.

13 '조리된 닭고기'라는 의미이므로 과거분사로, '소리치는 소년'이라는 의미이므로 현재분사로 명사를 수식하는 것이 적절하다.

14 모두 과거를 나타내는 어구와 함께 쓰여 과거동사가 들어가야 하지만, ②번은 현재완료 시제가 쓰인다. ① found ② has read ③ went ④ took ⑤ raised 혹은 had가 쓰일 수 있다.

15 'Chris라고 이름 지어진 소년'이므로 과거분사로, (2) '고장 난 냉장고'이므로 과거분사로, (3) '놀라움을 유발하는 소식'이므로 현재분사로 수식하는 것이 적절하다.

16 '추천된 책'이라고 하였으므로 과거분사로 book을 수식하는 것이 적절하다.

17 Mr. Smith has taught English to me since last year.라고 써도 좋다..

18 흥미를 유발하는 이야기들이므로 현재분사로 stories를 수식하는 것이 적절하다.

19 새로운 형태의 만화를 가리키는 대명사이다.

20 @는 형용사를 수식하는 부사로 쓰인 to부정사이다. ① 명사적 용법 중 목적격 보어 ② 명사적 용법 중 진주어 ③ 부사적 용법 중 목적 ④ 부사적 용법 중 형용사 수식 ⑤ 형용사적 용법으로 something을 수식

21 온라인에서 볼 수 있는 것은 웹툰이다.

22 동작이나 소리가 그림들이 생생하게 살아나게 한다.

23 만화영화는 모든 연령대의 사람들에게 매우 인기가 많다고 하였다.

24 만화를 제작하는 데 얼마만큼의 시간이 소요되는지는 위 글을 읽고 알 수 없다.

25 글쓴이가 좋아하는 캐릭터는 유머 있고 친절하지만 똑똑하지 않고 가끔 문제를 일으킨다는 연결이 자연스럽다. 따라서 However가 적절하다.

26 글쓴이가 '기영'을 좋아하는 이유는 모든 것의 긍정적인 측면을 바라보고 항상 남을 도우려 애쓰기 때문이라고 하였다.

---

01 No, he hasn't.

02 It's an animated movie about a teenager's feelings.

03 It can help him understand his feelings better.

04 (1)번 문장은 Amelia가 캐나다에 가 본 적이 있다는 경험을 나타내고. (2)번 문장은 Amelia가 캐나다로 가고 없다는 결과를 나타낸다.

05 I have lost my favorite book.

06 The crying boy ate five boiled eggs.

07 have had, have not had   08 a shaking voice

09 It is from *Black Rubber Shoes*.

10 He is humorous and kind. However, he is not very smart and sometimes causes trouble.

11 Artists have used this type of cartoon to make fun of well-known people.

12 Various types of cartoons and their roles

13 a gag cartoon, makes you laugh, a caricature, a comic strip, amusing

14 They have drawn a caricature to make fun of well-known people.

01 Kevin은 "Shining Days"를 보지 않았다.

02 "Shining Days"는 십대의 감정에 관한 것이다.

03 "Shining Days"는 Kevin이 자기의 감정들을 더욱 잘 이해할 수 있게 도와줄 수 있다.

04 현재완료 시제에서 '~에 가 본 적이 있다'는 have been to로 나타내고 '~에 가고 없다'는 'have gone to'로 나타내 는 것에 유의한다.

05 내가 가장 좋아하는 책을 잃어버리고 여전히 가지고 있지 않다고 하였으므로 현재완료 시제를 이용하여 책을 잃어버린 상황이 지속되고 있음을 말할 수 있다.

06 '울고 있는 소년'이므로 crying이 boy를 수식하고, 삶은 달걀은 '삶아진 달걀'인 boiled egg로 써서 문장을 만들 수 있다.

07 had를 대신하여 eaten을 써도 좋다.

08 '떨리는 목소리'라고 하였으므로 현재분사로 voice를 수식하는 것이 적절하다.

09 '검정고무신' 만화의 캐릭터이다.

10 캐릭터는 유머 있고 친절하지만 별로 똑똑하지 않고 가끔씩 말썽을 일으킨다고 하였다.

11 미술가들은 과거부터 지금까지 유명한 사람들을 풍자하기 위해 이런 종류의 만화를 그려왔다는 것이므로 현재완료 시제를 이용하여 하나의 문장으로 쓸 수 있다.

12 '다양한 종류의 만화와 그것들의 역할'이 글의 제목이 될 수 있다.

13 위 글에서 만화의 종류는 세 가지가 제시되어 있으며 그 종류는 개그 만화, 캐리커처, 그리고 연재만화이다.

14 미술가들은 유명한 사람들을 풍자하기 위해서 캐리커처를 그려 왔다.

|모범답안|

01 (A) down   (B) ups and downs
(C) watching the animated movie "Shining Days"
(D) a teenager's feelings

02 Iron Man, Tales of Suspense, a genius scientist, owns a weapon company, invented a suit of armor to save his life, Iron Man, he is very rich and is the leader of the superhero team, the Avengers

01 오늘 나는 별일 없이 우울했다. 요즘, 내 감정이 많이 바뀌었다. 그 때 Jane이 내게 다가왔고 많은 십대들이 기분에 기복을 갖는다고 이야기하며 내 기분을 이해해 주었다. 내 감정을 더욱 잘 이해하기 위해, 그녀는 만화 영화 "Shining Days"를 볼 것을 제안하였다. 그녀는 이 영화가 십대의 기분에 관한 것이라고 설명해 주었다. 이 영화는 괜찮은 것 같았고, 그래서 나는 이 영화를 곧 보기로 결정했다.

01 ④

02 (1) Jake played the role of Santa Clause in the play.
(2) I feel angry when people make fun of me.
(3) Cut the vegetables into small pieces.

03 (1) The soccer team members have a common goal.
(2) It is fun to learn English with animated movies.
(3) There are ups and downs in life.

04 (1) amusing   (2) probably   (3) movement
(4) publish   05 ①   06 ④

07 nacho chips / spread / some ham, onions, and peppers / cheese, about 12 minutes

08 ups and downs   09 ⑤   10 ②

11 Do you know how to use the machine?

12 ⑤   13 ④   14 ⑤   15 ④

16 These expressions are often used in spoken English.

17 ⑤   18 (A) laugh   (B) saying   (C) are

19 They have made them for hundreds of years.

20 ⑤   21 ⑤   22 ②

01 가르치고 배우는 과정을 가리키는 말은 education(교육)이다.

02 play the role: 역할을 하다, make fun of: ~을 놀리다, cut A into pieces ~A를 조각으로 자르다

03 common: 공통의, animated movie: 만화영화, ups and downs: 기복

04 movement: 움직임, amusing: 재미있는, 즐거운, publish: 출판하다, probably: 아마도

05 (A)는 도와주겠다는 표현으로 이와 바꾸어 쓸 수 있는 표현은 ①번이다. 나머지는 모두 도움을 요청하는 표현이다.

06 can't wait to ~: ~가 기대되다 = look forward to

09 주어진 문장은 "Shining Days"에 관해 설명하는 문장으로 ⓔ번이 적절하다.

10 Kevin의 Nothing serious.라는 말을 통해 심각한 문제가 아니라는 것을 알 수 있다.

12 ⑤ Emily와 Tony는 좌석을 선택한 후 표 값을 지불해야 한다.

13 현재완료 시제에서 부정어와 함께 쓰여 '아직'이라는 의미를 나타내는 것은 yet이다.

14 주어진 문장의 밑줄 친 부분은 '재활용을 위한 쓰레기통'이라는 의미로 쓰이는 동명사이다. 모두 현재분사이지만, ⑤번은 '잠자는 용도로 쓰이는 가방', 즉 '침낭'이라는 의미로 쓰이는 동명사이다.

15 danger는 '예상되지 않는' 것이므로 과거분사 unexpected로 수식하는 것이 적절하다.

16 구어체 언어란 일상 대화에서 쓰이는 말투를 의미한다. 따라서 과거분사 spoken으로 English를 수식하여 문장을 완성하는 것이 적절하다.

17 만화는 정보를 더 분명하고 학습하기 쉽게 만들어 준다는 것이 자연스럽다. more difficult → easier

18 (A) 사역동사의 목적격 보어로 동사원형이 쓰인다. (B) 캐릭터는 우스꽝스러운 행동이나 말을 함으로써 사람들을 웃게 만드는 것이므로 doing과 병렬로 연결되는 것이 자연스럽다. (C) 수의 일치의 대상이 some parts이므로 복수 동사를 쓰는 것이 적절하다.

19 사람들은 수 백 년 동안 만화를 만들어왔다고 하였다.

20 만화는 정보를 더 분명하게 만들어 준다고 하였으므로 ⑤번이 글의 내용과 일치한다.

21 글쓴이는 미래에 새로운 형태의 만화가 나타날지도 모른다고 하였다.

22 온라인에서 출판되는 특성상 언제 어디서든 웹툰을 읽을 수 있다는 강점이 있다.

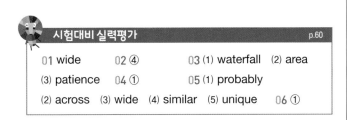

Lesson 8
Viva, South America!

시험대비 실력평가   p.60

01 wide   02 ④   03 (1) waterfall   (2) area
(3) patience   04 ①   05 (1) probably
(2) across   (3) wide   (4) similar   (5) unique   06 ①

01 주어진 관계는 반의어 관계를 나타낸다. wide: 넓은, narrow: 좁은

02 ④번 문장에서 wonder는 '경이, 놀라움'이란 뜻으로 쓰였다.

03 waterfall: 폭포, area: 지역, patience: 참을성

04 화내지 않고 침착함을 유지하는 능력을 가리키는 말은 patience(인내심)이다.

05 similar: 비슷한, unique: 독특한, probably: 아마도, wide: 넓은, across: 건너서

06 contain: 포함하다, ~이 들어 있다

서술형 시험대비   p.61

01 tourist
02 (1) outer space   (2) waterfall   (3) contain
03 (1) all year round   (2) went away   (3) by myself
    (4) social studies   (5) is full of   (6) throw a party
04 (1) The price of the potatoes is 250 won per 100 grams.
    (2) The climate of the Sahara Desert is very hot and dry.
    (3) You can find koalas and kangaroos on this continent.
05 (1) This region is humid all year round.
    (2) There is a big mountain range on the eastern side of Korea.
    (3) The stadium was full of excited soccer fans.
    (4) By the way, do you know who directed the movie?

01 주어진 관계는 동사와 그 동사의 동작을 행하는 사람의 관계이다. tour: 여행하다, tourist: 관광객

02 outer space: 우주 공간, waterfall: 폭포, contain: 포함하다

03 go away 없어지다, all year round 일 년 내내, 연중, be full of ~으로 가득하다, by oneself 혼자서, 홀로, social studies 사회(과목), throw a party: 파티를 열다

04 per: ~당, climate: 기후, continent: 대륙

교과서 Conversation

핵심 Check   p.62~63

1 (1) Do you know / throw
   (2) how old this building
2 (1) You know what / surprising
   (2) heard / can't

교과서 대화문 익히기

Check(√) True or False   p.64

1 F   2 T   3 T   4 F

교과서 확인학습   p.66~67

Communication: Listen – Dialog 1
tomato soup / happy / By the way, where, grown / somewhere / South America / How / social studies

Communication: Listen – Dialog 2
took / traveled, by herself / surprise / especially, pyramids / Are there / above sea level / can't believe it

Communication: Listen More
How was / fantastic / closed, riding / To be honest, scared / how fast, is / no idea / as fast as / surprising / ride / sign, after / maybe

Communicate: Speak
what the capital of Peru is / no idea / know

Wrap Up – Listening ❺
puppy / Where / heard, uncle

Wrap Up – Listening ❻
won first prize / quiet, shy / joined, has changed / join, too

시험대비 기본평가   p.68

01 ②, ④
02 I was told that he got the puppy from his uncle.
03 I can't believe it.   04 ⑤

11

01 (A)는 알고 있음을 묻고 있으므로 이와 같은 의도를 나타내는
　　것은 ②, ④번이다.

04 위 대화를 통해 연극 동아리가 바뀌었는지는 알 수 없다.

01 do you know where the tomato was first grown?

02 ②, ④　　　　03 ⑤　　　　04 ⑤

05 ⑤　　　　06 ③

07 Do you know how fast this roller coaster is?

08 ④　　　　09 (D) → (B) → (C) → (A)

02 이어지는 대답으로 보아 빈칸에는 어떻게 알게 되었는지를 묻는
　　질문이 알맞다.

03 이탈리아에서 무엇이 처음에 재배되었는지는 알 수 없다.

04 (A)와 나머지 표현은 모두 놀라움을 표현하지만 ⑤번은 안도감
　　을 표현한다.

05 Brian은 해발 3,800미터 정도에 위치한 몇몇 피라미드가 있다
　　는 것을 믿지 않았다는 설명은 대화의 내용과 일치하지 않는다.

06 (A) while ~ing: ~하는 동안, (B) scared: 무서워하는, 겁먹
　　은, (C) That's surprising.: 정말 놀랍다.

07 간접의문문의 어순으로 '의문사+주어+동사' 순서가 되어야 한
　　다.

08 알고 있음을 대답할 때 'Yes, I do.'로 대답한다.

09 (D) 인상 깊었던 사진 설명 → (B) 피라미드에 대한 질문 →
　　(C) 대답 및 구체적 설명 → (A) 놀라움 표현

01 herself

02 They are talking about the pictures that[which]
　　Ms. Song took in South America.

03 He got a puppy.

04 She wants to get a puppy.

05 (A) Sumin　　(B) quiet and shy
　　(C) joining the drama club

06 (C) → (B) → (D) → (A) → (E)

01 by oneself: 혼자서, 홀로

02 Jenny와 Brian은 송 선생님이 남아메리카에서 찍은 사진들에
　　대해 이야기하고 있다.

03 Junha는 그의 삼촌으로부터 강아지를 얻었다.

04 민지는 강아지를 갖고 싶어 한다.

05 오늘 나는 말하기 대회 우승자가 수민이라는 것을 들었다. 나는
　　많이 놀랐다. 그녀는 작년의 그녀가 아니었다. 작년에, 그녀는
　　매우 조용하고 수줍음이 많았었다. 그러나 그녀는 올해 연극 동
　　아리에 가입한 후 많이 변화였다. 나는 수민이처럼 좀 더 적극적

이고 자신감 있는 사람이 되고 싶다.

06 (C) 알고 있는지 질문 → (B) 추측 → (D) 정확한 설명 →
　　(A) 어떻게 알았는지 질문 → (E) 대답

Grammar

1 (1) the funniest boy　(2) the highest mountain

2 (1) whether　(2) when he left　(3) how tall he is

01 (1) what is she → what she is

　　(2) how did she break → how she broke

　　(3) the famousest → the most famous

　　(4) busiest → the busiest

02 (1) the cheapest　(2) the most interesting

　　(3) the biggest　(4) the most difficult

　　(5) the heaviest

03 (1) Tell me why he came late.

　　(2) Can you tell me where she is going?

　　(3) Do you remember when the boy went out?

　　(4) June doesn't know who built the house.

　　(5) Do you know who came in?

01 (1), (2) 간접의문문의 어순은 '의문사+주어+동사'이다. (3)
　　famous는 -ous로 끝나는 2음절 단어이므로 the most를 써서
　　최상급을 만든다. (4) 형용사의 최상급은 정관사 the와 함께 쓰
　　이는 것이 일반적이다.

02 cheap, big, heavy는 –est를 써서 최상급을 만들고, 3음절 이
　　상의 형용사인 interesting, difficult는 the most를 써서 최상
　　급을 만든다.

03 (1), (2), (3) 간접의문문의 어순인 '의문사+주어+동사'의 어순
　　임을 기억하자. (4), (5) 의문사가 주어 역할을 하는 의문대명사
　　인 경우 '의문사+동사' 어순이 가능하므로 이에 유의한다.

01 ④　　　　02 ④　　　　03 ③

04 Branda tried to guess if they needed her help.

05 ④

06 That is not the easiest job in the world.

07 ⑤　　　　08 bigger / big / the biggest

09 ⑤   10 ⑤   11 ③   12 ④

13 (that) health is the most important thing

14 more diligent   15 ③

16 David is the best student in our school.

17 ③   18 ②   19 the laziest animal

20 where he works   21 ⑤   22 ⑤

23 I wonder who made the decision.

24 How do you think we can get to the park?

01 모두 the most로 최상급을 만들지만 simple의 최상급은 simplest이다.

02 remember의 목적어 역할을 하는 간접의문문이 오는 것이 적절하다. 간접의문문의 어순은 '의문사+주어+동사'이다.

03 최상급과 같은 표현은 '부정 주어+so[as] 원급 as'이다. '어떠한 소녀도 Jessica만큼 영리하지 않다.'는 뜻이다.

04 의문사가 없는 의문문의 간접의문문은 if나 whether를 써서 나타낼 수 있다. 따라서 if를 대신하여 whether를 써도 무방하다. try to V: ~하려고 애쓰다

05 간접의문문의 어순은 '의문사+주어+동사'이다. 따라서 ④번이 적절하다.

06 easy의 최상급은 easiest이다.

07 간접의문문을 만들 수 없는 것은 that이다.

08 비교급과 원급을 이용하여 최상급을 나타내는 문장은 '비교급+than any other 단수 명사', '부정 주어+as[so] 원급 as'이다.

09 주어진 문장의 if는 '~인지 아닌지'라고 해석되는 명사절 접속사로 쓰인 if로 의문사가 없는 문장의 간접의문문을 이끈다. 따라서 ⑤번이 옳다. 나머지는 모두 부사절 접속사의 if로 '~라면'이라고 해석된다.

10 believe는 간접의문문의 의문사를 문두로 보내는 동사이므로 Who do you believe made the cookies yesterday?가 적절하다.

11 주어진 문장을 영어로 쓰면 Who is the funniest character in the movie?이다.

12 모두 최상급의 의미를 갖지만 ④번은 '그녀의 목소리는 우리 반에 있는 다른 모든 목소리만큼 아름답다.'라는 의미의 동등비교이다.

13 important는 3음절 이상의 형용사이므로 최상급을 만들 때 the most를 사용한다.

14 '부정 주어+비교급+than'을 이용하여 최상급을 나타낸다.

15 간접의문문에서 의문대명사가 쓰인 경우 '의문사+동사'의 어순이 가능하다. '내가 지금껏 방문해 본 호텔 중에서 가장 편안하다'는 의미가 적절하므로 최상급을 쓴다.

16 good의 최상급은 best이다

17 pretty의 최상급은 prettiest이다.

18 최상급의 의미를 갖는 것은 '부정 주어+비교급 than'이다.

19 lazy의 최상급은 laziest이다.

20 대답으로 미루어 보아 그가 어디에서 일하는지 알고 싶다고 말했음을 알 수 있다.

21 의문사가 없는 문장의 간접의문문은 if 혹은 whether를 써서 만든다.

22 clean의 최상급은 cleanest이다.

23 who는 의문사이자 주어 역할을 동시에 하는 의문대명사이다.

24 think는 간접의문문의 의문사를 문두로 보낸다.

서술형 시험대비   p.78~79

01 the longest, longer

02 (1) Can I ask if you are mad at me?

   (2) Do you know where Tom lives?

   (3) Can you tell me who she is?

   (4) I wonder what happened to you.

   (5) Please tell me why he broke the promise..

   (6) When do you think the book will be published?

   (7) Let me know if[whether] she is going to tell him the truth.

03 the bravest boy

04 (1) the worst   (2) the best   (3) worse

05 where he is going

06 February is the shortest month of the year.

07 the most popular

08 Let me introduce the most famous places in Korea.

09 who thinks him a thief

10 the most creative person   11 how old he is

12 Where is the coldest city on earth?

13 is more important than education / is as important as education / more important than any other thing / more important than all the other things

14 Who do you think she is?

15 where Emily is going, if[whether] Emily is going there to see a movie

01 비교급을 이용하여 최상급을 나타내는 문장은 '비교급+than any other 단수 명사'이다.

02 의문사가 있는 의문문의 간접의문문은 '의문사+주어+동사'의 어순이며, 의문사가 없는 경우 if나 whether를 써서 간접의문문을 만들 수 있다. think, believe, guess와 같은 동사는 간접의문문의 의문사를 문두로 배치한다.

03 brave의 최상급은 bravest이다.

04 네 개의 식당 중 식당 B가 가장 좋은 평점을 받았으며, 식당 C가 가장 낮은 평점을 기록하고 있다. good-better-best, bad-worse-worst를 활용하여 문장을 완성한다.

05 그가 어디로 가고 있는지는 모르지만 나중에 말해 줄 것이라고

생각한다는 대답이 적절하다. 대답은 간접의문문의 어순인 '의문사+주어+동사'에 맞게 완성한다.

06 short의 최상급은 shortest이다.

07 popular의 최상급은 the most를 사용한다.

08 famous의 최상급은 the most를 사용하여 만든다.

09 '누가 그를 도둑이라고 생각하는지 궁금하다.'는 의미이다. 여기서 who는 의문대명사이므로 '의문사+동사' 어순임에 유의한다.

10 '창의적인'이란 의미의 creative는 the most를 사용하여 최상급을 만든다.

11 대답으로 미루어 보아 그가 몇 살인지 아는지 묻는 것이 적절하다.

12 cold의 최상급은 the coldest이다.

13 비교급으로 최상급의 의미를 갖는 것은 '비교급 than any other 단수 명사', 혹은 '비교급 than all the other 복수 명사', '부정 주어 비교급 than'이다. 원급을 이용하여 최상급을 의미를 나타낼 때에는, '부정 주어 as 원급 as'로 쓸 수 있다.

14 think가 있는 문장에서는 간접의문문의 의문사를 문두에 배치한다.

15 의문사가 있는 문장의 간접의문문은 '의문사+주어+동사'의 어순이며 의문사가 없는 경우 'if' 혹은 'whether'를 이용하여 간접의문문을 만들 수 있다.

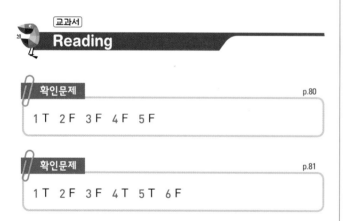

교과서 Reading

확인문제 p.80

1 T 2 F 3 F 4 F 5 F

확인문제 p.81

1 T 2 F 3 F 4 T 5 T 6 F

교과서 확인학습 A p.82~83

01 where the driest desert
02 the highest
03 they are both
04 is full of, that
05 the driest desert
06 it gets, at all
07 is so dry that
08 what scientists do
09 similar to, they prepare for trips
10 one of the best places
11 see the world's highest
12 It, high
13 cover, patience, luck
14 named after, who, flew
15 still get to, by
16 runs across, through
17 travels from, flows into
18 is interesting
19 no bridges
20 because it usually runs through
21 see the other side
22 swim in
23 home, that
24 the world's longest, range
25 how long the mountain range
26 about, long
27 contains, mountains
28 a third of the people
29 unique animals

교과서 확인학습 B p.84~85

1 Do you know where the driest desert on Earth is?
2 How about the highest waterfall?
3 Yes, they are both in South America.
4 This continent is full of natural wonders that will surprise you.
5 The Atacama is the driest desert on Earth.
6 In some parts, it gets almost no rain at all — only 1–3 millimeters per year!
7 The ground in some areas is so dry that no plants can grow.
8 Do you know what scientists do in such a dry place?
9 The soil in this desert is very similar to the soil on Mars, so they prepare for trips to outer space.
10 The Atacama is also one of the best places on Earth to watch stars.
11 If you go to Venezuela, you can see the world's highest waterfall.
12 It is 979 meters high.
13 Clouds often cover the top, so you need patience and a little luck to get a good view.
14 Actually, the waterfall is named after Jimmie Angel, a pilot from the United States who first flew over the waterfall in 1933.
15 You can still get to the top of the beautiful waterfall only by plane.
16 The Amazon runs across the continent through seven countries.
17 It travels from Peru in the west and flows into the Atlantic Ocean.
18 The Amazon River is interesting in many ways.
19 For the most part, it has no bridges.
20 That is because it usually runs through rainforests and wet areas, not cities or towns.
21 Also, in many places the river is very wide, so you cannot see the other side!

22 You probably do not want to swim in this river.

23 It is home to some very big snakes and fish that eat meat.

24 The Andes are the world's longest mountain range.

25 Do you know how long the mountain range is?

26 It is about 7,000 kilometers long!

27 It also contains the highest mountains outside of Asia.

28 About a third of the people in South America live in the Andes.

29 Many unique animals also live there.

시험대비 실력평가 p.86~89

01 ④	02 continent	03 ⑤	04 ⑤

05 It is in South America.　　06 ⑤

07 He first flew over the waterfall in 1933.　08 ④

09 interesting　　10 ③　　11 ③

12 It starts from Peru.　　13 ①　　14 ①

15 ③　　16 ⑤

17 It's because the ground in some areas is so dry.

18 ③　　19 ③

20 He was a pilot from the United States who first flew over the waterfall in 1933.　　21 ④

22 Because it is home to some very big snakes and fish that eat meat.

23 Do you know how long the mountain range is?

24 ①　　25 ⑤

01 원인과 결과를 이끄는 'so ~ that' 구문이다.

02 '바다에 의해 둘러싸인 큰 땅 덩어리'는 '대륙(continent)'이다.

03 아타카마 사막의 토양은 화성의 토양과 아주 비슷해서, 과학자들은 이곳에서 우주로의 여행을 준비한다고 하였다.

04 'one of the 최상급+복수 명사'이다.

05 아타카마 사막은 남아메리카에 있다고 하였다.

06 빈칸 (A)에는 전치사 after가 들어간다. ① turn off: ~을 끄다 ② be busy with: ~하느라 바쁘다 ③ be full of: ~으로 가득 차다 ④ be good at: ~을 잘하다 ⑤ look after: ~을 돌보다

07 그는 1933년에 처음으로 폭포 너머 비행을 하였다.

08 구름 꼭대기 부분을 구름이 자주 에워싸기 때문에 멋진 경치를 보려면 인내심과 약간의 운이 필요하다고 하였다.

09 흥미를 유발하는 것이므로 현재분사를 쓰는 것이 적절하다.

10 unique는 '독특한'이란 의미이다. 따라서 ③번이 적절하다.

---

11 강이 너무 넓어서 그 건너편을 볼 수조차 없는 곳이 있다고 하였다.

12 서쪽의 페루에서 시작한다고 하였다.

13 산맥의 길이는 7천 킬로미터라고 하였다.

14 사물을 선행사로 취하는 주격 관계대명사가 쓰이는 것이 적절하다.

15 ③번 다음 문장의 they는 주어진 문장의 scientists를 가리키는 말이다.

16 별을 관찰하기에 최고의 장소라고 나와 있을 뿐, 얼마나 많은 별을 관찰할 수 있는지는 나와 있지 않다.

17 토양이 너무 건조해서 식물이 자랄 수 없다고 하였다.

18 (A)는 '경치, 전망'이라는 의미로 쓰였다. ③ 경치, 전망 ①, ②, ④, ⑤ 견해

19 구름이 꼭대기 부분을 자주 에워싸기 때문에 원할 때 언제든 폭포의 멋진 경치를 보는 것은 불가능하다.

20 그는 미국의 비행사로, 1933년에 처음으로 폭포 너머 비행을 한 사람이다.

21 (A) run across: ~을 가로질러 흐르다 (B) 뒤 문장이 앞 문장에 대한 원인을 이끌고 있으므로 That's because (C) 강의 반대편을 볼 수 없다는 의미이므로 나머지 하나를 가리키는 the other를 쓴다. another는 여러 개 중 하나를 가리킬 때 쓴다.

22 아마존강은 몇몇 아주 큰 뱀과 고기를 먹는 물고기들의 서식지이므로 이곳에서 헤엄치는 것은 위험하다.

23 how가 long을 수식하는 것이므로 붙여 써야 한다.

24 (B)는 '대략'이란 의미로 쓰였다. 따라서 Roughly가 가장 적절하다.

25 글쓴이가 폭포에 어떻게 갔는지는 글을 읽고 알 수 없다.

서술형 시험대비 p.90~91

01 dry

02 Because it gets almost no rain at all - only 1–3 millimeters per year.

03 is drier than

04 the driest, similar to, Mars, to watch stars

05 We can see the driest desert on Earth and the highest waterfall in South America.

06 It got its name after Jimmie Angel, a pilot from the United States who first flew over the waterfall in 1933.

07 It's because clouds often cover the top.

08 highest, pilot, plane　　09 It is 979 meters high.

10 [C]–[B]–[A]

11 what the longest mountain range / longer than

12 Do you know how long the mountain range is?

13 how wide the Amazon River is / wide, see

14 It flows into the Atlantic Ocean.

01 너무 건조해서 식물들이 자랄 수 없다는 의미이다. driest의 원급인 dry를 쓸 수 있다.

02 연간 강수량이 1~3mm밖에 안될 정도로 비가 내리지 않기 때문이다.

03 부정 주어와 비교급을 이용하여 최상급을 나타내는 문장을 만들 수 있다.

04 아타카마 사막은 지구상에서 가장 건조한 사막이고, 그것의 토양은 화성의 토양과 매우 유사하다. 또한 그곳은 별을 관찰하기에 최고의 장소 중 하나이다.

05 지구에서 가장 건조한 사막과 가장 높은 폭포를 남아메리카에서 볼 수 있다.

06 폭포의 이름은 1933년에 처음으로 폭포 너머 비행을 한 미국의 비행사 Jimmie Angel에게서 이름을 따온 것이다.

07 구름이 꼭대기 부분을 자주 에워싸기 때문에 멋진 경치를 보려면 인내심과 약간의 운이 필요하다고 하였다.

08 앙헬 폭포는 지구에서 가장 높은 폭포이고 어느 미국인 비행사의 이름을 땄다. 오직 비행기로만 정상에 닿을 수 있다.

09 앙헬 폭포는 높이가 979m라고 하였다.

10 [C]에서 It이 지칭하는 것은 아마존강이며, 일곱 개의 나라를 거쳐 대륙을 가로지를 때 가장 먼저 서쪽 페루에서 시작한다는 것이다. [B] 아마존강에는 다리가 없는데 그 이유를 말하는 문장이 [A]에서 이어지고 있다.

11 대답으로 미루어 보아 세상에서 가장 긴 산맥이 무엇인지 아느냐는 질문을 완성하는 것이 적절하다. 비교급을 이용하여 최상급의 의미를 나타낼 수 있다.

12 간접의문문을 이용하여 문장을 만들 수 있다. 간접의문문의 어순은 '의문사+주어+동사' 어순임에 유의하자.

13 아마존강이 얼마나 넓은지 묻는 말에 '너무 넓어서 건너편을 볼 수 없을 정도'라고 답할 수 있다. too ~ to V: 너무 ~해서 V할 수 없는

14 아마존강은 대서양으로 흘러간다고 하였다.

영역별 핵심문제
p.93~97

01 impatient 02 ②   03 ④   04 ④

05 ②   06 (1) named after

(2) throw[give, have, hold], party   (3) To be honest

07 (A) the tomato soup

(C) the tomato came from South America

08 do you know where the tomato was first grown?

09 ⑤   10 It goes as fast as 140 km per hour.

11 (A) 140 km per hour   (B) 8 p.m   12 ④

13 (A) by   (B) What   (C) can't

14 (A) pictures of beautiful places in South America

(B) the pictures of pyramids

(C) some pyramids are about 3,800 meters

above sea level

15 ③   16 ③   17 ④, ⑤   18 ⑤

19 Do you remember the happiest moment of your

life?

20 ②   21 ④   22 ④

23 in the town is as[so] wise as

24 if[whether] Paul is free

25 I wonder if[whether] you found what you were

looking for.

26 Thursday was the worst day of the week for me.

27 Do you know where the driest desert on Earth is?

28 ⑤   29 ①   30 ④   31 ②

32 ④   33 It is in Bolivia.

01 주어진 관계는 반의어 관계를 나타낸다. patient: 인내심 있는, impatient: 인내심 없는

02 특히 직업으로 항공기 조종 장치를 작동하는 사람을 가리키는 말은 pilot(조종사)이다. crew: 승무원, steward: 스튜어드

03 scared; 겁먹은, 무서워하는

04 주어진 문장과 나머지는 모두 '흐르다'는 의미를 나타내지만 ④번은 '분출'을 나타낸다.

05 ride: 타다

06 name after ~을 따라 이름 짓다, throw[give, have, hold] a party 파티를 열다, to be honest 솔직히 말하면

08 간접의문문으로 '의문사+주어+동사'의 순서가 알맞다.

12 종하는 처음에는 무서웠지만 나중에는 신나했으므로 scared(무서운)에서 pleased(기쁜)가 적절하다. disappointed: 실망한, fearful: 무서운

13 (A) by oneself: 혼자서, (B) What a surprise!: 그것 참 놀랍구나! (C) I can't believe it.: 정말 놀랍다.

14 나는 송 선생님께서 지난여름에 혼자 남아메리카로 여행을 다녀오셨다는 것이 인상 깊었다. 나는 그녀가 정말로 용감했다고 생각했다. 선생님은 남아메리카의 아름다운 장소들의 사진들을 보여주셨다. 나는 피라미드 사진이 정말 좋았다. 선생님께서 몇몇 피라미드는 해발 3,800미터 정도에 위치하고 있다고 설명하셨다. 이것은 매우 흥미로웠으며 나는 언젠가 그곳을 방문하기로 결심했다.

15 주어진 단어를 영어로 쓰면 'He is the most boring person that I have ever met.'이다.

16 주어진 문장의 밑줄 친 부분은 간접의문문을 이끌며 '누구'라고 해석되는 의문대명사이다. 따라서 ③번이 답이다. 나머지는 모

두 관계대명사이다.

17 주어진 문장은 '정직보다 더 귀중한 것은 없다'는 의미이다. 최상급의 의미를 갖는 문장으로, '비교급 than any other 단수 명사'와 같다.

18 '누가 너를 파티에 초대했는지'라고 하였으므로 의문대명사 who를 사용하여 간접의문문을 만든다.

19 happy의 최상급은 the happiest이다.

20 형용사의 최상급은 정관사 the와 함께 쓰인다.

21 주어진 문장은 부정 주어와 원급을 이용하여 최상급을 나타내고 있다. 따라서 최상급 혹은 '비교급 than all the other 복수 명사'가 빈칸에 들어갈 수 있다.

22 delicious의 최상급은 the most delicious이다.

23 부정 주어와 원급을 이용하여 최상급을 나타내는 문장이다.

24 if를 대신하여 whether를 써도 좋다.

25 의문사가 없는 문장의 간접의문문은 if나 whether를 이용하여 만든다.

26 bad의 최상급은 worst이다.

27 간접의문문의 어순은 '의문사+주어+동사'이다.

28 과학자들이 아타카마 사막에서 연구하는 이유는 그곳의 토양이 화성의 토양과 비슷하기 때문이다. different from → similar to

29 아타카마 사막은 너무 건조해서 식물이 자랄 수 없다고 하였다.

30 많은 관광객들이 사진을 찍기 위해서 우유니를 방문하고, 당신이 찍는 모든 사진이 아름다운 예술 작품이 될 것이라고 하였으므로 ④번이 옳다.

31 (A)는 '일년 내내'라는 의미이다. ① 돌고 돌아 ② 일 년 내내 ③ 모든 너의 노력 ④ 여러 번 되풀이하여 ⑤ 자주, 매번

32 (B)는 '~하기 위해서'라고 해석되며 to부정사의 부사적 용법 중 목적으로 쓰였다. ① 명사적 용법 중 목적어 ② 진주어 ③ 형용사적 용법 ④ 부사적 용법 중 목적 ⑤ 부사적 용법 중 감정의 원인

33 세계에서 가장 큰 소금 평원은 볼리비아에 있다.

단원별 예상문제　　　　　p.98~101

01 ②　　　02 ⑤　　　03 To be honest
04 ②　　　05 ⑤　　　06 By the way
07 It came from South America.
08 Ms. Song, her social studies teacher, taught it to her.
09 Which country do you want to visit?
10 ⑤　　11 ④　　12 ④　　13 ⑤
14 What do you think she is doing?　　15 ①
16 Please tell me if[whether] she told you her number.　　17 ④
18 the Atacama　　19 ⑤　　20 ③
21 the driest desert, prepare space trips, watch stars
22 ②　　　　23 patience　　　24 ③
25 It runs through seven countries.

01 이어지는 대화에서 특히 피라미드 사진이 마음에 들었다고 설명하고 있으므로 주어진 문장은 (B)에 들어가는 것이 적절하다.

02 위 대화를 통해 Ms. Song이 남아메리카에서 얼마나 오랫동안 머물렀는지는 알 수 없다.

04 몰랐던 사실에 대해 놀라움을 나타내는 ②번이 적절하다.

05 하나와 종하는 저녁 8시 이후에 탈수 없기 때문에 다음에 타기로 했다.

07 토마토는 남아메리카에서 왔다.

08 송 선생님께서 수진에게 토마토의 산지에 대해 가르쳐 주셨다.

10 Brian은 브라질이 남아메리카에서 가장 큰 국가라는 사실에 깜짝 놀랐다.

11 모두 'est'를 붙여서 최상급을 만들 수 있지만, helpful은 most를 붙여서 최상급을 만든다.

12 의문사가 없는 문장의 간접의문문이므로 if 혹은 whether를 사용하여 간접의문문을 만들 수 있다.

13 모두 최상급의 의미를 갖지만 ⑤번은 '너의 조언은 다른 어떤 조언보다 더 도움이 되지는 않는다.'는 의미이다.

14 동사 think는 간접의문문의 의문사를 문두로 보낸다.

15 'one of the 최상급+복수 명사'를 써서 '가장 ~한 것 중 하나'를 나타낸다.

16 의문사가 없는 의문문의 간접의문문은 if나 whether를 써서 만든다.

17 최상급의 의미를 갖는 '비교급 than any other 단수 명사'이다.

18 아타카마 사막을 의미한다.

19 밑줄 친 (B)는 places를 수식하는 형용사적 용법으로 쓰인 to부정사이다. ① 명사적 용법 중 목적어 ② 진주어 ③ 부사적 용법 중 목적 ④ 감정의 원인 ⑤ 형용사적 용법

20 과학자들은 아타카마 사막에서 우주로의 여행을 준비하고 있다고 하였다. 과학자들이 아타카마 사막으로 여행을 가는 것은 아니다.

21 지구에서 가장 건조한 사막인 아타카마 사막은 우주여행을 준비하고 별을 관찰하기에 좋은 장소이다.

22 앞 문장의 결과를 이끄는 문장이므로 so가 적절하다.

23 화를 내지 않고 차분함을 유지하는 능력은 '인내심'이다.

24 구름 때문에 앙헬 폭포의 정상에서 좋은 경관을 보기 힘들 수 있다고 하였다.

25 아마존강은 일곱 개의 나라를 거쳐 흐른다고 하였다.

01 Sumin won the contest.

02 She was very quiet and shy (last year).

03 She joined the drama club this year.

04 how much water you drink

05 (1) I'd like to know if[whether] you are comfortable.

   (2) I wonder when you came home.

06 (1) the smartest   (2) the noisiest

07 (1) Playing tennis is the most exciting sport

   (2) No other sport is as[so] exciting as playing

    tennis

08 the driest desert on Earth, the highest waterfall

09 (A) They prepare for trips to outer space.

   (B) the soil in the Atacama is very similar to the

    soil on Mars

10 수천 년 전에 있던 물이 모두 말라서 생겼다.

11 It's because the salt flat makes any tourist a

   great photographer.

12 (1) under sea level → above sea level

   (2) during a certain period → all year round

   (3) the most visited natural wonder → one of the

    most visited natural wonders

01 수민이가 말하기 대회에서 우승했다.

02 수민이는 작년에 매우 조용하고 수줍음이 많았다.

03 수민이는 올해 연극 동아리에 가입했다.

04 대답으로 미루어 보아 하루에 물을 얼마나 마시는지가 궁금하다
는 말이 들어가는 것이 적절하다. 간접의문문의 어순에 유의하
여 'how much water you drink'라고 쓴다.

05 의문사가 없는 의문문의 간접의문문은 if나 whether를 써서 만
든다. 의문사가 있는 경우 '의문사+주어+동사' 어순임에 유의한
다.

06 smart와 noisy의 최상급은 각각 the smartest, the noisiest
이다.

07 부정 주어와 원급을 이용하여 최상급의 의미를 나타낼 수 있다.

08 지구에서 가장 건조한 사막과 가장 높은 폭포를 가리키는 대명
사이다.

09 과학자들은 화성의 토양과 비슷한 아타카마 사막에서 우주로의
여행을 준비한다고 하였다.

10 우유니는 소금 평원으로, 수천 년 전에 있던 물이 모두 말라서
생긴 것이다.

11 사실, 그 솔트 플랫은 어떤 방문객도 훌륭한 사진작가로 만들기
때문에 우유니에서 찍은 모든 사진이 아름다운 예술 작품이 될
것이라고 하였다.

12 (1) 우유니 소금 평원은 해저가 아닌 해발 약 3,656 미터에 위

치해 있다. (2) 이곳은 일 년 내내 방문할 수 있다. (3) 남아메리
카에서 가장 방문이 많은 곳 중 하나이고 유일한 곳은 아니다.

|모범답안|

01 (A) social studies   (B) where

   (C) Italy or somewhere in Europe

   (D) the tomato came from South America

02 Gwanak Mountain, my family, 632 meters high,

   the south of Seoul, the bridges over the Han

   River, all my stress went away

01 나는 아빠의 토마토 수프를 맛보았을 때 매우 행복했다. 그것은
매우 맛있었다. 나는 수프를 맛보았을 때, 나의 사회 선생님이신
송 선생님에게서 배운 것이 기억났다. 그녀는 내게 토마토가 어
디에서 처음 재배되었는지 알려주셨다. 나는 아빠에게 그가 이것
을 알고 있는지 모르는지 물어보았다. 처음에 아빠는 토마토가
이탈리아나 유럽 어딘가에서 왔다고 추측했다. 나는 아빠에게 토
마토가 남아메리카에서 왔다고 말했다. 나는 내가 선생님에게서
배운 것을 아빠와 공유했을 때 내 스스로가 자랑스러웠다.

01 ②

02 (1) sunrise   (2) view   (3) Mars   (4) scared

   (5) wonders   03 ①

04 (1) A number of works of art were stolen.

   (2) Amsterdam is 4 meters below sea level.

05 (C) → (B) → (D) → (A)   06 ⓓ → ⓐ → ⓒ → ⓔ → ⓑ

07 ②   08 ⑤

09 (A) By   (B) How   (C) learned   10 ③

11 (1) The mountain range is home to many unique

    plants and animals.

   (2) At first, I couldn't understand him at all.

   (3) To be honest, I want to stay (at) home and

    watch TV.

12 (1) Whales   (2) natural   (3) contain   13 ④

14 ③, ④   15 ⑤

16 Singapore is one of the most interesting places

   that I've ever visited.

17 (1) Do you know why she is upset?

   (2) I wonder if[whether] he sings well.

18 ③   19 [B] - [A] - [C]   20 ①, ④

21 We can get there only by plane.   22 ⑤

23 ⑤   24 Because it usually runs through

   rainforests and wet areas, not cities or towns.

25 seven countries, bridges, snakes, fish

01 예를 들어 절벽이나 바위와 같은 높은 장소로부터 냇물 또는 강이 떨어지는 장소를 가리키는 말은 waterfall(폭포)이다.

02 wonder: 경이, 놀라움, sunrise: 일출, scared: 겁먹은, Mars: 화성, view: 전망

03 주어진 문장에서 wonder는 '경이, 놀라움'을 나타내며 이와 같은 의미를 나타내는 것은 ①번이다. 나머지 문장에서는 모두 '궁금해 하다'를 나타낸다.

05 (C) 알고 있는지 여부 질문 → (B) 대답 및 추가 질문 → (D) 대답 → (A) 반응

06 ⓓ 롤러코스터의 속도 설명 → ⓐ 놀라움 표현 → ⓒ 한 번 더 탈 것을 권유 → ⓔ 표지판 내용 설명 → ⓑ 반응

07 ① 일반적으로 말해서, ② 솔직히 말해서, ③ 엄밀히 말해서, ④ 대체로, ⑤ 개인적으로 말하면

08 롤러코스터는 8시까지 운영한다는 설명은 대화의 내용과 일치한다.

09 (A) By the way: 그런데, (B) 이어지는 대답으로 보아 어떻게 알았는지 질문해야 하므로 'How', (C) 알게 된 것을 설명하므로 learned가 적절하다.

10 수진은 송선생님에게서 사회를 배우고 있다는 설명이 대화의 내용과 일치한다.

11 unique: 독특한, at first: 처음에는, to be honest: 솔직히 말하면

12 whale: 고래, natural: 자연의, 천연의, contain: 포함하다

13 모두 '~인지 아닌지'라고 해석되는 명사절 접속사로 간접의문문을 이끈다. 하지만, ④번은 '~라면'이라고 해석되는 부사절 접속사이다.

14 이구아수 폭포는 세계에서 가장 넓은 폭포라는 의미이다. 최상급과 '비교급 than all the other 복수 명사'로 바꿔 쓸 수 있다.

15 who found your book이라고 쓰는 것이 적절하다.

16 one of the 최상급+복수 명사: ~ 중 가장 ~한 것들 중 하나

17 간접의문문의 어순은 '의문사+주어+동사'이며, 의문사가 없는 경우 'if(또는 whether)+주어+동사'의 어순으로 간접의문문을 만든다. (2) if를 대신하여 whether를 써도 좋다.

18 부정 주어와 비교급을 이용하여 최상급의 의미를 나타낼 수 있다.

19 가장 건조한 사막인 이유는 [B] 비가 1-3mm만 내리는 지역이 있을 정도로 비가 거의 오지 않기 때문이고 [A] 토양이 건조해서 어떤 식물도 자랄 수가 없지만 과학자들이 이곳에서 무슨 일을 하고 있다. [C] 그들이 하는 일은 우주로의 여행을 준비하는 것이다.

20 폭포의 높이와 이름의 기원이 언급되어 있다.

21 비행기를 이용해서만 폭포의 정상에 갈 수 있다고 하였다.

22 Jimmie Angel이 폭포 너머를 비행할 때 몇 살이었는지는 위 글을 읽고 답할 수 없다.

23 사람들은 사진을 찍기 위해서 우유니를 방문하는데, 이곳에서 사진을 찍는 어떤 방문객도 훌륭한 사진작가가 될 수 있는 이유가 ⑤번이 이끄는 문장에서 제시되고 있다.

24 아마존강은 대개 도시나 마을이 아닌 열대우림과 습지를 지나 흐르기 때문에 강의 대부분에 다리가 없다고 하였다.

25 아마존강은 남아메리카의 일곱 개 나라를 거쳐 흐르고 강 위에 다리가 없는 경우가 대부분이며 아주 큰 뱀과 고기를 먹는 물고기가 그 강에 살고 있다.

The Two Stones

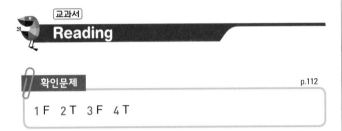

교과서 Reading

확인문제 p.112

1 F 2 T 3 F 4 T

확인문제 p.113

1 F 2 T 3 T 4 F

교과서 확인학습 A p.114~115

01 Two Stones

02 Characters, Money Lender, Narrator

03 ago, village, there lived

04 had to borrow, million, from

05 the money lender, asked for, to pay back, allow, anymore

06 no

07 servant instead

09 to be, servant

10 either, thank you

11 prison

12 let's play, put

13 One, the other, pick

14 happens if

15 Then, servant

16 mean, How terrible

17 if, pick

18 free, doesn't have to

19 doesn't play, with

20 *loudly*, Then, prison

21 Prison

22 *picks up, looks carefully at*

23 *to herself*, picked up

24 make, become, should

25 Stop and think

26 cannot pick

27 drops, right away

28 dropped

29 okay

30 Show us the stone

31 which one

32 *to herself*, cannot tell, trick

33 *shows everyone the white stone*

34 *celebrating*

35 picked, free

36 Good thinking, saved

교과서 확인학습 B p.116~117

1 The Two Stones

2 Characters: Father, Daughter, Money Lender, Friends, Narrator

3 Narrator: A long time ago, in a small village in South America, there lived a farmer and his daughter.

4 The farmer was poor, and had to borrow three million pesos from a money lender.

5 But the money lender was not kind, and when the farmer asked for one month to pay back the money, she didn't allow him anymore time.

6 Money Lender: You have no money? That's okay.

7 Your daughter will become my servant instead.

8 Father and Daughter: Oh, no!

9 Daughter: I don't want to be your servant.

10 Father: I don't want that, either! *(to Money Lender)* No, thank you.

11 Money Lender: Do you want to go to prison?

12 Then, let's play a game. I will put two stones in a bag.

13 One is white, and the other is black. Your daughter will pick one.

14 Daughter: What happens if I pick the white one?

15 Money Lender: Then you will be my servant.

16 Friends: Oh, no! She's mean. How terrible!

17 Daughter: What happens if I pick the black one?

18 Money Lender: Then you will be free, and your father doesn't have to pay back my money..

19 Father: What happens if she doesn't play this game with you?

20 Money Lender: *(loudly)* Then you will go to prison!

21 Now I want to go to school and become a better person.

21 Father, Daughter, and Friends: Oh, no! Prison!

22 *(Money Lender picks up two stones. Daughter looks carefully at her.)*

23 Daughter: *(to herself)* Oh! She has picked up two white stones!

24 She will make me become her servant. What should I do?

25 Narrator: Stop and think. What should she do?

26 She cannot pick a black one.

27 *(Daughter picks a stone from the bag. She drops it right away.)*

28 Daughter: Oh, no! I'm sorry, I've dropped it. *(to Money Lender)* But it's okay.

29 Show us the stone in the bag.

30 Then we will know which one I picked.

31 Money Lender: *(to herself)* I cannot tell them about my trick! Oh, no!

32 *(Money Lender shows everyone the white stone. Friends and Father start celebrating.)*

33 Friends: She picked the black one! They are free!

34 Narrator: Good thinking has saved Father and Daughter!

서술형 실전문제   p.118~120

01 (1) servants   (2) pay back   (3) pick   (4) right away
   (5) instead   (6) borrow   (7) mean

02 (1) trick   (2) mean   (3) save   (4) borrow

03 (1) One, the other   (2) one   (3) me do
   (4) which one   (5) has saved

04 (1) He has served this school for twenty years.
   (2) He has two balls. One is white and the other is red.

05 (1) I don't know what Sarah wanted me to do.
   (2) Will you tell me if[whether] you want to go shopping with me?
   (3) What do you think he wants?
   (4) Let me know if[whether] you will go there.

06 there lived a farmer and his daughter.

07 servant

08 is in a small village in South America

09 want, to be your servant

10 One is white, and the other is black.

11 How terrible it is!

12 your father doesn't have to pay back my money.

13 She will make me become her servant.

14 Show the stone in the bag to us.

15 ①, ④
   (1) ① If the farmer's daughter doesn't play the game with money lender, the farmer will go to prison.
   (2) ④ Actually the farmer's daughter picked a white stone.

01 instead: 대신에, borrow: 빌리다, right away: 즉시, 바로, mean: 사악한, 못된, servant: 하인, pick: 고르다, pay back: (돈을) 갚다

02 save: (목숨을) 구하다, borrow: 빌리다, mean: 사악한, 못된, trick; 속임수

03 (1) 가리키는 대상이 두 개일 때, 하나는 one, 다른 하나는 the other로 지칭한다. (2) one은 앞 문장에 사용된 것을 가리키는 부정대명사이다. (3) 사역동사 'make'의 목적어와 목적격보어

로 동사원형이 적절하다. (4) which one you want to have는 간접의문문으로 동사 Tell의 목적어 역할을 한다. (5) So far(지금까지)로 보아 현재완료 시제가 적절하다.

04 (1) 현재완료에서 'for+기간 명사', 'since+시간 명사' (2) one ~ the other ...: (둘 중에서) 하나는 ~, 다른 하나는

05 간접의문문의 어순은 '의문사+주어+동사'이다. 의문사가 없을 경우에는 의문사 대신에 if나 whether를 쓴다. 또한 의문사가 주어일 경우에는 '의문사+동사'의 어순이 되는 것에 주의한다. 주절에 think 동사가 있는 경우 의문사가 문장의 맨 앞으로 나간다는 것에도 주의한다.

06 there lived+주어: ~가 살았다

07 servant: 하인 / 직업이 다른 사람의 집안일을 하는 것이고, 종종 그 집에서 사는 사람

08 이야기의 배경은 어디인가? 이야기의 배경은 남아메리카의 작은 마을이다.

09 (A)의 대명사 'that'은 '자신의 딸이 대부업자의 하인이 되는 것'을 가리킨다.

10 가리키는 대상이 두 개일 때, 하나는 one, 다른 하나는 the other로 지칭한다.

11 형용사 'terrible'을 이용한 감탄문은 'How+형용사+주어+동사!' 어순을 취한다. 문장에서 주어는 앞에 언급된 상황을 가리키는 it을 사용하고 be동사는 is를 쓴다.

12 '~할 필요가 없다'는 'don't[doesn't] have to'를 사용하고, '(돈을) 갚다'는 'pay back'을 사용한다.

13 '사역동사(make)+목적어(me)+동사원형(become)' 형태를 사용한다.

14 '수여동사(show)+직접목적어+전치사(to)+간접목적어'인 3형식으로 문장을 전환할 수 있다.

15 ① 농부의 딸이 대부업자와 게임을 하지 않으면 농부가 감옥에 가게 된다. ④ 대부업자가 두 개의 흰 돌을 가방에 넣었기 때문에 실제로 농부의 딸은 흰 돌을 집은 것이다.

단원별 예상문제   p.121~124

01 ④   02 ⑤   03 ②

04 (1) carefully   (2) borrow   05 (c)elebrate

06 ③   07 ①   08 ③

09 (1) You can choose one or the other of the two rooms.
   (2) I'm not sure if[whether] he will come or not.

10 Characters   11 ②   12 ②

13 ⑤   14 ④   15 ③

16 She should pick the black stone.

17 ②   18 ④   19 black

20 dropped, picked, right away   21 ⑤

01 character는 '등장인물'이라는 뜻으로 나머지는 모두 연극의 배역과 관련된 표현들이다. ① lead role: 주연 ② villain: 악역 ③ cameo: 카메오(유명인이 잠시 출연하는 역할) ⑤ bit part: 단역

02 '누군가 무언가를 했을 때 그것을 해도 좋고 어떤 문제도 없는 것'은 허락되는 것이다.

03 anymore (부) (부정문·의문문에서) 지금은, 이제는 (더 이상) (= any longer)

04 (1) carefully: 주의 깊게 (2) borrow: 빌리다

05 '특별한 행사나 누군가의 성공을 기념하기 위해 즐거운 것을 하다'를 뜻하는 것은 'celebrate(축하하다)'가 적절하다.

06 ① 저도 역시 Jack을 좋아하지 않아요. ② 크게 말하지 않으면 들리지 않는다. ③ trick: 속임수, 그것은 단지 그녀의 속임수입니다. ④ 경찰은 그를 투옥했다. ⑤ 그 사람은 비열하고 조심성이 없으며 어리석습니다.

07 부정문이므로 either가 적절하다.

08 ① She picked the[a] black one. ② Why do you think she left the party so early? ④ I have two sisters. One is older than me and the other is younger than me. ⑤ How nice the old lady is!

09 (1) one ~ the other ...: (둘 중에서) 하나는 ~, 다른 하나는 … (2) 의문사가 없는 간접의문문은 의문사 대신에 if나 whether를 쓴다. 이 문장에서 that을 쓰면 그 의미가 어색하며 뒤에 나오는 or not과도 어울리지 않는다.

10 영화, 연극 또는 이야기에서 그려지는[묘사되는] 사람

11 '~해야 한다'는 의미로 'have to+동사원형'을 사용한다.

12 보기 ②번의 'lend'는 '(돈을) 빌려주다'는 의미로 본문의 내용과 일치하지 않는다.

13 빈칸은 농부 친구들의 대사로 빈칸 뒤에 'How terrible!'이라고 말하고 있으므로 빈칸에는 '대부업자'에 대한 부정적인 의미인 '못된, 비열한'이 적절하다.

14 제시문은 '두 개의 돌을 가방에 넣을 것이다'라는 뜻으로 (④)번 뒤에 'one ~, the other ~'가 나오므로 (④)가 적절하다.

15 본문은 농부가 돈을 갖지 못하자 대부업자가 게임을 제안하며 농부의 딸을 자신의 하인으로 삼고자 하는 갈등 부분이다.

16 질문: 대부업자의 하인이 되지 않으려면 농부의 딸은 어떤 색깔의 돌을 뽑아야 하는가?

17 제시문은 '대부업자가 두 개의 돌을 집는다. 딸이 주의 깊게 그녀를 본다.'는 의미로 (②) 뒤의 딸의 대사에서 '그녀가 두 개의 흰 돌을 집었어!'라는 내용이 나오므로 (②)가 적절하다.

18 딸이 아버지에게 하는 말이 아니라 대부업자에게 하는 말이므로 ④번에 들어갈 지시문은 'to Money Lender'이 적절하다.

19 빈칸은 친구들의 대사이기 때문에, 가방에 흰 돌이 남아 있는 것을 보고 친구들은 농부의 딸이 검은 돌을 집었다고 생각하는 것이 적절하다.

20 농부의 딸이 대부업자의 가방에 두 개의 흰색 돌이 있다는 것을 알았을 때 무엇을 했는가? / that she picked from the bag은 목적격 관계대명사절로 선행사인 the stone을 수식하는 역할을 한다.

21 본문 내용은 대부업자가 게임을 제시하고 흰 돌 두 개를 가방에 넣는 절정(Climax) 부분에서 갈등이 해결되는 결말 부분(Solution)이다.

22 ⓓ의 대사에 'She's mean.'이라고 3인칭을 사용하고 있으므로 대부업자와 이야기를 직접 나누고 있는 '아버지와 딸'이 아닌 친구들이라는 것을 알 수 있다.

23 돈이 없다면 대신에 당신 딸은 내 하인이 될 것이라는 대안을 제시하는 instead가 적절하다.

24 밑줄 (B)는 '그녀는 야비해'라는 정보로 보아 게임을 자신에게 유리하게 바꿀 수 있다고 추측할 수 있다.

교과서 파헤치기

단어 TEST Step 1   p.02

01 요리사	02 오염시키다	03 끓이다, 끓다
04 상영 시간	05 아마도	06 매력적인
07 나타나다, 등장하다		08 기계
09 교육	10 붓다	11 선택하다, 고르다
12 마지막으로	13 창의적인, 독창적인	
14 움직임	15 공통의	16 살아 있는
17 재미있는, 즐거운	18 접시	19 맛보다, 먹다
20 개발하다, 만들다	21 간단한, 단순한	22 출판하다
23 평소의, 보통의	24 조리법, 비법	25 ~ 중에
26 계속 ~이다	27 어리석은	28 유명한, 잘 알려진
29 자외선 차단제	30 번역하다	31 고르다, 선택하다
32 캐리커처, (풍자) 만화		33 만화영화
34 만화가	35 ~에 대한 돈을 내다	
36 ~에게 금방 눈에 띄다, ~에게 분명히 보이다		
37 ~을 놀리다	38 ~가 기대되다	39 기복
40 조심하다	41 A를 조각으로 자르다	
42 역할을 하다	43 합쳐지다	

단어 TEST Step 2   p.03

01 appear	02 chef	03 pollute
04 translate	05 creative	06 develop
07 cartoonist	08 dirty	09 alive
10 education	11 publish	12 fry
13 lastly	14 usual	15 pour
16 among	17 sunscreen	18 machine
19 showtime	20 silly	21 boil
22 simple	23 box office	24 common
25 animated movie		26 choose
27 recipe	28 pepper	29 plate
30 taste	31 well-known	32 probably
33 fascinating	34 movement	35 watch out
36 play a role	37 be made into	38 take a look
39 can't wait to	40 ups and downs	
41 make fun of	42 pay for	43 of all ages

단어 TEST Step 3   p.04

1 movement, 움직임   2 usual, 평소의, 보통의
3 showtime, 상영 시간   4 amusing, 재미있는, 즐거운
5 education, 교육   6 appear, 나타나다   7 silly, 어리석은
8 develop, 개발하다, 만들다   9 fascinating, 매력적인

---

10 translate, 번역하다   11 fry, 볶다, 튀기다
12 remain, 계속 ~이다   13 caricature, 풍자문화
14 publish, 출판하다   15 sunscreen, 자외선 차단제
16 chef, 요리사

대화문 TEST Step 1   p.05~06

Communication: Listen – Dialog 1

look down / serious, Sometimes, a lot / teens, ups and downs / really / Have you watched, animated movie / I haven't, Why, ask / teenager's feelings, will help, understand, better / sounds, watch

Communication: Listen – Dialog 2

look at, line / ticket machine, Let's buy, from, machine / how to use the machine / select, showtime / watch, what / select, choose, seats / sit in the back / problem, Lastly, pay for / simple

Communication: Listen More

Have you ever made / No, I haven't / how to make / Sounds / First, put, on, plate, spread / help, with / Next, peppers / Add, bake for about, oven / can't wait to taste

Communicate: Speak

how to, fried rice / cut, into / next / Put, fry, with rice / simple

Wrap Up – Listening ❺

Have, been to / have, Actually, every year / you've climbed, haven't you / twice

Wrap Up – Listening ❻

how to draw, First, circle, Next, 'draw, color, draw, circle, Lastly, make

대화문 TEST Step 2   p.07~08

Communication: Listen – Dialog 1

Jane: Kevin, you look down.

Kevin: Nothing serious. Sometimes my feelings change a lot.

Jane: I understand. Many teens have ups and downs in their feelings.

Kevin: Oh, really?

Jane: Have you watched the animated movie "Shining Days"?

Kevin: No, I haven't. Why do you ask?

Jane: It is about a teenager's feelings. It will help you understand your feelings better.

Kevin: That sounds good! I'll watch it.

Communication: Listen – Dialog 2

Emily: Oh, look at the long line at the box office.

Tony: Yeah, there's a ticket machine over there. Let's buy the tickets from the machine.

Emily: All right. Do you know how to use the machine?

Tony: Sure. It's easy. First, select a movie and a showtime.

Emily: Okay. We can watch the seven o'clock show. Then what?

Tony: Well, select the number of tickets and choose our seats.

Emily: Okay. Two tickets, and I want to sit in the back.

Tony: No problem. Lastly, pay for the tickets.

Emily: It's very simple.

Communication: Listen More

Suji: Good morning, Chef Garcia!

Garcia: Hello, Suji. Have you ever made nacho pizza?

Suji: Nacho pizza? No, I haven't.

Garcia: Kids will love it, and I'll tell you how to make it.

Suji: Sounds good!

Garcia: It's easy to make. First, put nacho chips on a plate and spread pizza sauce on them.

Suji: Okay. Let me help you with the pizza sauce.

Garcia: Thanks. Next, put some ham, onions, and peppers on top.

Suji: Okay. Then?

Garcia: Add cheese and bake for about 12 minutes in the oven.

Suji: I can't wait to taste it!

Communicate: Speak

Anna: Do you know how to make fried rice?

Jinsu: Sure. It's easy. First, cut the vegetables into small pieces.

Anna: Okay. What do you do next?

Jinsu: Put some oil in the pan. Then, fry the vegetables with rice.

Anna: Wow, it's really simple.

Wrap Up – Listening ⑤

Judy: Have you ever been to Sokcho?

Minsu: Yes, I have. Actually my uncle lives there, so I visit him every year.

Judy: Really? Then, you've climbed Mt. Seorak, haven't you?

Minsu: Yes, I've climbed to the top of the mountain twice.

Wrap Up – Listening ⑥

Mike: Today, I'll tell you how to draw a bear's face.

First, draw a big circle for the face. Next, make two circles on top of the face. After that, draw two circles for its eyes and color them black. Then, draw a small circle for the nose. Lastly, make a mouth.

본문 TEST Step 1   p.09~10

01 Both, Land   02 laugh, saw, above
03 so, successful   04 who make cartoons
05 catch, make, laugh, creative
06 have made, for hundreds
07 types, cartoons different roles
08 One, is, a few   09 is, called
10 makes, character, laugh, saying
11 Another, is called
12 parts, different, bigger, usual
13 at, on, right   14 Which parts, jump out
15 have used, make fun
16 several, come together, strip
17 have been, for, years   18 just amusing stories
19 have also used, education
20 make, clearer, easier, learn
21 have probably seen
22 have surely seen, animated
23 popular among, all ages
24 added to, come alive
25 develop fascinating, interesting, through
26 type, was developed   27 is called
28 are published, read, on
29 popular, them, even, into
30 forms, may appear
31 different, exciting, remain, relax

본문 TEST Step 2   p.11~12

01 Land
02 laugh when, saw, above
03 so, cartoonist, successful
04 who make cartoons
05 to catch, make you laugh, creative drawings
06 have made, for hundreds of years
07 many types of cartoons, different roles
08 One form, is, a few words
09 is sometimes called
10 makes a funny character, makes, laugh, doing, saying

11 Another, is called

12 some parts, are different, bigger than usual

13 Look at, on   14 Which parts, jump out

15 have used, to make fun of well-known people

16 several, come together, a comic strip

17 have been, for many years

18 just amusing stories

19 have also used, for education

20 make, clearer, easier to learn

21 have probably seen

22 have surely seen, animated movies, too

23 popular among people of all ages

24 Movement, are added to, come alive

25 develop fascinating characters, interesting, through

26 type of, was developed

27 is called

28 are published, read them, on

29 popular, them are, made into

30 forms, may appear

31 different, exciting than, remain, laugh, relax, learn

20 만화는 정보를 더 명료하고 더 배우기 쉽게 만들 수 있다.

21 여러분은 아마 만화 역사책이나 과학책을 본 적이 있을 것이다.

22 여러분은 많은 만화영화도 당연히 봤을 것이다.

23 이것들은 모든 연령대의 사람들에게 매우 인기가 많다.

24 동작이나 소리가 그림에 더해져서 그림들이 생생하게 살아난다.

25 미술가들과 작가들은 매력적인 캐릭터를 개발하고 만화영화 제작을 통해 재미있는 이야기를 들려준다.

26 1990년대에 새로운 형식의 만화가 개발되었다.

27 그건 웹툰이라고 불린다.

28 웹툰은 온라인으로 출판되기 때문에 여러분이 휴대 전화나 컴퓨터로 언제 어디서나 볼 수 있다.

29 그것은 매우 인기가 있고, 그들 가운데 일부는 심지어 텔레비전 드라마나 영화로 만들어지기도 한다.

30 미래에는 새로운 형태의 만화가 나타날지도 모른다.

31 그것은 지금과는 다르고 한층 더 재미있겠지만, 한 가지는 같을 것이다. 그것은 우리가 웃고, 쉬고, 배우도록 도와줄 것이다.

1 배다! 육지다!

2 위의 만화를 보고 웃었는가?

3 그랬다면 그 만화가는 성공했다.

4 만화가들은 만화를 만드는 사람들이다.

5 그들은 여러분의 관심을 끌고, 대개는 간단한 말과 독창적인 그림으로 여러분을 웃게 하고 싶어 한다.

6 사람들은 수백 년 동안 만화를 만들어 왔다.

7 만화에는 많은 종류가 있으며, 그것들은 다양한 역할을 한다.

8 만화의 한 형태로 몇 마디 말을 쓴 그림이 있다.

9 간혹 그것은 '개그 만화'라고 불린다.

10 만화가는 웃긴 캐릭터를 만들고, 그 캐릭터는 우스꽝스러운 행동이나 말을 함으로써 여러분을 웃게 만든다.

11 다른 종류의 만화는 캐리커처라고 불린다.

12 캐리커처에서 캐릭터의 어떤 부분은 평소와 다르거나 더 크다.

13 오른쪽의 그림을 보아라.

14 남자 얼굴의 어떤 부분이 여러분에게 분명히 보이는가?

15 미술가들은 유명한 사람들을 풍자하기 위해 이런 종류의 만화를 그려 왔다.

16 몇 가지 만화 그림이 모여서 이야기를 들려주게 되면, 그것이 연재만화가 된다.

17 연재만화는 여러 해 동안 신문에 실려 왔다.

18 그것들은 종종 그저 재미있는 이야기이다.

19 사람들은 연재만화를 교육용으로 사용해 오기도 했다.

1 Boat! Land!

2 Did you laugh when you saw the cartoon above?

3 If so, the cartoonist was successful.

4 Cartoonists are the people who make cartoons.

5 They want to catch your interest, and usually, make you laugh with simple language and creative drawings.

6 People have made cartoons for hundreds of years.

7 There are many types of cartoons, and they play different roles.

8 One form of cartoon is a picture with a few words.

9 It is sometimes called a "gag cartoon."

10 The cartoonist makes a funny character, and the character makes you laugh by doing or saying silly things.

11 Another type of cartoon is called a caricature.

12 In a caricature, some parts of a character are different or bigger than usual.

13 Look at the picture on the right.

14 Which parts of the man's face jump out at you?

15 Artists have used this type of cartoon to make fun of well-known people.

16 When several cartoon pictures come together and tell a story, we have a comic strip.

17 Comic strips have been in newspapers for many years.

18 They are often just amusing stories.

19 People have also used comic strips for education.

20 Comics can make information clearer and easier to learn.

21 You have probably seen comic history or science books.

22 You have surely seen many cartoon movies, or animated movies, too.

23 These are very popular among people of all ages.

24 Movement and sounds are added to pictures, so they come alive.

25 Artists and writers can develop fascinating characters and tell interesting stories through animation.

26 In the 1990s, a new type of cartoon was developed.

27 It is called a webtoon.

28 Webtoons are published online, so you can read them anytime, anywhere on your phone or computer.

29 They are very popular, and some of them are even made into TV dramas or movies.

30 New forms of cartoons may appear in the future.

31 They could be different and even more exciting than now, but one thing will remain the same: they will help us laugh, relax, and learn.

My Speaking Portfolio – Step 3

1. Here, useful tip

2. washed, many times

3. warm, washing powder

4. Then, leave, for seven minutes

5. Lastly, out of, them

6. look like

My Writing Portfolio

1. Cartoon Character

2. favorite cartoon character

3. elementary school, humorous, kind

4. However, causes trouble

5. because, bright side, tries to, others

Words in Action B

1. Animated Movie

2. to build, in the forest

3. soon suffer from, pollution

4. makes a suggestion

5. reach an agreement to create

My Speaking Portfolio – Step 3

1. Here is a useful tip for you.

2. I've washed my sneakers this way many times.

3. First, put the sneakers, warm water, and washing powder in a plastic bag.

4. Then close the bag and leave it for seven minutes.

5. Lastly, take the sneakers out of the bag and wash them.

6. They'll look like new sneakers.

My Writing Portfolio

1. Giyeong, My Favorite Cartoon Character

2. My favorite cartoon character is Giyeong of *Black Rubber Shoes*.

3. He is an elementary school student. He is humorous and kind.

4. However, he is not very smart and sometimes causes trouble.

5. I like him because he looks on the bright side of everything and always tries to help others.

Words in Action B

1. The Best Animated Movie for Children's Education

2. Animals welcome the city's plan to build an amusement park in the forest.

3. However, they soon suffer from serious pollution.

4. An old elephant makes a suggestion.

5. The animals and the city reach an agreement to create a better world for everyone.

15 waterfall, 폭포   16 bridge, 다리

단어 TEST Step 1   p.21

01 조종사	02 해돋이, 일출	03 이익, 혜택
04 준비하다	05 다리	06 지역
07 ~당, ~마다	08 자연의, 천연의	09 아마도
10 수도	11 전망	12 대륙
13 겁먹은, 무서워하는		14 비슷한, 유사한
15 환상적인, 엄청난	16 흐르다	17 수줍은, 부끄럼 타는
18 자외선 차단제	19 산맥	20 독특한
21 폭포	22 흙, 토양	23 대양
24 경이, 놀라움	25 인내심	26 예술품, 미술품
27 우주, 외계	28 특히	29 기원, 원산
30 열대 우림	31 포함하다	32 해수면
33 ~을 통하여	34 넓은	35 없어지다
36 ~와 비슷하다	37 솔직히 말하면	38 일 년 내내, 연중
39 ~으로 가득하다	40 ~을 따라 이름 짓다	
41 혼자서, 홀로	42 파티를 열다	43 그건 그렇고

단어 TEST Step 2   p.22

01 prepare	02 benefit	03 view
04 wide	05 capital	06 wonder
07 bridge	08 origin	09 patience
10 waterfall	11 especially	12 sunrise
13 tourist	14 sunscreen	15 fantastic
16 unique	17 flow	18 Mars
19 shy	20 mountain range	
21 similar	22 through	23 soil
24 continent	25 per	26 area
27 sea level	28 scared	29 natural
30 contain	31 probably	32 rainforest
33 ocean	34 across	35 name after
36 by the way	37 go away	38 all year round
39 be full of	40 be similar to	41 to be honest
42 throw a party	43 by oneself	

단어 TEST Step 3   p.23

1 prepare, 준비하다   2 benefit, 이익   3 area, 지역

4 rainforest, 열대 우림   5 continent, 대륙

6 across, 건너서, 가로질러   7 wonder, 경이, 놀라움

8 patience, 인내심   9 soil, 토양, 흙

10 natural, 천연의, 자연의   11 desert, 사막

12 wide, 넓은   13 origin, 기원   14 pilot, 조종사

대화문 TEST Step 1   p.24~25

Communication: Listen – Dialog 1

tomato soup / happy, like / By the way, where, was first grown / somewhere in Europe / came from South America / How / social studies

Communication: Listen – Dialog 2

Did, see, took / What / traveled around, by herself / surprise / showed us pictures, especially, pyramids / Are there, South America / about, above sea level / can't believe it

Communication: Listen More

How was / fantastic, really enjoyed / closed, while riding / To be honest, scared at first / how fast, is / no idea / as fast as / surprising / Let's ride / sign, after / maybe next time

Communicate: Speak

what the capital of Peru is / no idea / didn't know

Wrap Up – Listening ❺

got a puppy / Where, pet shop / heard, uncle / want, too

Wrap Up – Listening ❻

won first prize / quiet, shy / joined, has changed a lot / want to join, too

대화문 TEST Step 2   p.26~27

Communication: Listen – Dialog 1

Sujin: Dad, I like this tomato soup.

Dad: I'm happy you like it.

Sujin: By the way, do you know where the tomato was first grown?

Dad: Italy or somewhere in Europe?

Sujin: No, the tomato came from South America.

Dad: Really? How did you know that?

Sujin: I learned it from Ms. Song, my social studies teacher.

Dad: That's good.

Communication: Listen – Dialog 2

Jenny: Did you see the pictures Ms. Song took?

Brian: What pictures?

Jenny: She traveled around South America by herself last summer.

Brian: Really? What a surprise!

Jenny: She showed us pictures of beautiful places. I especially liked the pictures of pyramids.

Brian: Are there pyramids in South America?

Jenny: Yes. She said some pyramids are about 3,800 meters above sea level.

Brian: I can't believe it.

Communication: Listen More

Hana: How was the roller coaster ride, Jongha?

Jongha: It was fantastic. I really enjoyed it.

Hana: Ha ha. You closed your eyes while riding.

Jongha: Did you see? To be honest, I was really scared at first.

Hana: Do you know how fast this roller coaster is?

Jongha: I have no idea.

Hana: It goes as fast as 140 km per hour.

Jongha: Wow! That's surprising!

Hana: Let's ride it one more time!

Jongha: Look at the sign. We can't ride it after 8 p.m.

Hana: Oh, maybe next time.

Communicate: Speak

Amy: Do you know what the capital of Peru is?

Jinsu: I have no idea. What is it?

Amy: It's Lima.

Jinsu: I didn't know that.

Wrap Up – Listening ❺

Jack: Do you know Junha got a puppy?

Minji: No. Where did he get it? From a pet shop?

Jack: No. I heard he got the puppy from his uncle.

Minji: I want one, too.

Wrap Up – Listening ❻

Mike: Do you know Sumin won first prize at the speech contest?

Sue: I can't believe it. She was very quiet and shy last year.

Mike: Yeah. She joined the drama club this year, and she has changed a lot.

Sue: I see. I want to join the club, too.

본문 TEST Step 1   p.28~29

01 where, driest desert   02 about the highest
03 they, both, South
04 full, wonders that, surprise
05 the driest desert   06 parts, gets, all, per
07 areas, so, that, grow

---

08 what scientists, such, dry
09 similar, so, prepare, outer
10 one, best places, watch
11 If, to, world's highest   12 meters high
13 cover, patience, luck, view
14 named after, flew over   15 get to, top, by
16 runs across, through   17 travels from, flows into
18 interesting in, ways   19 most, no bridges
20 because, runs through, wet
21 places, wide, other side
22 probably, swim in
23 home, that, meat
24 the world's longest, range
25 how long, mountain range
26 about, long
27 contains, mountains outside
28 About, third, people   29 unique, also live

본문 TEST Step 2   p.30~31

01 where the driest desert
02 about the highest waterfall
03 they are both
04 is full of, that will surprise
05 the driest desert   06 it gets, at all, per year
07 is so dry that, can grow
08 what scientists do, such a dry place
09 similar to, they prepare for trips, outer space
10 one of the best places, to watch stars
11 see the world's highest waterfall
12 It, meters high
13 cover, patience, luck, good view
14 named after, who, flew
15 still get to, only by plane
16 runs across, through
17 travels from, flows into, Atlantic Ocean
18 is interesting, many ways
19 no bridges
20 because it usually runs through, wet areas
21 see the other side   22 probably, swim in
23 home, that
24 the world's longest mountain range
25 how long the mountain range
26 about, long
27 contains, mountains outside
28 a third of the people, live in
29 unique animals, live there

1 여러분은 지구에서 가장 건조한 사막이 어디인지 알고 있나요?

2 가장 높은 폭포는 어떠한가요?

3 그렇습니다, 그것들은 둘 다 남아메리카에 있습니다.

4 이 대륙은 여러분을 놀라게 할 자연 경관으로 가득하답니다.

5 아타카마 사막은 지구에서 가장 건조한 사막입니다.

6 몇몇 지역은 비가 전혀 오지 않아서, 연간 강수량이 1~3mm에 그칩니다!

7 어떤 지역의 토양은 너무 건조해서 어떤 식물도 자랄 수가 없습니다.

8 이처럼 건조한 곳에서 과학자들이 무슨 일을 하는지 알고 있나요?

9 이 사막의 토양은 화성의 토양과 아주 비슷해서, 그들은 우주로의 여행을 준비합니다.

10 또한 아타카마 사막은 지구에서 별을 관측하기에 가장 좋은 장소 가운데 하나이기도 합니다.

11 여러분이 베네수엘라에 간다면, 세계에서 가장 높은 폭포를 볼 수 있을 것입니다.

12 그것은 높이가 979m입니다.

13 구름이 꼭대기 부분을 자주 에워싸기 때문에, 멋진 경치를 보려면 인내심과 약간의 운이 필요합니다.

14 사실 그 폭포는 1933년에 처음으로 폭포 너머 비행을 한 미국의 비행사 Jimmie Angel에게서 이름을 따왔습니다.

15 여전히 비행기로만 그 아름다운 폭포의 꼭대기에 갈 수 있습니다.

16 아마존강은 일곱 개의 나라를 거쳐 대륙을 가로질러 흐릅니다.

17 그것은 서쪽의 페루에서 시작하여 대서양으로 흘러갑니다.

18 아마존강은 많은 점에서 흥미롭습니다.

19 강의 대부분에는 다리가 없습니다.

20 그것은 강이 대개 도시나 마을이 아닌, 열대 우림과 습지를 지나 흐르기 때문입니다.

21 또한 많은 곳에서 강이 너무 넓어서 그 건너편을 볼 수조차 없습니다!

22 여러분은 아마도 이 강에서 헤엄치고 싶지 않을 것입니다.

23 이곳은 몇몇 아주 큰 뱀과 고기를 먹는 물고기들의 서식지입니다.

24 안데스 산맥은 세계에서 가장 긴 산맥입니다.

25 여러분은 그 산맥의 길이가 얼마인지 아시나요?

26 그것은 약 7,000km입니다.

27 또한 그곳에는 아시아 외의 지역에서 가장 높은 산이 있습니다.

28 남아메리카 인구의 3분의 1 정도가 안데스 산맥에 살고 있습니다.

29 그리고 독특한 동물들이 많이 서식하고 있기도 합니다.

1 Do you know where the driest desert on Earth is?

2 How about the highest waterfall?

3 Yes, they are both in South America.

4 This continent is full of natural wonders that will surprise you.

5 The Atacama is the driest desert on Earth.

6 In some parts, it gets almost no rain at all — only 1-3 millimeters per year!

7 The ground in some areas is so dry that no plants can grow.

8 Do you know what scientists do in such a dry place?

9 The soil in this desert is very similar to the soil on Mars, so they prepare for trips to outer space.

10 The Atacama is also one of the best places on Earth to watch stars.

11 If you go to Venezuela, you can see the world's highest waterfall.

12 It is 979 meters high.

13 Clouds often cover the top, so you need patience and a little luck to get a good view.

14 Actually, the waterfall is named after Jimmie Angel, a pilot from the United States who first flew over the waterfall in 1933.

15 You can still get to the top of the beautiful waterfall only by plane.

16 The Amazon runs across the continent through seven countries.

17 It travels from Peru in the west and flows into the Atlantic Ocean.

18 The Amazon River is interesting in many ways.

19 For the most part, it has no bridges.

20 That is because it usually runs through rainforests and wet areas, not cities or towns.

21 Also, in many places the river is very wide, so you cannot see the other side!

22 You probably do not want to swim in this river.

23 It is home to some very big snakes and fish that eat meat.

24 The Andes are the world's longest mountain range.

25 Do you know how long the mountain range is?

26 It is about 7,000 kilometers long!

27 It also contains the highest mountains outside of Asia.

28 About a third of the people in South America live in the Andes.

29 Many unique animals also live there.

My Speaking Portfolio
1. Which country, to visit
2. where Brazil is
3. in South America, the biggest country
4. What a surprise, the first thing
5. to see, from

My Writing Portfolio
1. Day, Nature
2. went to, with
3. sits in, meters high
4. was surprised at
5. brown rocks, green trees
6. My trip to, made me feel
7. felt like, went away

Wrap Up - Reading
1. the world's largest
2. Thousands of year, all dried up
3. is left about, above sea level
4. one of the most visited natural wonders
5. All year round, unique natural beauty
6. In fact, makes, tourist
7. Every picture, take, beautiful work of art

Wrap Up - Reading
1. Salar de Uyuni in Bolivia is the world's largest salt flat.
2. Thousands of years ago, there was water, but it all dried up.
3. Now, a large salt desert is left about 3,656 meters above sea level.
4. Salar de Uyuni is one of the most visited natural wonders of South America, too.
5. All year round a lot of people visit this place to take pictures of its unique natural beauty.
6. In fact, the salt flat makes any tourist a great photographer.
7. Every picture you take in Salar de Uyuni will be a beautiful work of art!

My Speaking Portfolio
1. A: Which country do you want to visit?
2. B: Brazil. Do you know where Brazil is?
3. A: Yes, I do. It's in South America. Do you know that Brazil is the biggest country in South America?
4. B: What a surprise! I didn't know that. So, what's the first thing you want to see in Brazil?
5. A: I want to see Iguazu Falls from the sky.

My Writing Portfolio
1. A Day in Nature
2. I went to Kaieteur Falls with my family.
3. The waterfall sits in the Amazon Rainforest in Guyana, and it is 226 meters high.
4. I was surprised at the size of the waterfall.
5. I could see the brown rocks and green trees there.
6. My trip to Kaieteur Falls made me feel good.
7. I felt like all my stress went away.

Lesson S

단어 TEST Step 1   p.40

01 고르다	02 축하하다
03 (부정문에서) 역시, 또한	
04 일어나다, 생기다, 발생하다	05 속임수
06 비열한, 못된	07 빌리다	08 주의 깊게
09 백만	10 지금은, 이제는 (더 이상)
11 하인	12 해설자, 내레이터	13 가난한
14 대신에	15 큰소리로	16 감옥
17 (목숨을) 구하다	18 허락하다, 허가하다
19 끔찍한	20 등장인물	21 떨어뜨리다
22 ~할 필요가 없다	23 대부업자	24 (돈을) 갚다
25 즉시, 바로	26 중얼거리다	27 혼잣말로

단어 TEST Step 2   p.41

01 poor	02 borrow	03 drop
04 million	05 carefully	06 save
07 trick	08 narrator	09 terrible
10 happen	11 allow	12 instead
13 pick	14 loudly	15 character
16 mean	17 anymore	18 prison
19 servant	20 either	21 celebrate
22 right away	23 say to oneself	24 money lender
25 pay back	26 to oneself	
27 don't[doesn't] have to		

단어 TEST Step 3   p.42

1 instead, 대신에   2 trick, 속임수   3 pick, 고르다
4 mean, 비열한, 못된   5 borrow, 빌리다
6 character, 등장인물   7 happen, 발생하다, 일어나다
8 narrator, 해설자, 내레이터   9 prison, 감옥
10 save, (목숨을) 구하다   11 celebrate, 축하하다
12 servant, 하인

본문 TEST Step 1   p.43~44

01 Two Stones
02 Characters, Money Lender, Narrator
03 ago, village, there lived
04 had, borrow, million, from
05 for, pay, allow, anymore

06 have no
07 become, servant instead
08 Daughter, no   09 to be, servant
10 want, either, thank   11 to go, prison
12 let's play, put   13 One, the other, pick
14 happens if, one   15 Then, be, servant
16 mean, How terrible   17 What, if, pick
18 free, have, pay back   19 happens, doesn't, with
20 *loudly*, Then, prison
21 Daughter, Friends, Prison
22 *picks up, carefully at*
23 *to herself*, picked up 24 make, become, should
25 Stop, think, should   26 cannot pick, one
27 *from, drops, right away* 28 sorry, dropped
29 But, okay   30 Show us, stone
31 which one, picked
32 *to herself*, cannot, trick
33 *shows everyone, stone*
34 *start celebrating*   35 picked, one, free
36 Good thinking, saved

본문 TEST Step 2   p.45~46

01 Two Stones
02 Characters, Money Lender, Narrator
03 long time ago, village, there lived
04 had to borrow, million, from, money lender
05 the money lender, asked for, to pay back, allow, anymore   06 have no
07 will become, servant instead
08 no   09 to be, servant
10 either, thank you   11 go to prison
12 let's play, put
13 One, the other, pick one
14 happens if, pick   15 Then, will be, servant
16 mean, How terrible   17 if, pick
18 free, doesn't have to pay back
19 happens, doesn't play, with
20 *loudly*, Then, prison 21 Prison
22 *picks up, looks carefully at*
23 *to herself*, picked up, white stones
24 make, become, What should
25 Stop and think   26 cannot pick
27 drops, right away   28 dropped
29 okay   30 Show us the stone
31 which one I picked
32 *to herself*, cannot tell, trick

31

33 *shows everyone the white stone*
34 *start celebrating*   35 picked, free
36 Good thinking, saved

32 (대부업자는 모두에게 흰 돌을 보여 준다. 친구들과 아버지는
   축하하기 시작한다.)
33 친구들: 그녀는 검은 돌을 집었어! 그들은 자유야!
34 해설자: 현명한 생각이 아버지와 딸을 구했습니다!

1 두 개의 돌
2 등장인물: 아버지, 딸, 대부업자, 친구들, 해설자
3 해설자: 오래 전 남아메리카의 작은 마을에 농부와 그의 딸이
   살았습니다.
4 농부는 가난했고, 대부업자로부터 3백만 페소를 빌려야
   했습니다.
5 하지만 대부업자는 친절하지 않았고, 농부가 돈을 갚을 때까지
   한 달을 기다려 달라고 하자, 더 이상의 시간을 허락   해 주지
   않았습니다.
6 대부업자: 돈이 없다는 거죠? 좋아요
7 대신 당신 딸이 내 하녀가 돼야겠네요.
8 아버지와 딸: 오, 안 돼!
9 딸: 저는 당신의 하녀가 되고 싶지 않아요.
10 아버지: 나도 그것을 원하지 않아! (대부업자에게) 사양하겠습니다.
11 대부업자: 감옥에 가고 싶은가요?
12 그렇다면, 게임을 하나 합시다. 내가 가방에 돌 두 개를
   넣겠어요.
13 하나는 흰색이고, 다른 하나는 검은색이죠. 당신 딸이
   하나를 집을 거예요.
14 딸: 제가 흰 돌을 집으면 어떻게 되죠?
15 대부업자: 그러면 넌 내 하녀가 될 거야.
16 친구들: 오, 안 돼! 그녀는 야비해. 정말 끔찍해!
17 딸: 제가 검은 돌을 집으면 어떻게 되죠?
18 대부업자: 그러면 넌 자유로워질 것이고, 네 아버지는 내 돈을
   갚을 필요가 없어.
19 아버지: 내 딸이 당신과 이 게임을 하지 않으면 어떻게 되죠?
20 대부업자: (큰소리로) 그러면 당신은 감옥에 가게 되겠죠!
21 아버지, 딸, 친구들: 오, 안 돼! 감옥이라니!
22 (대부업자는 두 개의 돌을 집는다. 딸은 주의 깊게 그녀를 본다.)
23 딸: (혼잣말로) 오! 그녀는 두 개의 흰 돌을 집었어!
24 그녀는 나를 자신의 하녀로 만들 거야. 어떻게 하면 좋지?
25 해설자: 가만히 생각해 보세요. 그녀는 어떻게 하면 좋을까요?
26 그녀는 검은 돌을 집을 수 없어요.
27 (딸은 가방에서 돌을 하나 집는다. 그녀는 그것을 바로
   떨어뜨린다.)
28 딸: 오, 안 돼! 미안해요, 제가 돌을 떨어뜨렸어요. (대부업자에게)
   하지만 괜찮아요.
29 가방에 있는 돌을 우리에게 보여주세요.
30 그러면 제가 무엇을 집었는지 우리가 알게 될 테니까요.
31 대부업자: (혼잣말로) 그들에게 내 속임수를 말할 수 없어! 오,
   안 돼!

1 The Two Stones
2 Characters: Father, Daughter, Money Lender,
   Friends, Narrator
3 Narrator: A long time ago, in a small village in
   South America, there lived a farmer and his
   daughter.
4 The farmer was poor, and had to borrow three
   million pesos from a money lender.
5 But the money lender was not kind, and when the
   farmer asked for one month to pay back the
   money, she didn't allow him anymore time.
6 Money Lender: You have no money? That's okay.
7 Your daughter will become my servant instead.
8 Father and Daughter: Oh, no!
9 Daughter: I don't want to be your servant.
10 Father: I don't want that, either! (to Money Lender)
   No, thank you.
11 Money Lender: Do you want to go to prison?
12 Then, let's play a game. I will put two stones in a
   bag.
13 One is white, and the other is black. Your
   daughter will pick one.
14 Daughter: What happens if I pick the white one?
15 Money Lender: Then you will be my servant.
16 Friends: Oh, no! She's mean. How terrible!
17 Daughter: What happens if I pick the black one?
18 Money Lender: Then you will be free, and your
   father doesn't have to pay back my money.
19 Father: What happens if she doesn't play this
   game with you?
20 Money Lender: (loudly) Then you will go to prison!
21 Father, Daughter, and Friends: Oh, no! Prison!
22 (Money Lender picks up two stones. Daughter
   looks carefully at her.)
23 Daughter: (to herself) Oh! She has picked up two
   white stones!
24 She will make me become her servant. What
   should I do?
25 Narrator: Stop and think. What should she do?
26 She cannot pick a black one.

27 *(Daughter picks a stone from the bag. She drops it right away.)*

28 Daughter: Oh, no! I'm sorry, I've dropped it. *(to Money Lender)* But it's okay.

29 Show us the stone in the bag.

30 Then we will know which one I picked.

31 Money Lender: *(to herself)* I cannot tell them about my trick! Oh, no!

32 *(Money Lender shows everyone the white stone. Friends and Father start celebrating.)*

33 Friends: She picked the black one! They are free!

34 Narrator: Good thinking has saved Father and Daughter!

MEMO

MEMO

MEMO

적중 100

영어 기출 문제집

정답 및 해설

천재 | 이재영